The SHAPERS *of*

AMERICAN FICTION

Books by

GEORGE SNELL

THE SHAPERS OF AMERICAN FICTION

AND—IF MAN TRIUMPH

THE GREAT ADAM

ROOT, HOG, AND DIE

The SHAPERS *of* AMERICAN FICTION

1798-1947

By GEORGE SNELL

COOPER SQUARE PUBLISHERS, INC.

New York • 1961

Printed in U.S.A. by
NOBLE OFFSET PRINTERS, INC.
NEW YORK 3, N. Y.

To FRED T. MARSH

CONTENTS

8 *Contents*

ACKNOWLEDGMENTS

Some chapters of this book have appeared, usually in a different form, in *The Yale Review, University of Kansas City Review, Arizona Quarterly, Modern Language Quarterly, College English* and *The Western Review.*

The author acknowledges permissions for the more extensive quotations as follows:

BIERCE, AMBROSE: from *The Cynic's Word Book.* By permission of Albert Boni.

BROOKS, VAN WYCK: from *Opinions of Oliver Allston* and *The World of Washington Irving.* By permission of E. P. Dutton & Co., Inc.

BROWNELL, WILLIAM CRARY: from *American Prose Masters.* By permission of Charles Scribner's Sons.

CALDWELL, ERSKINE: from *Tobacco Road; God's Little Acre,* "A Day's Wooing" in *Jackpot,* "Candy-man Beechum" in *Jackpot,* and "Kneel to the Rising Sun" in *Kneel to the Rising Sun.* By permission of Duell, Sloan and Pearce.

CATHER, WILLA: from Preface to *Alexander's Bridge.* By permission of Houghton, Mifflin Company.

DOS PASSOS, JOHN: from *Manhattan Transfer.* By permission of John Dos Passos.

DREISER, THEODORE: from *Hey, Rub-a-Dub-Dub* and *The Financier.* By permission of Mrs. Theodore Dreiser. And from *The Bulwark.* By permission of Doubleday & Company, Inc.

FAULKNER, WILLIAM: from *Absalom, Absalom, As I Lay Dying,* and from "A Rose for Emily" and "That Evening Sun Go Down" in *These Thirteen.* By permission of Random House.

FARRELL, JAMES T.: from *A Note on Literary Criticism, The*

League of Frightened Philistines, Judgment Day, and *Bernard Clare.* By permission of Vanguard Press.

FISHER, VARDIS: from *In Tragic Life,* and *Dark Bridwell.* By permission of The Caxton Printers, Ltd. And from *The Neurotic Nightingale.* By permission of Harry W. Schwartz.

HEARN, LAFCADIO: from *Chita.* By permission of Harper and Brothers. And from *Books and Habits.* By permission of Dodd, Mead & Company.

HEMINGWAY, ERNEST: from *In Our Time, Death in the Afternoon, The Sun Also Rises, A Farewell To Arms, To Have and To Have Not, For Whom The Bell Tolls, The Green Hills of Africa,* "The Gambler, the Nun and the Radio," "A Natural History of the Dead," and "The Snows of Kilimanjaro" in *Fifth Column and the First Forty-nine.* By permission of Charles Scribner's Sons.

JAMES, HENRY: from *Letters* and from *The Golden Bowl.* By permission of Charles Scribner's Sons.

STEINBECK, JOHN: from *Cup of Gold, The Pastures of Heaven,* and *Tortilla Flat.* By permission of The Viking Press, Inc.

TWAIN, MARK: from *Life on the Mississippi* and from *Huckleberry Finn.* By permission of Harper and Brothers.

WHARTON, EDITH: from *The House of Mirth, The Age of Innocence* and from *The Writing of Fiction.* By permission of Charles Scribner's Sons.

WOLFE, THOMAS: from *You Can't Go Home Again.* By permission of Harper and Brothers. And from *Look Homeward, Angel.* By permission of Charles Scribner's Sons.

PREFACE

AMERICAN FICTION is not much more than a hundred and fifty years old; and during at least the first half-century of its existence it was subservient to the fashions and subject matter of English and Continental models. By the time Hawthorne and Melville appeared, it had begun to sever the umbilical cord; when the twentieth century dawned, it had become largely indigenous. For the last three or four decades it has been admittedly the most lively and puissant literature in the world. There seems little question but that today the tables are turned; from being imitators we have become the imitated, and the strength of American literature has been stimulating to the imaginative talents of other lands.

This record of the development of American fiction is meant to give a comprehensive view of that change which has come over our literature. It attempts to provide an insight into the stages of growth, as it traces the forms of our fiction from its weak, imitative beginnings to its present eminence and originality. If the record dwells at greater length on the major contemporary figures, that is because our living novelists and short-story writers represent American fiction at the full tide. But it is necessary, in order to understand the emergence of these powerfully influential writers, to know what their inheritance has been.

For the sake of convenience, rather than for any other reason, the record separates these products of the American imagination into four characteristic channels. It is apparent that our early storytellers worked largely from British models, but at the same time they were shapers, in the sense that they took the foreign forms and cast them in new molds. These shapers, Cooper, Brown, Irving and Howells, launched four types of fiction in America. And, with due allowance for the elasticity of categories, it is possible to trace distinct "lines of inheritance" in methods and moods through the work of their successors. These four categories I have named the Romantic, the Apocalyptic, the Temperamentist and the Realistic. This book thus naturally divides itself into four sections, each of which starts with its progenitive author and progresses to the major contemporaries in its category.

It is worth repeating, however, that this division, and its argument, are more matters of convenience than anything, because it is obviously impossible to pigeonhole anything so Protean as the creative spirit. I think that it does enable one to summarize in a useful fashion the results of what are unquestionably dominant tendencies in American fiction. It is worthwhile to trace, for example, points at which the imagination of a Brockden Brown and a William Faulkner coincide. Besides, it has been the usual practice for a long while to note the development of American naturalism out of Howells' tepid realism, and the worth of this notation is so evident that a similar examination of other tendencies in fiction is immediately indicated. But again I emphasize that it is not the book's intention to insist upon arbitrary systems and definitions, but merely to use them as aids toward illumination.

It will be seen that I do not attempt a comprehensive history of our literature, and that this record covers only the work of outstanding writers of imaginative prose. Some of that work is examined closely, and the position of each writer considered is summarized in its relation to the mainstream of American fiction. There is more attention given, in general, to the overall significance of each writer and less to an intensive critique of individual works. If there is any bias to be detected in my interpretations, I trust it derives from my sympathy with the dominant modes of contemporary expression, and not from any real prejudice for or against any of the four categories of fiction. My intention was that these chapters should exhibit only the spirit of enthusiasm and inquiry which I believe to be the *sine qua non* of creative criticism, and that they form a stimulating examination into the means by which our current writers have arrived at what they are, by surveying what they have done. Undoubtedly by understanding their inheritance we can better understand their performance. And ultimately we may have grounds for forecasting what they, and their own inheritors, will do.

It is one of my hopes that this record may lead interested readers, not specialists, to consult some of our older novelists and short-story writers, and that the net result of my discussion shall be a livelier appreciation of the forces shaping the entire course of imaginative prose writing in America.

San Francisco
January, 1947

G. S.

The SHAPERS *of*

AMERICAN FICTION

ROMANTICS

J. FENIMORE COOPER
Shaper of American Romance

How COMPLETELY most prodigious creators in fiction are aware of the inherent meaning of their work is a question difficult to decide. Most of them, probably, are only partially conscious on this point, which only a later, contemplative criticism can deduce. Also, few of the great proliferators have been artists on purpose, though some of them created with serious intentions. We recall Hugo, Dumas, Scott, Dickens, as such gigantic machines lavishly pouring out creation, but we do not think of them as artists. In Henry James's opinion, "for the most part these loose and easy producers, the great resounding improvvisatori, have not, in general, ended by imposing themselves." Perhaps not, but from Fielding on, the loose and easy producers have had and largely held their audiences. Certainly Cooper was one of America's greatest "improvvisatori." That he was also an artist, in special instances, can be demonstrated. That he was, further, a conscious if unassuming novelist at all times can easily be seen upon examination of the many prefaces to the novels, from *Precaution* to *The Ways of the Hour*.

Cooper's chief claim upon our attention is the germinative power of his method and content. The shaping influence of the Cooper tradition (it could become a tradition only through a recognizable operation) is obvious. No other American romancer has risen to Cooper's eminence, but countless imitative practitioners have built upon his foundations; and though there are many essential differences between Cooper's method and attitudes and those of today's commercial romancer, the similarities

15

prove how seminal the shaper's influence has been. And after all, it is not the innovator's fault if his method has been preempted by hacks and his system reduced to a money-making formula. If a *Saturday Evening Post* writer could produce a true Cooper romance, we would entertain a higher opinion of commercial fiction.

The screen that stands between us and the America of the early nineteenth century has hampered the communication of Cooper's special qualities. It is the same obstruction of changed modes in etymology, moral dispositions and social emphases which cuts us off from any preceding epoch. We can, however, triumph over this obstacle as easily in the case of Cooper as in that of Jonson or Pope, or the writers of any other age. For the beauties are there which invite us to seek and do the recreative act which all reading in the literature of the past requires. This cannot be said of the whole of Cooper's enormous output, but it is certainly true of the major works. The special interest which attaches to novels carefully constructed, "achieving closeness and weight," in Henry James's phrase, is lacking; but the lasting values of richly conceived overall portrayals of a time and place, and the qualities of vivid life, are everywhere. These excellences were so apparent and powerful that they have profoundly influenced the shape of the American novel from Cooper's day to our own.

Still, it is not true that Cooper, any more than Irving or Howells or Brockden Brown, was a fresh spring in himself. The waters that enlivened him sprang again out of European soil. Scott's vogue was already great when Cooper wrote *The Spy*, and that novel owes as much for manner and inspiration to Scott as *Wieland* does to *The Castle of Otranto*. But the remarkable difference is there: Cooper went directly to his American experience and observation, and relied upon an unassailable empiricism, for his background and his story. One could have expected this of him, if one had had any way of foreseeing the irascible champion of all things American (and by inversion their bitterest critic) the he was to become in middle life. Cooper was hyperconscious of his Americanism if not of his art, a circumstance which, however, insured that art against meretriciousness. He thus escaped the pitfalls that opened immediately in the paths of Brown and Poe, and wrote the first genuinely "American" novels.

It is true that the most successful among them do not deal with contemporary events; the novels that do, like *Ways of the Hour* and *The Monikins*, are comparative failures. It seems almost as though Cooper was unable to look directly at experience; that when he attempted it, his personal prejudices always transformed the story-teller into the teacher. However, even the most "historical" of his novels, we must remember, were inspired by events which had occurred practically within his lifetime. Leatherstocking's adventures were being enacted in real life not long before Cooper committed them to paper. Commenting on his failures, Cooper noted wistfully that his "historical romances" had never found great favor with the public; and he was thinking then of such tales as *Lionel Lincoln* and *The Wept of Wish-ton-Wish*, which dealt with colonial New England and King Philip's War, places and events that he had not known first-hand. For them he collected material and worked up his subject—somewhat in the manner to be used by Zola for his documentary novels. The creative spark failed to ignite, equally in the case of novels based on events too remote and those too near.

His interest in the immediate past, as well as his general technique, obviously owe a great deal to the example of Scott. Although in later life it irked Cooper to be called the "American Scott," he never denied the obligation, and indeed it would have been impossible. However, there is no sedulous imitation to be traced; Scott's influence seems to have been stimulative and even competitive. For example, we have the anecdote that on reading Scott's sea story, *The Pirate*, Cooper exclaimed that he could write a better. He rightly contended that his own early life as a sailor entitled him to write more authentically of the sea. The result was *The Pilot*, undoubtedly the first authentic American sea novel, and still a fine instance of the genre. Neither Melville nor Conrad ever did anything more striking, and though the philosophical overtones of a *Nigger of the Narcissus* or a

Moby Dick are absent in Cooper's novel, it is doubtful if any other sea story surpasses it for fidelity to the peculiar argot of the sea and a certain vast beauty and grandeur in description.

His attitude toward Scott shows also his formal opinion of historical faithfulness in fiction. Once, in Paris, he was asked what he thought of Walter Scott, and whether he considered *Ivanhoe* an "indifferent" book. "A little surprised at such a question," he says, "I told my litterateur that *Ivanhoe* appeared to me to be very unequal, the first half being incomparably the best, but that as a whole I thought it stood quite at the head of the particular sort of romance to which it belonged. *The Antiquary* and *Guy Mannering*, for instance, were both much nearer perfection, and on the whole I thought both better books; but *Ivanhoe*, especially at its commencement, was a noble poem. But did I not condemn the want of historical truth in its pictures? I did not consider *Ivanhoe* as intended to be history; it was a work of the imagination, in which all the fidelity that was requisite was enough to be probable and natural, and that requisite I thought it possessed in an eminent degree. . . . Nothing could *seem* more true than Scott's pictures."

Whatever may be said in detraction of *The Last of the Mohicans*, *The Pathfinder* and *The Deerslayer*, it cannot be denied that they are faithful to probability in the broadest sense. But in a more restricted sense, we would quarrel with Cooper's contention that Scott's novels "seem" true; they, like Cooper's, have the immediate effect of artificiality because of their unmitigated romanticism, their inflated rhetoric and their convention of a two-dimensional quality in the essential characterizations. It is upon the large sweep of canvas that Scott and Cooper were verisimilitudinarian, and by reason of this we can still grant them some pretensions to realism.

Still, enough credit has scarcely been allowed Cooper for the frequently penetrating psychological analysis bestowed upon his characters. Of all his novels, *Lionel Lincoln* shows the greatest depth of insight and a seriousness of interpretation lacking in the better known works. It may be said that this novel is a precursor of the many studies of morbidity in the New England temperament, brought to a higher degree of development by Hawthorne, Miss Jewett, Mrs. Freeman and Edith Wharton. In many respects it is the best of Cooper's novels, despite its melodrama and overweighted historical intention. In any case, it was the first novel about the American Revolution to deal accurately and impartially with that upheaval, and it is to Cooper's credit that he was able to take an objective stand on an issue that was obviously close to his heart.

The book's gloominess militated against its initial success with the public that had recently devoured the fresh romances of *The Spy*, *The Pioneers* and *The Pilot*. His readers could not assimilate the many forbidding characteristics of a work which deals with a hereditary strain of insanity, a double infidelity and an idiot bastard, and which displays an Elizabethan freedom of expression throughout. Besides, the historical episodes and the story proper are not fused with uniform success. In spite of this drawback, the novel stands out clearly as one of Cooper's great achievements. If it were only for the character of Polwarth, *Lionel Lincoln* would head the Cooper list; for in this redoubtable gourmand we have a full-size and lifelike figure, surpassing even Natty Bumppo in fidelity to life. He speaks with an authentic wit and aplomb reminiscent of Congreve and Sheridan. As an instance, on an evening when Polwarth and Lionel are rowing across Naragasket Bay with the ill-fated Lexington expedition of General Gage, Polwarth delivers himself of the following whimsical sentiments:

" 'There are moments when I could fancy the life of a sailor,' he said, leaning indolently back, and playing with one hand in the water. 'This pulling about in boats is easy work, and must be capital assistance for heavy digestion, inasmuch as it furnishes air with as little violent exercise as may be. Your marine should lead a merry life of it!'

" 'They are said to murmur at the clashing of their duties with those of the sea-officers,' said Lionel; 'and I have often heard them complain of a want of room to make use of their legs.'

" 'Humph!' ejaculated Polwarth; 'the leg is a part of a man for which I see less actual necessity than for any other portion of his frame. I often think there has been a sad mistake in the formation of the animal; as, for instance, one can be a very good waterman, as you see, without legs—a good fiddler, a first-rate tailor, a lawyer, a doctor, a parson, a very tolerable cook, and, in short, anything but a dancing-master. I see no use in a leg, unless it be to have the gout; at any rate, a leg of twelve inches is as good as one a mile long, and the saving might be appropriated to the nobler parts of the animal, such as the brain and the stomach.' "

Polwarth goes on to rhapsodize about Agnes Danforth, with whom he is in love: " 'Ah! she is a girl of a million! her very acids are sweet! the spices were not forgotten when the dough of her composition was mixed; would that she were here—five minutes of moonshine to a man in love is worth a whole summer of a broiling sun; 'twould be a master-stroke to entice her into one of our picturesque marches; your partisan is the man to take everything by surprise—women and fortifications! Where now are your companies of the line; your artillery and dragoons; your engineers and staff? nightcapped and snoring to a man, while we enjoy here the very dessert of existence—I wish I could hear a nightingale.' "

If the Falstaffian Polwarth supplies the humor, Ralph, the demonic old man whose ubiquitous presence dominates the tale, serves as the rigorous New England conscience of the protagonists. He is possessed of an unsleeping moral sense, and through it Cooper manages to convey an unexpected preoccupation with problems of good and evil. As Ralph says, " 'The propensities of the mind, in its infancy and in its maturity, are but a span apart; the amount of human knowledge is but to know how much we are under the dominion of our passions; and he who has learned by experience how to smother the volcano, and he who never felt its fires, are surely fit associates.' " The problem faced by the aged Ralph is how to reconcile the results of his youthful passions and their evil consequences for his son Lionel. Hence, in this novel we have the first fictional study of the effects of ancestral sin, familiar now as almost obsessive among New England novelists.

Though Lionel is shown as a healthy individual, a young British Major but a Bostonian by birth, the ancestral taint sometimes comes to the fore; and Cooper is able to delve into it with much pre-Freudian accuracy. Lionel's schizophrenia is perfectly apparent in such a description as this: "Perhaps there was something a little romantic, if not diseased, in the mind of Lionel that caused him to derive a secret pleasure from the hidden movements he contemplated. He was certainly not entirely free from a touch of that melancholy and morbid humor which has been mentioned as the characteristic of his race, nor did he always feel the less happy because he was a little miserable. However, either by his activity of intellect or that excellent training in life he had undergone, by being required to act early for himself, he had so far succeeded in quelling the evil spirit within him, as to render its influence quite imperceptible to others, and nearly to himself."

There are abundant evidences of Cooper's descriptive power and narrative generalship throughout. His picture of the opening shots fired at the Battle of Concord is masterly. "The columns opened for the sake of ease, and each man was permitted to consult his own convenience, provided he preserved his appointed situation, and kept even pace with his comrades. In this manner the detachment advanced swiftly, a general silence pervading the whole, as the spirits of the men settled into that deep sobriety which denotes much earnestness of purpose. At first, the whole country appeared buried in a general sleep; but as they proceeded, the barking of dogs, and the tread of the soldiery, drew the inhabitants of the farmhouses to their windows, who gazed in mute wonder at the passing spectacle, across which the mellow light of the moon cast a glow of brilliancy. Lionel had turned his head from studying the surprise depicted in the faces of the members of one of these disturbed families, when the deep tones of a distant church bell came sweeping down the valley in which they marched, ringing peal on peal, in the quick, spirit-stirring sounds of an alarm. The men raised their heads in wondering attention, as they advanced; but it was not long before the reports of firearms were heard echoing among the hills, and bell began to answer bell in every direction, until the sounds blended with the murmurs of the night air, or were lost in the distance. The whole country was now filled with every organ of sound that the means of the people furnished, or their ingenuity could devise, to call the population to arms. Fires blazed along the heights, the bellowing of the conches and horns mingled with the rattling of the muskets and the varied tones of the bells, while the swift clattering of horses' hoofs began to be heard, as if their riders were dashing furiously along the flanks of the party."

Nothing could be more effective than the use of contrast consistently throughout the novel, a juxtaposition exemplified most forcibly in the scene where the idiot, Job Pray, lies a victim both of starvation and smallpox, set against the blazing extravagance of Province House where Gage, Clinton and Burgoyne are banqueting. *Lionel Lincoln* deserves to be better known; it displays a maturity superior to any other American novel published prior to its time.

II

Of recent years, in fact since the re-publication (1928) of the *Gleanings in Europe* series, edited by Robert E. Spiller, Cooper's extraordinary capabilities as an amateur sociologist have begun to receive the attention they merit. Where, in his art, he failed to achieve the amalgamation of these social observations with story proper, he succeeded brilliantly in his travel sketches. They are undoubtedly the most penetrating analyses of customs, politics and theories of government which the time produced; many of them have special relevance for us today. When other men of letters in America were content to accept the patronizing attitude of England as regards their achievements in government and the arts, Cooper was a staunch and sometimes violent partisan for democratic culture. The *Gleanings in Europe* letters indicate how warmly he loved the Jeffersonian ideals which, even in his lifetime, were giving way to oligarchical and authoritarian methodology in both political and esthetic fields. The concepts of the Revolution were already breaking down, Cooper saw, and he spent the latter half of his life attempting to revivify them. This not only cost him most of the public favor he had previously enjoyed, but did irreparable harm to his art. *The Deerslayer* and *The Pathfinder* only excepted, all the novels from *The Bravo* to his last, *The Ways of the Hour*, suffered from the vigor of his didactic purpose. There is never a fusion of character and incident with thesis and program. Cooper failed, as our militant propaganda novelists of the 1930's failed, whenever he tried to unite fiction and doctrinaire exposition.

The Heidenmauer frankly states its didactic intention. "Our object has been to show the reluctant manner in which the mind of man abandons old, and receives new, impressions." From the publication of this novel until the close of his life, Cooper was far more interested in assuming the mantle of prophet and teacher than in creating fiction. His observations in Europe convinced him that the dangers of the aristocratic tradition were insidious and that the imitation of Continental manners by Americans was likely to negate the efforts of the egalitarian party that formed the early democracy. The social concepts of America and Europe must first be clearly defined, then kept entirely separate. He conceived it his duty to do this for his countrymen, at the same time that he spoke to Europe in defense of democratic principles. He called for a militant nationalism, seeing that the new world was still subservient to the old. "The practise of deferring to foreign opinion," he said, "is dangerous to the institutions of the country."

Though Cooper was an ardent democrat, he was far from holding that "all men are created equal."[1] In fact, he often showed himself to be intolerant of the "vulgarians of taste" and in general of the common run of humanity. He always required that he be considered an "American gentleman" as well as a democrat. Here is his definition of republican government: "All that democracy means is as equal a participation in rights as is practicable; and to pretend that social equality is a condition of popular institutions, is to assume that the latter are destruc-

---

[1] In this connection, Lounsbury acutely observes, "He was an aristocrat in feeling, and a democrat by conviction."

tive of civilization, for, as nothing is more self-evident than the impossibility of raising all men to the highest standards of tastes and refinement, the alternative would be to reduce the entire community to the lowest."

Thus, in some sense, Cooper was effective in shaping not only the form of the romance, and that taste which called it forth, but the general American attitude toward American institutions. The innumerable polemics in which he engaged during the last part of his life made him at once the feared and execrated defender of revolutionary ideals. While Irving and Hawthorne dabbled very slightly in these matters, Cooper stopped nowhere short of the limit. Irving's urbane comments on English life and his gentle contrasting of it with American, Hawthorne's quiet absorption in moral dubieties through a shadowy, half-timid symbolism, were not Cooper's method. When he thought something, he stated it flatly, with an aggressiveness most readers mistook for truculence. For him the best defense was a savage offense. In the polite literary climate where Irving, Halleck and Paulding basked, this was hardly tolerated. Cooper became one of the most maligned men of his time. The loss of his public, together with the sense of being misunderstood, was reflected in the dry, argumentative productions of his later years. Such novels as *Satanstoe* and the other Littlepage chronicles, and *The Crater* and *Afloat and Ashore* abound with forthright essays in no way assimilated in the fictional fabric; and this inordinate sermonizing probably did as much as anything to alienate his readers; it would have done so, no doubt, even if its subject matter had been more generally acceptable.

Yet by dint of indefatigable repetition, Cooper made his opinions tell. Libel actions brought by him against newspapers were invariably won. His criticism of American institutions has been borne out, though most of his own generation regarded him until the end as a wrong-headed, self-constituted Jeremiah. Actually, he was better informed and shrewder than any other social critic of his time, as is amply proven by his voluminous essays, from *Notions of the Americans* to *The American Democrat*. His prophecies regarding the population of the United States fifty years after his day were fulfilled almost to the letter. In reference to slavery, he showed himself possessed of ultimate judgment: "The time must come when American slavery shall cease, and when that day shall arrive (unless early and effectual means are devised to obviate it), two races will exist in the same region, whose feelings will be embittered by inextinguishable hatred, and who carry, on their faces, the respective stamps of their factions. The struggle that will follow will necessarily be a war of extermination. The evil day may be delayed, but can scarcely be averted." However romantic Cooper may have been as an artist, as a social observer he was certainly the sternest realist of his generation.

III

That there is much genuine poetry in Cooper, together with a fully developed consciousness of the poetic effects to be obtained in the novel, can easily be demonstrated. The two most "poetic" of the thirty-three novels are *The Prairie* and *The Water-Witch*. Stylistically, *The Prairie* is probably the finest of them all. For felicity of invention and whimsical fantasy *The Water-Witch* is easily its peer; but in the former there is a sustained atmosphere of brooding beauty and a relation of incident and character to background that foreshadows the work of the English bucolic novelists. Cooper's usual practice of opening a novel with the appearance of a figure moving in a landscape was followed scrupulously by Hardy. The Cooper style, at its best, is by no means inferior to that of George Eliot. Besides, Cooper is always able to evoke the unusual image, to plan scenes that stick in the memory, and to do this with a very fine economy of means. Early in *The Prairie*, Leatherstocking is introduced to the party of emigrants: "The sun had fallen below the crest of the nearest wave of the prairie, leaving the usual rich and glowing train on its track. In the center of this flood of fiery light a human form appeared, drawn against the gilded background as distinctly, and seeming as palpable, as though it would come within the grasp of any extended hand. The figure was colossal;

the attitude musing and melancholy; and the situation directly in the route of the travellers. But imbedded, as it was, in its setting of garish light, it was impossible to distinguish its just proportions or true character."

Cooper's prose can be finely balanced and almost sensuous; in *The Prairie* it most often is. "It was now in the first watch of the night; and the pale, quivering, and deceptive light from a new moon was playing over the endless waves of the prairie, tipping the swells with gleams of brightness and leaving the interval land in deep shadow. Accustomed to scenes of solitude like the present, the old man, as he left the encampment, proceeded alone into the waste, like a bold vessel leaving its haven to enter on the trackless field of the ocean."

Throughout this novel, Leatherstocking now an old man, is presented with moving fidelity and appositeness. The closing scenes contain probably the most powerful and restrained writing to be found in Cooper. Leatherstocking "had hunted with the tribe in the spring, and even throughout most of the summer; when his limbs suddenly refused to perform their customary offices. A sympathizing weakness took possession of all his faculties; and the Pawnees believed that they were going to lose, in this unexpected manner, a sage and counsellor whom they had begun both to love and respect. But, as we have already said, the immortal occupant seemed unwilling to desert its tenement. The lamp of life flickered, without becoming extinguished." As the old man lies on his deathbed, he says to his friend Middleton, " 'I am at the close of many weary days, but there is not one among them all that I could wish to overlook. I remember you, with the whole of your company; ay, and your gran'ther, that went before you. I am glad that you have come back upon these plains, for I had need of one who speaks the English, since little faith can be put in the traders of these regions. Will you do a favor to an old and dying man?'

" 'Name it,' said Middleton; 'it shall be done.'

" 'It is a far journey to send such trifles,' resumed the old man, who spoke at short intervals, as strength and breath permitted; 'a far and weary journey is the same; but kindnesses and friendships are things not to be forgotten. There is a settlement among the Otsego hills—'

" 'I know the place,' interrupted Middleton, observing that he spoke with increasing difficulty; 'proceed to tell me what you would have done.' "

He is told to send the old hunter's rifle, pouch and horn for the sake of love to the Otsego settlement (a whimsical notion, for this was Cooper's own home); and then there is another of those brilliant scenes in which not only this novel but all of Cooper's abound.

"The trapper had remained nearly motionless for an hour. His eyes alone had occasionally opened and shut. When opened, his gaze seemed fastened on the clouds which hung around the western horizon, reflecting the bright colors, and giving form and loveliness to the glorious tints of the American sunset. The hour —the calm beauty of the season—the occasion, all conspired to fill the spectators with solemn awe. Suddenly, while musing on the remarkable position in which he was placed, Middleton felt the hand which he held grasp his own with incredible power, and the old man, supported on either side by his friends, rose upright to his feet. For a moment he looked about him, as if to invite all in presence to listen (the lingering remnant of human frailty), and then, with a fine military elevation of the head, and with a voice that might be heard in every part of that numerous assembly, he pronounced the word—

" 'Here!' "

So, with something of a flourish, closes the career of Natty Bumppo, certainly one of the great creations of American fiction. Not Hawthorne, Irving, Poe or Brown approached this achievement. Of all the "shapers," Cooper alone entered that realm of the creative imagination in which a whole people unconsciously owns a small share. For what he lacked in concentration of effect, artistic purpose and purely technical ability, Cooper easily made up in sheer imaginative power. It was not for nothing that whole generations have kept his work alive and gone on to imitate him to the last installment of our popular magazines.

THE ROMANTIC NOVEL
Coda

IF COOPER was the first romantic novelist in America, he was also the greatest, and none of his successors has managed to extend the frontiers of the sentimental or adventure novel beyond what had been done in the "Leatherstocking Tales." There have been innumerable romancers, and a few of them contributed new material or treated Cooper's own themes individually; and some of their books are undoubtedly worth reading. By and large, it might be said that the American imagination has been most fruitful in the romantic field; but it has not been most incisive there. The romantic novel on all its levels, the cheapest and most illiterate to the more respectable and technically competent, has been numerically by far the predominant type of our fiction. In Europe, at about the time Scott ceased writing, the romantic imagination was on the wane, to be followed at once by an era of realism; on this side of the Atlantic romanticism continued to flourish for nearly half a century. As Carl Van Doren has pointed out, this may have been due to the existence of a vast frontier in which the mysterious and unknown were still to be encountered. Our literary artists could still look to the horizon and realize that there were realms of the imagination not yet explored. But of course even after the conquest of all the frontiers, romance continued to hold sway. And it will undoubtedly continue to do so on the lower levels of men's imagination. As long as there is a public that wishes to escape the reality of the mundane life it knows, there will be stories written to assist that escape.

And yet romantic fiction of the better sort need by no means offer an "escape from reality." Cooper's novels were based on solid fact, and the interpretation of reality as he conceived it gave his pictures their aura of romance. *The Pathfinder* might not, in real life, have been so willing to renounce the girl he loved; but he certainly would have been the kind of woodsman Cooper made him. The superimposition upon pragmatic conditions of an ideal behavior is the usual rational of good romance. In bad romantic fiction we usually have only the ideal behavior.

"Popular fiction," the term used nowadays to denote this type of writing, is itself a revealing phrase. The fiction is usually popular in direct ratio to its dramatic idealization of life; and frequently the least intense imagination is capable of creating it. But this need not be the case; it has happened more than once that a first-rate creative talent has been joined to a temperament incapable of clinical views. Its product is romantic fiction of respectable caliber.

In William Gilmore Simms's *The Yamasee* (1835), for example, there is a wealth of excellently conceived documentation, overlaid with a plot reminiscent of *The Last of the Mohicans*. It is a story of the Yamasee Indian uprising against the white settlers of Charleston in 1715; and its admirable background of tribal customs, chants and dances encompasses a whole mythology. Simms had made himself familiar with the frontier Indian, probably even more thoroughly than had Cooper, and his filling-in of the scenes with authentic lore gave his novel a verity which supported its narrative and made it a memorable work of romance.

The Indian was one of the great themes for our early romantic novel; and as Cooper had demonstrated, the sea was another. *The Water-Witch, The Pilot, Afloat and Ashore,* all remain the best of their genre; but in 1840 another story-teller appeared with *Two Years Before the Mast,* to prove that there was ample room for further interpretation. Richard Henry Dana had made the voyage he described in this book, and it was essentially a transcript from his own experience, idealized to the extent that it could be taken as a traveler's projection of desirable adventure. So much so that it is supposed to have been the cause of Herman Melville's taking to the sea. It has the breadth and intensity of a novel, and a sturdy kind of realism to serve as a solid base for the essentially romantic chronicle of events. *Two Years Before the Mast* readily takes its place as a classic among narratives of the sea after Cooper and Melville.

As an example of the novel dealing sentimentally with the

Negro, one would first cite *Uncle Tom's Cabin* (1852) by that inveterate sentimentalist, Harriet Beecher Stowe. This work probably had the most sensational reception and the greatest practical influence of any novel ever published. It sold into the millions and was read throughout the world. It became, in fact, a part of American folklore, and its Topsy, Little Eva, Simon Legree and Uncle Tom are characters that have left the realm of literature and entered the domain of folk inheritance. Here again a first-rate imagination, crippled by sentimentality, was nevertheless stirred deeply enough to create a memorable tract. The idealized picture of the old plantation, and the rendering of a system of racial tyranny, at once caught the fancy of the popular mind. But it was as a topical story that the novel had its success; and today the book lives only as a memory, as the womb from which sprang a bit of folklore.

Interest in the events of other ages, previously rewarded by the literature of history, called forth in the nineteenth century fictional recreations. From the beginning these were romantic in character. It is possible to write historical novels unglazed by sentimentality, as Flaubert's *Salammbo* shows, but in America at least, from the earliest to the latest, such novels seem to have existed largely for the sake of romanticizing the past. From *Ben Hur* (1884) to *Anthony Adverse* and *Gone with the Wind*, these "historical novels" have been grandiose, full-blown, and heavily overwrought with idealization. As literature, they fall between the stools of history and fiction. But they continue to be written, and indeed form the greatest proportion of romantic novels today. In the last twenty years or so there has been an increasingly noticeable tendency among writers of romance to recreate the past with a measure of sobriety. Kenneth Roberts' series of novels about the American Revolution, and particularly his *Northwest Passage*, is among the most noteworthy, and lively plot interest is supplemented by a good deal of sound scholarship in the customs and obscure forces at work in the era. Walter D. Edmonds' historical novels, like *Rome Haul*, have a similar basis of fact, glazed with romance. Earlier than either of these novelists, Joseph Hergesheimer, in *Java Head, Balisand* and other historical romances, undertook to recreate sections of the American past, with interesting results. The popularity of these books paved the way for the deluge of such fiction as has come to be one of the staples of each publishing season. On a somewhat higher level, and of a different genre, the verse novel, like Stephen Vincent Benet's *John Brown's Body*, is another type of historical romance with justifiable pretensions to serious critical attention.

By and large, however, romantic fiction in America has been fanciful, extravagant and unreal; it appeals to our love of the chimerical; it is the stuff of which Hollywood fables are made. And until our mass culture arrives at a condition of greater enlightenment, there is no doubt but that novels filled with surprising incident, adventure and a set of imposed idealizations will constitute the principal fare of the "average reader."

APOCALYPTICS

CHARLES BROCKDEN BROWN

THE HISTORY of the novel in America dates from 1798, the year in which Charles Brockden Brown published *Wieland*. In the century and a half that has elapsed, the novel has undergone Protean transformations; it has found new shapes and explored ever-wider ranges of human experience; it has taken various directions and appeared often to have reached limits in depth and breadth; but it continues to flourish and to find variations hitherto unexpected. It has long since severed the umbilical tie that held it to England, yet it has absorbed continuously from Europe without losing its own special qualities. The perfectly indigenous American novel has not, of course, been written and never can be. But there is a sense in which the "American novel" is as distinct and separable an entity as the "Russian novel" or the "French novel."

This could not have been said in Brockden Brown's time. Even after his work was done, and after Irving and Cooper had done theirs, the American novel had not come entirely into existence, although it was showing unmistakable signs of life. But the history of the novel in America is something different from the "American novel," and Brown's is the first name to be encountered in that history. There had been other romancers before him, but no one who was, first and last, a writer; and no novelist whose work is still read today. *Wieland* may not be a great reading experience, but it is a novel that continues to be read, and it is the first novel published by an American, possessing qualities which recommend it to a serious critical consideration.

Brown has this further distinction: he was the shaper of a tradition which affected writers greater than he and which continues today to fructify some of our most serious fiction. It is no accident that we are able to trace back to him an apocalyptical vision, culminating in the novels of William Faulkner, which has been a preoccupation of the American imagination from *Wieland* to *Absalom, Absalom!* It is worthwhile to search for the causes of this preoccupation, an apparent "sport" in the development of American fiction yet in reality an integral part of the American creative imagination equally nourished by a dark strain in our life and by the private tendencies of men of genius able to express it. In Brown we discover foreshadowed all the demonic, macabre or apocalyptic idiosyncrasies of what, to employ an inexact but useful term, amounts to a school in the American novel.

Twenty years after the Revolution, the American republic had become sufficiently self-conscious and self-confident to launch a tentative literature. Without doubt its beginnings were imitative, timid, and on the whole, inauspicious. It so happened that Brown was the man, selected by a coalition of fortuitous circumstances, to become the first professional novelist. Born of Quaker parents, he was a sickly child who exhibited all the characteristics of introversion; almost from infancy he avoided company, shut himself up with books and spent his time in pleasant day-dreaming. His family was well off enough to send him to the best tutor in Philadelphia, Robert Proud, who is remembered today as a particularly liberal and "advanced" pedagogue. Brown's father intended him for the law, and the young man actually practiced at the Bar for a brief time, but he had already formed strong intentions to earn a living by writing, and as soon as possible he set about his life career. His first important work, published when he was twenty-six, was a dialogue on the Rights of Women. This broadside, *Alcuin*, (1797), shows evidences of its author's youth as well as a certain indebtedness to the explosive new ideals of the French Revolution. The alarm with which such views was greeted can be detected in Prescott's remarks, written a generation later: "It exhibits the crude and fanciful speculations of a theorist who, in his dreams of optimism, charges exclusively on human institutions the imperfections necessarily incident to human nature." Among other things, the young man called for equal suffrage, more justice and greater educational opportunities for women: modest enough demands, one would think. At any rate, on the authority of Prescott, *Alcuin* "made little impression on the public; it found few purchasers, and made, it may be presumed, still fewer converts."

This tendency toward liberalism vanished henceforth from Brown's writings; he became an ardent Federalist, and within a few years, upon founding *The Literary Magazine and American Register*, could make the following eminently "safe" announcement: "In an age like this, when the foundations of religion and morality have been so boldly attacked, it seems necessary, in announcing a work of this nature, to be particularly explicit as to the path which the editor means to pursue. He, therefore, avows himself to be, without equivocation or reserve, the ardent friend and the willing champion of the Christian religion. Christian piety he reveres as the highest excellence of human beings; and the amplest reward he can seek for his labor is the consciousness of having in some degree, however inconsiderable, contributed to recommend the practice of religious duties. As in the conduct of this work a supreme regard will be paid to the interests of religion and morality, he will scrupulously guard against all that dishonors and impairs that principle. Everything that savors of indelicacy and licentiousness will be rigorously proscribed. His poetical pieces may be dull, but they shall at least be free from voluptuousness or sensuality; and his prose, whether seconded or not by genius and knowledge, shall scrupulously aim at the promotion of public and private virtue."

Perhaps he found it necessary to make these avowals, with the consciousness of the bloody sensationalism of *Wieland* and *Ormond* still upon him. It must be remembered, however, that all of Brown's novels were written in his youth; that they were produced within a period of only three or four years, and that his interest in them had largely died by the time he was thirty. In 1803 he wrote, "I am far from wishing that my readers should judge of my exertions by my former ones. I have written much, but take much blame to myself for something which I have written and take no praise for anything. I should enjoy a larger share of my own respect, at the present moment, if nothing had ever flowed from my pen, the production of which could be traced to me. A variety of causes induce me to form such a wish, but I am particularly influenced by the consideration that time can scarcely fail of enlarging and refining the powers of a man; while the world is sure to judge of his capabilities and principles at fifty by what he has written at fifteen."

It is remarkable that in his twenties Brown was capable of turning out six long novels, at a white heat of inspiration, which emerge from the mass of contemporary romances and which possess an individuality and a kind of tortured strength that carries over with unquestionable power and firmness even to a generation such as ours. One of them at least (*Arthur Mervyn*) is as good as anything of the same type written anywhere, and all of them contain passages that are unequaled in our literature for the unusual effects at which they aim. Brown himself may have wished to repudiate them, but their effect on the work of Poe, Hawthorne, Melville, Simms, Hearn, Bierce and Faulkner has produced one of the important, if narrow, currents of American literature.

Two immediate circumstances conspired to bring about the creation of the Brown novels. The first was Brown's peculiar sort of morbidity in temperament. A depression of spirits suffered all his life probably had its origin in his lifelong consumption. There are numerous references to it throughout his letters and journals. In one place he asks, "When have I known that lightness and vivacity of mind which the divine flow of health, even in calamity, produces in some men, and would produce in me, no doubt; at least, when not soured by misfortune? Never; scarcely ever; not longer than an half-hour at a time, since I have called myself a man." Also he was extraordinarily sensitive to personal rebuffs, imagining them where they were not intended, and prone to self-reviling upon very little provocation. In this connection, a remarkably enlightening letter to a friend, subsequently his biographer, has been discovered by the Historical Society of Pennsylvania:

Philadelphia, Jan'y 1, 1798.

To William Dunlap, Care of Dunlap & Judah, Pearl St., New York.

It is nearly twelve months since I parted from you. I believe I have not written to you nor you written to me since. How shall I account for your silence? The task is an easy one. I was not an object of sufficient importance to justify the trouble. My infirmities & follies were too rooted for you to hope their cure. . . . I lived with you six months. During that time you, no doubt, scrutinized my conduct & character with accuracy. You must have formed some conclusions respecting me, but you thought proper to be silent respecting them. . . . I revere your rectitude, my friend, in as great a degree as I detest my own imbecility: but it is allowable for me to question the propriety of your decision.

Communication, it appears to me, was your duty. Whatever was my depravity, it did not sink me below deserving a mere verbal effort for my restoration. . . .

I think upon the life of last winter with self-loathing almost insupportable. Alas! my friend, few consolations of a self-approving mind have fallen to my lot. . . . I am sometimes apt to think that few human beings have drunk so deeply of the cup of self-abhorrence as I have. . . . As I am, you despise me. I shall die, as I have lived, a victim to perverse and incurable habits. My progress in knowledge has enlightened my judgment, without adding to my power. . . .

C. B. BROWN

It is clear, though, that such moods were the result only of an insane hyper-sensitivity. Brown, according to all testimony, was a perfectly normal person in all outward respects—a model of moral rectitude, an affectionate husband and father, and an indefatigable worker. Nevertheless he was constantly preoccupied with morbid fancies, saw death not far off, and perhaps consciously, during his youth, paraded the "melancholia" then fashionable in some circles.

This habit of mind served to make Brown especially susceptible to the spell of the "Gothic" romance which at about this time suddenly found favor in Europe. This is the second contingency that prompted the creation of *Wieland* and the other novels. *Caleb Williams, The Monk, The Mysteries of Udolpho* and *The Castle of Otranto*, all coming within a few years, made a powerful impression on him. The extravagant melodrama and pseudo mystery with which they abound, their stage properties of dismal corridors, unmentionable crimes, malignant spirits, dank tarns and haunted castles stimulated his imagination to an unusual degree. He set himself to the creation of a Gothic novel that would put America on the literary map with a vengeance, and in *Wieland* very nearly succeeded. In his own opinion, however, he was not successful. After the book had appeared he modestly wrote, "When a mental comparison is made between this and the mass of novels, I am inclined to be pleased with my own production. But when the objects of comparison are changed, and I revolve the transcendant merits of *Caleb Williams*, my pleasure is diminished, and is preserved from a total extinction only by the reflection that this performance is the first." So he went on, in *Ormond*, to cap the climax with a remarkably apt imitation of Godwin's novel. The plot and manner of *Ormond* are sufficiently Godwinian, but it is the worst of Brown's works in this vein and only a little better than his last two novels, written in a different tradition: *Clara Howard* and *Jane Talbot*—oppressively sentimental tales, tedious almost beyond belief.

But coming from an American, *Wieland* was, at least, fresh and powerful; and, for all its laborious prose, highfalutin phraseology, redundant and turgid rhetoric, not lacking in drama or even in power of characterization. It has also a mordant analytical quality in its delineation of fanatic tendencies among the outlandish protagonists, better developed in the third novel, *Arthur Mervyn*. The plot of *Wieland* revolves about ventriloquism, then in vogue, and its horrors result from the immoral use of his ventriloquist powers by the demonic practical joker, Carwin. Wieland is made to murder his wife and family at the bidding of disembodied voices, and through several hundred pages of spiritual anguish and bloody violence, the secret of Carwin's "joke" is withheld. To say the least, the denouement when it comes is something of a let-down. However, for the readers of Brown's time, ventriloquism, second sight, mesmerism and like fake "sciences" were held in some esteem. No doubt *Wieland* seemed based on sound doctrine.

What interest us here is not the extravagance of Brown's subject matter, but his manner, which, especially in *Wieland* but
also in *Arthur Mervyn* and *Edgar Huntly*, possessed germinative
qualities for his successors. Compare, for example, the general
tone and style of Poe's "The Case of M. Valdemar" with whole
passages in *Wieland*, like this: "Meanwhile, the disease thus wonderfully generated betrayed more terrible symptoms. Fever and
delirium terminated in lethargic slumber, which, in the course of
two hours, gave place to death; yet not till insupportable exhala-
tions and crawling putrefaction had driven from his chamber and
the house everyone whom their duty did not detain. Such was the
end of my father."

Poe's dramatic manipulation and subject matter in many of
the *Tales of the Grotesque and Arabesque* bear unmistakable
similarity to *Wieland*. Here is the description of Wieland's final
attack on his wife: "She returned with a light; I led the way to
the chamber; she looked round her; she lifted the curtain of the
bed; she saw nothing. At length she fixed inquiring eyes upon me.
The light now enabled her to discover in my visage what darkness had hitherto concealed . . . she said in a tremulous voice,
'Wieland! you are not well; what ails you? Can I do nothing for
you?' That accents and looks so winning should disarm me of
my resolution, was to be expected. My thoughts were thrown
anew into anarchy. I spread my hand before my eyes, that I
might not see her, and answered only by groans. . . . 'My friend!
my soul's friend! tell me thy cause of grief. Do I not merit to
partake with thee in thy cares? Am I not thy wife?'

"This was too much. I broke from her embrace. . . . 'I brought
thee hither to fulfill a divine command. I am appointed thy de-
stroyer, and destroy thee I must.' Saying this, I seized her wrists.
She shrieked aloud, and endeavored to free herself from my
grasp; but her efforts were in vain. . . . Till her breath was
stopped she shrieked for help—for mercy. When she could
speak no longer, her gestures, her looks, appealed to my compassion. My accursed hand was irresolute and tremulous. I meant
thy death to be sudden, thy struggles to be brief. Alas! my heart
was infirm; my resolves mutable. Thrice I slackened my grasp,

and life kept its hold, though in the midst of pangs. Her eyeballs started from their sockets. Grimness and distortion took place of all that used to bewitch me into transport, and subdue me into reverence. . . . This was a moment of triumph. Thus had I successfully subdued the stubbornness of human passions; the victim which had been demanded was given; the deed was done past recall."

The macabre love-in-death themes ("Ligeia," "Morella") that fascinated Poe are also fully foreshadowed. After murdering his wife, Wieland experiences transports very similar to those of Poe's pathological heroes. "I lifted the corpse in my arms and laid it on the bed. I gazed upon it with delight. Such was the elation of my thoughts that I even broke into laughter. I clapped my hands and exclaimed, 'It is done! My sacred duty is fulfilled. To what have I sacrificed, O my God; thy last and best gift, my wife!'. . . . I thought upon what I had done as a sacrifice to duty, and *was calm*." Poe was able to inject into equally diabolic action a quality of cold deliberation and to surround it with an aura of distorted moral earnestness quite beyond Brown's reach; but the germ evidently is here.

The following comment might very well have been written with Poe in mind: "His great object seems to be exhibit the soul in scenes of extraordinary interest. For this purpose striking and perilous situations are devised, or circumstances of strong moral excitement, a troubled conscience, partial gleams of insanity, or bodings of imaginary evil which haunt the soul, and force it into all the agonies of terror. . . . We are constantly struck with the strange contrast of over-passion and over-reasoning;"[1] but actually, it is a discussion of Brown. With some modifications, it is a comment that might equally apply to the whole school of apocalyptical writers from Brown to Thomas Wolfe.

Brown's best novel, *Arthur Mervyn*, while perhaps only a second-rate work, is an astonishing production if we take properly into account the fact that it was composed in a kind of vacuum, by a man who willed it into existence without the peculiar bene-

---

[1] W. H. Prescott, in *The Library of American Biography.*

fits of an active milieu which could both evoke and nourish it. What, can we conceive, would Flaubert have been able to do had he worked in complete spiritual isolation, a pioneer without public, confreres, or the ferment of ideas on technique and subject that surrounded his productive years? Brown had no props except the pale assistance of distant and unpromising predecessors like Godwin and Mrs. Radcliffe. He worked utterly alone. And yet he was able to write an *Arthur Mervyn*, a novel that certainly surpasses most of its models and may be favorably compared with almost any novel of its genre in Europe.

The incidental theme of *Arthur Mervyn*, a plague of yellow fever which struck Philadelphia in 1793, brings up comparisons with DeFoe's account of a similar pestilence in London; but the identities go somewhat deeper than this. The dry and factual tone of DeFoe's fictions is often reflected in Brown's descriptions, as well as the overwhelming succession of repetitious incident. The air of improvisation lies upon *Arthur Mervyn* as it does upon *Roxana* or *Moll Flanders,* and there is not a little of the picaresque about Mervyn's peripatetic, hairbreadth adventures.

Throughout this novel there are flashes of psychological penetration that anticipate the later and more accomplished novelists. To his contemporaries Brown was, in fact, noted for profundity, most of which seems to us now only the result of perhaps intentional obscurantism. Even several decades after his death our criticism was unequal to plumbing these muddy depths. Prescott, for example, believed that, "Like the productions of Coleridge, or Wordsworth, (Brown's) seem to rely on deeper sensibilities than most men possess, and tax the reasoning powers more severely than is agreeable to readers who resort to works of fiction only as an epicurean indulgence." [2] But there are passages of insight such as that in which Mervyn tells of Betty Lawrence's attitude toward him: "Me she hated, because she was conscious of having injured me, because she knew that I held her in contempt, and because I had detected her in an illicit intercourse with

---

[2] *Op. cit.*

the son of a neighbor." Or take this excerpt from the confession of the suicidal Welbeck: "One evening, as I traversed the bank of the creek, these dismal meditations were uncommonly intense. They at length terminated in a resolution to throw myself in the stream. The first impulse was to rush instantly to my death; but the remembrance of papers, lying at my lodgings, which might unfold more than I desired to the curiosity of survivors, induced me to postpone this catastrophe till the next morning.

"My purpose being formed, *I found my heart lightened of its usual weight. By you it will be thought strange, but it is nevertheless true, that I derived from this new prospect not only tranquillity but cheerfulness.* I hastened home." (Italics mine.) This, in spite of its brevity and catch-as-catch-can manner, is worthy of Dostoevsky. Again, Mervyn is delineated as a wholly self-conscious agent quite aware of his psychological peculiarities. "The constitution of my mind is doubtless singular and perverse; yet that opinion, perhaps, is the fruit of my ignorance. It may by no means be uncommon for men to *fashion* their conclusions in opposition to evidence and *probability*, and so as to feed their malice and subvert their happiness. Thus it was, in an eminent degree, in my case."

The principal objections to be raised against the novel are its implausibility, overwhelming employment of coincidence, and general lack of distinction in style. As an instance of fantastic improbability and lack of human significance, here is the thumbnail story of the life of a minor character, Clavering, who appears briefly and then is not heard of again (a fault evident throughout the work; characters are introduced, then summarily dropped, with inconsequential effect in *Arthur Mervyn* and all the other novels). "He gave no distinct account of his family, but stated, in loose terms, that they were residents in England, high-born and wealthy. That they had denied him the woman whom he loved and banished him to America, under penalty of death if he should dare to return, and that they had refused him all means of subsistence in a foreign land. He predicted, in his wild and declamatory way, his own death."

The overabundant surprises and twists of plot hinge almost

wholly on coincidence. Young Mervyn, after his father marries the bond-servant, Betty Lawrence, leaves the farm and goes to Philadelphia where, after sundry adventures, he encounters Welbeck, a mysterious person of great wealth. In the course of time Mervyn learns through a number of quite fortuitous accidents that Welbeck gained his wealth illegally, and that he has murdered a man. Mervyn apprehends him a few moments after the deed is committed, and Welbeck proceeds to tell the story of his life. It is an honest enough depiction of the degeneration of an essentially well-meaning man of weak will, though tinged with sentimentality and minimized in final effectiveness by melodramatic resolutions.

Brown could write good plain realism, and often does in this novel. Here is the account of Mervyn's accosting a beggarly youth sitting on a bench opposite a house about whose inmates Mervyn desires to secure information:

"I went up to him and, pointing to the house in question, asked him who lived there.

"He answered, 'Mr. Matthews.'

" 'What is his profession—his way of life?'

" 'A gentleman. He does nothing but walk about.'

" 'How long has he been married?'

" 'Married! He is not married as I know on. He never has been married. He is a bachelor.'

"This intelligence was unexpected. It made me pause to reflect whether I had not mistaken the house. This, however, seemed impossible. I renewed my questions.

" 'A bachelor, say you? Are you not mistaken?'

" 'No. It would be an odd thing if he was married. An old fellow, with one foot in the grave— Comical enough for him to *git* a *vife!*'

" 'An old man? Does he live alone? What is his family?'

" 'No, he does not live alone. He has a niece that lives with him. She is married, and her husband lives there too.'

" 'What is his name?'

" 'I don't know. I never heard it as I know on.'

" 'What is his trade?'

" 'He's a merchant; he keeps a store somewhere or other; but I don't know where.'

" 'How long has he been married?'

" 'About two years. They lost a child lately. The young woman was in a huge taking about it. They say she was quite crazy some days for the death of the child; and she is not quite out of *the dumps* yet. To be sure, the child was a sweet little thing; but they need not make such a rout about it. I'll war'n' they'll have enough of them before they die.' "

Probably the most successful single aspect of *Arthur Mervyn* is its remarkable picture of a city stricken by pestilence. Brown is here restrained and effective in his portrayal of a plague creeping across the town, of passers-by moving like ghosts along deserted streets, and a certain murky dread pervading the whole of Philadelphia. He can strike off in a scene the whole tone of the time. There is even a macabre humor (something rare in Brown) in such an episode as this: ". . . I approached a house the door of which was opened, and before which stood a vehicle, which I presently recognized to be a *hearse*.

"The driver was seated on it. I stood still to mark his visage, and to observe the course which he proposed to take. Presently a coffin, borne by two men, issued from the house. The driver was a negro; but his companions were white. Their features were marked by ferocious indifference to danger or pity. One of them, as he assisted in thrusting the coffin into the cavity prepared for it, said, 'I'll be damned if I think the poor dog was quite dead. It wasn't the *fever* that ailed him, but the sight of the girl and her mother on the floor. I wonder how they all got into that room. Whàt carried them there?'

"The other fellow surlily muttered, 'Their legs, to be sure.'

" 'And I thank them with all my heart; but, damn it, it wasn't right to put him in his coffin before the breath was fairly gone. I thought the last look he gave me told me to stay a few minutes.'

" 'Pshaw! He could not live. The sooner dead the better for him; as well as for us. Did you mark how he eyed us when we carried away his wife and daughter? I never cried in my life, since 1 was knee-high, but curse me if I ever felt in better tune for the business than just then. Hey!' continued he, looking up, and observing me standing a few paces distant, and listening to their discourse; 'what's wanted? Anybody dead?'"

Brown wrote rapidly and apparently never revised, but apart from haste and lack of respect for his medium, his conception of style placed him in the line of all apocalyptical writers from Sir Thomas Browne to Thomas Wolfe. Is it accidental that these writers invariably produce a luxuriant, involuted prose, or is there some indeterminate connection between their cast of mind, subject matter and its medium of expression? Browne, Coleridge, Melville, Poe, and in our day Faulkner and Wolfe, all formed themselves upon a style of sensuous splendor. Brockden Brown's writing is often bad because of it, but again he achieves striking effects by it. His prose is unwieldy when, instead of writing simply, "I was unhappy," he circumlocutes: "The condition of my mind was considerably remote from happiness"; or when for "I could strike a light," he writes, "by a common apparatus (tinderbox) that lay beside my bed I could instantly produce a light." On the other hand, compare such striking phrases as "His brain seemed to swell beyond its continent" and "What have I to do with that dauntless yet guiltless front? With that foolishly-confiding and obsequious, yet erect and unconquerable, spirit? Is there no means of evading your pursuit? Must I dip my hands, a second time, in blood; and dig for you a grave by the side of Watson?" with similar passages in Melville or Poe. The seed of the matter, and the pattern of the manner, in both Poe and Melville, it is not too fanciful to think, can be found in the first three novels of Brown.

Of the last three works, little need be said. *Edgar Huntly* attempted, it is true, to utilize the American Indian as a character, anticipating Cooper by a quarter of a century; but the result was unhappy. Brown's Indians are little more than animals. The framework of the novel rests upon the bizarre escapades of a sleepwalker and is entirely incredible, nor are there portraits of recognizable individuality, like Welbeck in *Arthur Mervyn*. After *Edgar Huntly* there was an interval of two years in which Brown devoted himself to journalism; *Clara Howard* was published in 1801 and *Jane Talbot* in 1804. Brown had by then regretted his earlier sensationalism, writing to his brother, "Your remarks upon the gloominess and out-of-nature incidents of 'Huntly,' if they be not just in their full extent, are doubtless such as most readers will make, which alone is a sufficient reason for dropping the doleful tone and assuming a cheerful one, or at least substituting moral causes and daily incidents in place of the prodigious or the singular. I shall not fall hereafter into that strain." But without the spur of dark deeds and that peculiar sort of morbidity which alone fired his imagination, he could not produce fiction of vitality. The final two attempts must have convinced him of this for, though he lived six years longer and wrote voluminously in his *Literary Magazine and American Register*, he produced nothing notable. Dying at thirty-nine, he had apparently said all that was in him; and it was considerable. A beginning had been made; the shape of American fiction had been set in at least one of its characteristic channels; and this was achievement of a significant order.

POE

The Terror of the Soul

A SMALL, delicate boy with somber eyes and a large head, living in Richmond in the 1820's, devoured Charles Brown's *Edgar Huntly* and *Wieland*, no doubt finding in them a peculiarly sympathetic savor. He was already familiar, too, with the Gothic tales of terror and mystery that had filtered into English literature from Germany; but to find that atmosphere of gloom and mystification transplanted to near-by Philadelphia must have set fire to his young imagination and given him the impetus to try his hand in the same genre. In the study of his foster father, young Poe became acquainted with the story of Brown's life and was given another reason for emulating his earlier countryman.[1]

If Brown was the earliest of our professional men of letters,

---

[1] Later in life Poe was to wander the same streets in which Brown had walked, the Philadelphia where the older man had composed his best work. Of that work Poe was to make a high estimate, placing it (with that of Hawthorne) above Cooper in permanent appeal. (See Poe's review of *Wyandotte*.)

Poe was to become, in the popular mind, the epitome of the writer, the very type of the man of genius living meagerly by his pen, suffering every form of trial, including that of near-starvation and contumely, misunderstood to the last, but triumphing *post mortem* in the achievement of world-wide fame and immortality. From the day when he quit West Point, every cent that he earned came by way of his writings. To a greater extent than any American, Poe may be said to have lived and died by his pen, literally dependent for his bread upon the product of his daily literary efforts. Those efforts included every form of composition, except the novel of manners, and in all of them he achieved preeminence. No other American writer has done enduring work in so many fields: poetry, fiction, criticism and philosophy; none has been so vigorously original in so many forms; and finally, though many have set out to win the attention of a majority of mankind, none has been so widely and continuously read as Poe, who, it might have been thought, addressed a small and special audience.[2]

Like Brown, Poe as a youth felt himself separated from the interests of the average boy, and with more cause. His position as an adopted son, living off the largesse of his wealthy foster father, with many of the apparent rights and privileges of a gentleman but without the actual possession of them; his tendency to bizarre attitudes in which John Allan would not support him; his propensity to daydream and to the composition of poetry— all these things tended to exacerbate a neuroticism that was congenital. Unstable emotionally, and with tendencies to extremes in conduct, Poe found himself out of step with his companions. His continual quarrels with his foster parent over money and school debts, his recurrent promises of reformation and the subsequent breaking of them, deepened the schism between himself and Allan, and finally forced him into the world on his own.

---

[2] For example, as Max Eastman has observed, Whitman celebrated the common man, wrote of things he believed would interest all, disregarded form, and his appeal today is almost wholly to the intellectual; Poe wrote exclusively of experience detached from normal life, was highly conscious of technique, and yet has been more thoroughly read than any other American author.

He was poorly equipped to fight a winning battle in the commercial world, and poetry certainly offered no means of livelihood. The publication of *Tamerlane and Other Poems* (1827) and *Al Aaraaf* (1829), as well as *Poems* (1831), proved conclusively that there was no paying market for such productions. The world seemed against him, and yet he was always conscious of superior powers and knew that one day the world would acclaim them. The inward-turning boy was proud; a mixture of humility and arrogance informed his attitude toward the society that would not give him his due.

There is something besides the traditional sense of estrangement from the world felt by sensitive adolescents in the poem of 1829, "Alone":

> From childhood's hour I have not been
> As others were—I have not seen
> As others saw—I could not bring
> My passions from a common spring—
> From the same source I have not taken
> My sorrow—I could not awaken
> My heart to joy at the same tone—
> And all I lov'd—*I* lov'd alone.
> *Then*—in my childhood—in the dawn
> Of a most stormy life—was drawn
> From ev'ry depth of good and ill
> The mystery which binds me still—
> From the torrent, or the fountain—
> From the red cliff of the mountain—
> From the sun that round me roll'd
> In its autumn tint of gold—
> From the lightning in the sky
> As it pass'd me flying by—
> From the thunder, and the storm—
> And the cloud that took the form
> (When the rest of Heaven was blue)
> Of a demon in my view.

Seldom has an obsession, largely unconscious, been given such clear acknowledgment. The sense of the poem casts an accurate and ominous chart of Poe's whole emotional life, and after we have discounted the element of posturing which inevitably figures in it, there is a strange and fearful individuality in its closing lines. The lonely boy who sometimes pretended to a mad gayety[3] and often posed as a young Southern aristocrat had a private vision of horror, unnamed and perhaps rationally unaccountable, but it was to be the touchstone of his future art.

In these same years that saw the early poems produced, Poe had turned toward fiction as a more likely means of livelihood, and in 1832 published five tales, none of them particularly good, but all original and all adumbrating the greater Poe to come. Their originality lay not so much in subject or style as in tone— a fierce, unholy humor as in the sadistic "A Bargain Lost," a morbid Gothicism as in "Metzengerstein." Brockden Brown might have written "A Tale of Jerusalem," and in fact had written "Thessalonica," a powerful historical story with which Poe was undoubtedly familiar.[4] Brown had written the first American short story, though it was more like a condensed novel; Irving had shown what could be done in the sketch; a greater master than either was trying his wings and soon proved that he had no peer in the rather circumscribed province he had marked out as his own. The short story as a distinctive American form in fiction was on its way.

In the next year, 1833, the *Baltimore Sunday Visiter* published a winning short story of a contest that had also included poetry; Poe's "MS. Found in a Bottle" won the fiction award; and though his poem, "The Coliseum," did not receive the prize, it would have won the poetry award had the judges wished to give both prizes to one author. The story, one of Poe's greatest, immediately attracted wide attention and gave him that delicious

---

[3] "Edgar, . . . exceptionally handsome, winning in manner, had become an imperious older boy, a capital horseman, fencer and shot and a leader of the other boys at his school in Richmond."—Van Wyck Brooks, *The World of Washington Irving.* © 1944 by E. P. Dutton & Co., Inc.

[4] The only particular case in which Poe can be seen to have copied Brown is in "The Pit and the Pendulum," where scenes and manner are very similar to Chapter 14 of *Edgar Huntly,* whose hero meets with a fate like Poe's hero, falls in a pit, believes he is to be buried alive, suffers thirst and experiences the terror of darkness and unusual surroundings.

first taste of the fame for which he craved insatiably all his life. It led him to believe that here, at least, was the way to make a living, though poetry was to continue as his real passion.[5] Fifty dollars for one story—that was more than he had realized from three books of poems.

Although "MS. Found in a Bottle" is ostensibly a story of terror, and although it has certain obvious parallels with Coleridge's "Rime of the Ancient Mariner," there is a good deal more in it than lies on the surface. Already Poe was investing his imaginative stories with symbolism, looking toward the day when he would produce those triumphs (for his time) of psychological allegory, "The Fall of the House of Usher," "Eleonora" and "Ulalume." In this early story, technically excellent as it is, the unity which later became a *sine qua non* of Poe's art is not so readily apparent; it is a straightforward, first-person narrative by a remarkably prosaic observer whose matter-of-fact reporting of wildly improbable events lends an air of probity and heightens the impact of the terrible. The story begins, reaches a climax, and ends. DeFoe might have written it, and in fact it does in some sense resemble in its dry reportorial method "The Apparition of Mrs. Veal." But this is the external aspect only; there is symbolism in it too, which in spite of Poe's often repeated diatribes against allegory, is frequently met with in his greater stories.

"MS. Found in a Bottle" may be read as a parable of man's passage through life. Its ominous opening phrases conceivably refer to the unknown beginnings of our life, and its gloomy, catastrophic closing tells of the unknowable aftermath of temporal experience. "Of my country and of my family I have little to say. Ill usage and length of years have driven me from the one, and estranged me from the other." In these words we have the sense of the prenatal enigma, of the inscrutable deeps out of which consciousness has emerged. The first paragraph then sketches in the character of the narrator as one with "a strong

---

[5] "With me poetry has not been a purpose, but a passion; and the passions should be held in reverence; they must not—they cannot at will be excited, with an eye to the paltry compensations, or the more paltry commendations, of mankind."—Preface to the *Poems* of 1845.

relish for physical philosophy (which) has, I fear, tinctured my mind with a very common error of this age—I mean the habit of referring occurrences, even the least susceptible of such reference, to the principles of that science," and immediately we are launched upon that voyage which ends in destruction or, at best, in a transition to some further stage, the nature of which is unguessable. The vessel is described in detail, and its immediate plunge into the terror of storm and mystery parallels the condition of man's journey into the confusions and alarms of life. The eventual appearance of the ghostly ship which runs down this vessel in the midst of the simoon may be construed as the awakening of our consciousness to the mystery of life, its indefinable intention and ultimately undecipherable destination. The narrator manages to climb aboard the ghost ship and later becomes aware that he is invisible to its wraithlike crew. The captain, who seems to represent a personified wisdom withheld from the narrator, has the "solemn dignity of a God. . . . Although in his appearance there is, to a casual observer, nothing which might bespeak him more or less than man—still a feeling of irrepressible reverence and awe mingled with the sensation of wonder with which I regarded him. In stature he is nearly my own height; that is, about five feet eight inches. He is of a well-knit and compact frame of body, neither robust nor remarkably otherwise. But it is in the singularity of the expression which reigns upon his face—it is the intense, the wonderful, the thrilling evidence of old age, so utter, so extreme, which excites within my spirit a sense—a sentiment ineffable. His forehead, although little wrinkled, seems to bear upon it the stamp of a myriad of years.—His gray hairs are records of the past, and his grayer eyes are Sybils of the future."

Doom is written on every lineament of these faces, and in every aspect of the ship; a current is drawing them on to some obscure but fearful fate; and the narrator is filled with a curiosity to know it. The secret of our existence seems about to be revealed. "It is evident that we are hurrying onwards to some exciting knowledge—some never-to-be-imparted secret, whose attainment is destruction." And the crew itself seems to anticipate the end. ". . . there is upon their countenances an expression more of the eagerness of hope than of the apathy of despair." But whatever the secret is, we do not discover it, and the story ends with the ship sucked down in a thundering whirlpool. Poe's reading of life is summed up in this dark parable perhaps more generally but also more comprehensively than in any later story.

A great deal has been written of Poe's theories of unity and brevity in connection with the poem and the short story, and of his definitions of imagination and reason or fancy. The latter stem certainly from Coleridge, but it is not so easy to trace the former. Aristotle's dicta regarding the unities must have played some part, but Poe's usage of the term "unity" differs in some essential respects from the classical ideal. In his own practice, beginning-middle-end was a concept usually embraced; and sometimes, but not always, the unities of time, place and action were observed. But frequently *tone* served as the only unifying medium; and, with Poe, unity and brevity were practically corollaries. Brevity as an active principle may have recommended itself through mere exigency, since Poe, with only one exception, wrote exclusively for magazines which did not encourage lengthy fiction. In the work excepted, the *Narrative of Arthur Gordon Pym*, the only unity to be found is that of tone, and this is not rigorously adhered to. Poe was notoriously not above erecting general systems upon particular examples, where the examples were his own work. It has often been pointed out that the "philosophy" of his composition is merely a rationalization of his own working principles; but this, also, is a generalization too inclusive to be accurate. Men of genius have often been blind to the excellences of methods other than their own, but Poe does not seem to have been one of them. He venerated Coleridge, greatly admired Dickens, was deeply affected by Shakespeare, and in general had a wide appreciation of all literary forms. Undoubtedly he preferred his own methods, but whether they or the system they demonstrated came first is an open question.

Another typical story type was included in the first group of tales to win publication, the type dubbed by Poe "grotesque." It is a descriptive term, for these stories are without exception little more than caricatures, written with a strange humor that is usually mechanical and seldom successful. "A Bargain Lost" (1832), later renamed "Bon-Bon," is a fair example. It tells of an encounter between the Devil and one Pierre Bon-Bon, a creature "barely three feet in height, and if his head was diminutively small, still it was impossible to behold the rotundity of his stomach without a sense of the magnificent bordering upon the sublime." He is noted for the restaurant he keeps and for his pretensions as a metaphysician and philosopher. In a heavy-handed satirical tone Poe makes fun of the Platonists, the Aristotelians, the Kantians, and the followers of other philosophical systems. Bon-Bon was a superlative cook, his *"pâtés à la fois* were beyond doubt immaculate; but what pen can do justice to his essays *sur la Nature*—his thoughts *sur l'Ame*—his observations *sur l'Esprit?* If his *omelettes*—if his *ficandeaux* were inestimable, what *litterateur* of that day would not have given twice as much for an *'Idée de Bon-Bon'* as for all the trash of all the *'Idées'* of all the rest of the savants?" The Devil, a lean and cadaverous individual, appears to this troglodytic scapegrace, and a conversation regarding the soul ensues. The Devil assures him that the soul exists, and enumerates a number of historical figures whose souls he has "shelled" from their bodies and pickled, toasted and consumed. Bon-Bon, who has been drinking during the interview and become quite fuddled, offers him his soul. But the Devil refuses, on the ground it would be ungentlemanly of him to take advantage of Bon-Bon while drunk. This is a not uncharacteristic demonstration of Poe's humor, such as it is. A number of other tales in this kind are no worse, some are perhaps better. "A Predicament," "Hop-Frog," "Loss of Breath" and their like are deliberate attempts at humorous writing, but they are too macabre, too cruel, or so outlandishly distorted as to have almost no human significance whatever. Some of them are technically excellent; "Hop-Frog" is probably as well constructed as "The Fall of the House of Usher," brief, unified, and tending to a single effect.

Unity and brevity in fiction were to become an obsession with Poe, and he never tired of reiterating their desirability. He was working toward a method in the early stories which would utilize to a maximum degree the effectiveness of both. Probably "Berenice" (1835) comes closer to it than any preceding story; he was developing and polishing here the materials of Brockden Brown, tightening the joins and adding a superstructure. Gruesome details, lavished on similar themes by Brown, began to have a coldly logical look that heightened their horror. Like Brown, Poe was interested in medical science and had made a study of the same books that fascinated the older writer. Anatomical details, especially those of a moribund nature, bodily decomposition, the charnel house, all exerted a profound impression on his mind and of course figure prominently in most of his stories. The exhuming of a beloved's body by a madman for the purpose of obtaining her teeth, upon which the maniac had had an insane fixation—this is the sort of theme toward which Poe naturally gravitated. He could be assured of a lively interest in it on the part of readers (the magazines were filled with similar stories), and its imagining was congenial to him in all respects. Madness by itself was a subject that fascinated him, for he knew there were strains of it in himself as there had been in his forebears and in his sister. Where his contemporaries were indeed writing of the terror of Germany, *he* wrote of that of his soul.[6]

Brown, when he wrote *Wieland*, dealt with themes not unlike these; but a comparison of their artistic depth is sufficient to show how much further Poe had pushed back the frontiers of American fiction. While at the bidding of disembodied voices Wieland had murdered his wife, and this set of essentially unbelievable circumstances had enabled Brown to deal with the horror theme, Poe's dying and dead heroines become the center of moral action which is always of consequence and often interpenetrated with psychological significance of a high order. The action of "Berenice" is perhaps the least involved, the most superficial, but even there it is the madness of the lover which engages our primary interest and is the center of meaning. In "Morella"

---

[6] "If in many of my productions terror has been the thesis, I maintain that terror is not of Germany but of the soul."—Preface to the *Tales*, 1840.

another type of death-and-rebirth receives treatment; and in "Ligeia" (1838) the same theme, that of metempsychosis or the transmigration of souls, is embodied in a story of unusual depth and high artistry. Read on any level, it is a powerful tale; examined closely, it yields an unusual amount of information regarding Poe's general method, and shows to what extent Poe had advanced the rudimentary handling of themes inherited from Brown and his progenitors.

The popular interpretation of "Ligeia" makes it simply a tale of the supernatural, in which Ligeia by the force of her will returns from death to displace the soul and inhabit the body of Rowena, the wife whom the narrator had married at Ligeia's death. Interpreted on this level, however, the story has certain flaws, ends on a climax, not a resolution, and hardly seems, by Poe's own admission,[7] entirely satisfactory. On the other hand, when interpreted as a story dictated by Poe's unconscious, that is, evolving out of certain undefined psychic attitudes, but shaped by Poe's astute artistry, "Ligeia" seems to be an allegory for belief in the impossibility of finding a substitute for a first love, when that love is obsessive; and the obliteration of the substitute in the lover's yearning memory of the first love.

The mad narrator of the story undoubtedly has murdered Rowena, and only a literal reading of the second part would give the impression that a transmigration of identities had actually oc-

---

[7] Replying to a criticism of Philip Pendleton Cooke, that the story did not conclude satisfactorily, Poe wrote: "Touching 'Ligeia' you are right—all right—throughout. The *gradual* perception of the fact that Ligeia lives again in the person of Rowena is a far loftier and more thrilling idea than the one I have embodied. It offers, in my opinion, the widest possible scope to the imagination—it might be rendered even sublime. And this idea was mine—had I never written before I should have adopted it—but there is 'Morella.' Do you remember there the *gradual* conviction on the part of the parent that the spirit of the first Morella tenants the person of the second? It was necessary, since 'Morella' was written, to modify 'Ligeia.' I was forced to be content with a sudden half-consciousness, on the part of the narrator, that Ligeia stood before him. One point I have not fully carried out—I should have intimated that the *will* did not perfect its intention—there should have been a relapse—a final one —and Ligeia (who had only succeeded in so much as to convey an idea of the truth to the narrator) should be at length entombed as Rowena—the bodily alterations having gradually faded away."

curred. Cunningly he admits "incipient madness" but his deeds are those of a hopeless megalomaniac, and his oblique admission: "I saw, or may have dreamed that I saw, fall within the goblet, as if from some invisible spring in the atmosphere of the room, three or four large drops of a brilliant and ruby colored fluid" is the damaging evidence that *he* has poisoned her, though in his hallucinatory frame of mind he may have thought, or at least wished us to think, that the poison was a magical distillation from the weird atmosphere of the room. He wishes for the return of Ligeia, he wills it, and in his madness it seems to him (and he attempts to persuade us too) that Rowena's death struggles are the wrestling of Ligeia's spirit in its endeavor to enter Rowena's body. When at last he is convinced that this ghastly drama is ended, total megalomania descends upon him, and the story closes as "inexpressible madness" seizes him, he "shrieks aloud" and asks," '. . . can I never—can I never be mistaken—these are the full, and the black, and the wild eyes—of my lost love—of the Lady—of the LADY LIGEIA.' "

Psychologically, "Ligeia" is sound. It anticipates Freud by nearly a century, and there is no question but that it is the ultimate expression of Poe's art, as it is the ultimate perfection of the sensational theme handled in so rudimentary a form by Brown. But there are other stories of even deeper psychological significance, and these followed directly upon the writing of "Ligeia."

For example, "William Wilson" (1839) was Poe's first study of the schizophrenic mind, a pioneering in the realm of abnormal psychology far in advance of the time. This somewhat rambling tale was undoubtedly the genesis of Stevenson's *Dr. Jekyll and Mr. Hyde*, and is hardly superior to it as art; but in "The Fall of the House of Usher" (1839), "Eleonora" (1842), and the poem "Ulalume" (1847), the theme receives very finished treatment, its significance largely concealed in "Usher," but nearly explicit in the others.

Superficially, "Usher" is only another story of premature burial; but while Poe was not above writing merely sensational stories on that plane ("The Facts in the Case of M. Valdemar," "The Premature Burial," "Dr. Tarr and Professor Fether," etc.), here we have an extremely subtle rendering of an attitude and a psychic condition with which Poe was intimately familiar, since it was his own. The gloomy, ruined House itself seems to be the tangible bodying forth of the psyche of Poe, just as it is identified by Usher with his own soul. Usher and his tendencies to self-annihilation, are the repressive factors within the human psyche; his sister Madeline, who is immured in the same house with him, represents that outward tendency, the positive pole of a divided ego, which suffers immolation at the hands of the negative personality. But she does not immediately die; prematurely buried, she breaks out of her coffin and the deep vault within the House, only to confront her oppressor, and upon the confrontation, to cause his death and her own. Shortly thereafter the house (with its symbolic division, "that once barely discernible fissure of which I have before spoken as extending from the roof of the building, in a zigzag direction, to the base,") breaks asunder and is swallowed up in "the deep and dank tarn" of oblivion. The split personality is mortally incapable of cohesion, of attaining that unity which Poe sought with indefatigable and fanatic purpose—an effort in which he failed in his life but succeeded in his art. "Usher," however, is the only story in which defeat is irremediably suffered and openly admitted. In "Ligeia," "Eleonora" and "Ulalume" the dualism is resolved or at least compensated for with completely satisfactory artistic effect.

All of these parables are indefinite and incomplete; nowhere in Poe will be found the explicit allegory of Hawthorne, and Poe's fulminations against allegory were doubtless sincere; but he could no more help writing into his stories and poems the basic psychopathology of his own nature than he could resist the effects of wine. Indefiniteness was, in fact, a prime tenet of his theory. Part of the poetic appeal of "Eleonora" and "Ulalume" is their vagueness and the sense that we have entered a dim, shadowy world where the half-seen is more effective than any stark revelation could be. "Eleonora," also, approached the prose-poem form of "Silence" and "Shadow," but it is certainly a well-balanced story too, with the elements of plot, the beginning, middle and end, and the brevity and unity inseparable from Poe's masterpieces. Eleonora herself represents to the narrator, her lover, a duality of natures and after her death reappears to him as Ermengarde, whom he marries. One of the original versions of the story contains direct evidence that Poe intended us to understand this reading: "I could not but dream as I gazed, enrapt, upon her alternate moods of melancholy and mirth, that two separate souls were enshrined within her." When Ermengarde arrives to replace the dead Eleonora, Poe formerly had: "And there was a wild delirium in the love I bore her when I started to see upon her countenance the identical transition from tears to smiles that I had wondered at in the long-lost Eleonora." He deleted these passages, increasing the indefiniteness but without changing the meaning. A balance is struck, and the dualism resolved in a "happy ending," endowing the story with all the elements, in the Poe lexicon, for a masterwork, including the circumstance of the death of a beautiful woman which, he contended, was the most poetical of all subjects—a notion peculiar to him, as it was the event he most dreaded in his personal life and the one that had on several occasions caused him the most anguish, first in the case of his mother, then of his foster mother, and finally of his wife.

The anguish of the latter loss probably impelled him to write "Ulalume," a poem not understood in its day but greatly influential in our time by its impressionism, its peculiar vagueness, and more than anything else because it, together with the whole body of his work, had such an electrifying effect upon Baudelaire and through him the whole school of French symbolists. But "Ulalume's" dialogue between its author and Psyche, his soul, is the furthest advance of Poe's psychoanalytical effort in poetry, sounding depths only exceeded in the best of his stories. It has been argued that this achievement was unconscious, but no one can doubt that Poe at least knew *his* self-consuming, perverse and maladjusted personality, and "Ulalume" was the cry *de profundis* of a shattered schizophrenic who had plumbed his private hell.

A year before he published "Eleonora" Poe discovered another type of fiction, discovered it in almost the absolute sense, for it was a genre that had never been worked in before. This was, of course, the "ratiocinative" or detective story. "The Murders in the Rue Morgue" (1841), with its Auguste Dupin, the cold, logical, ultra-rational mind, and his foil (Dr. Watson's precursor), was a brilliantly original achievement, whatever its deficiencies as a work of art. Poe certainly shaped the detective story; in fact, he may be said to have fashioned the mold from which all subsequent development in this form has come.

Another field in which he pioneered was that of pseudo "scientific" fiction, later exploited by Jules Verne, H. G. Wells and scores of lesser luminaries. "The Unparalleled Adventures of One Hans Pfaall," "The Balloon Hoax" and "Von Kempelen and His Discovery" were something new in fiction, while "Three Sundays in a Week" was undoubtedly the inspiration for the denouement of Verne's "Around the World in Eighty Days," and Smitherton's ingenuity provided the ammunition for Phileas Fogg's well-known *coup*.

But the psychological tale was always his forte, and he even anticipated, in "William Wilson" and the "Black Cat," the tales of conscience in which Hawthorne specialized. The rigid, agonizing guilt complex with which Hawthorne's figures are endowed cannot be found in Poe, but in the retributive justice paid out to these murderers turned madmen, it is not too difficult to see the same inexorable condemnation of sin. What interests Poe, however, is not evil *per se*, nor even the evil of the deed, but the horror that can be wrung from it. Poe accused Hawthorne of plagiarizing "William Wilson" in "Howe's Masquerade," but the latter appeared more than a year before Poe's story and the plagiarism, if any, must have been in the opposite direction. In many ways Hawthorne's writings parallel those of Poe, but the parallels are superficial. The "gloom" in both writers seems to be the principal element of similarity; but a closer inspection of Hawthorne's subjects and methods will show how widely the two differ, and how much more nearly Hawthorne stands in the Irving tradition, as later chapters will demonstrate.

Poe has often been regarded as a "sport" in American letters, fitting into no category and much more nearly aligned to what is commonly regarded as the French genius than to the American. In some respects this conception is sound; when we look back to the time of his appearance in American literature he may seem an anomaly; but there are good reasons for supposing that, outside of his time, he would not have been the force he undoubtedly was, or have written in the way he did. Actually, he worked in a tradition that had its preceptor and was to have its lineal descendants. Poe shaped the tradition, perhaps more strongly and certainly more constructively than the originator; but he was by no means a lonely, misunderstood and isolated artist. Neal, Simms, even J. P. Kennedy, had written tales in the manner of Blackwood, and the horror story was a marketable item in America long before Poe began to write. His handling of the theme, and his technical excellence in it, have preserved his work while the others' has perished; his methods fructified later workers in the same medium who were not so capable of a range of creative activity as he.

In considering Poe's versatility, his mastery in poetry, the short story and criticism, it is obvious that his range, in all these departments, was very narrow. He possessed a certain universality of interests, it is true, and under happier circumstances might have approached the Goethean ideal of a universal genius in letters; but the fact remains that the problems dealt with in his creative work are largely limited to private, personal, eccentric and morbid preoccupations with such subjects as madness, pathological manias, and bizarre and grotesque dramatic situations. His seventy-odd stories and sketches in prose include only seven that are not cast in the first-person narrative form.[8] Had he been a healthier man, had his interests extended to the world of normal human relationships, had he been better adjusted psychologically, socially and economically, it is just possible that, with his extraordinary technical equipment and the vigor and originality of his mind, Poe might have joined the small com-

---

[8] "The Masque of the Red Death," "The Power of Words," "The Colloquy of Monos and Una," "Eiros and Charmion," "A Tale of Jerusalem," "The Duc de L'Omelette," and "King Pest."

pany of universal artists. But then he would not have been Poe.
Within the circumscribed limits where he chose to work, he
was mining a characteristically American ore, a vein that seems
to have been peculiarly rich for a whole line of American writers
cf fiction. Was it the dark strain of Calvinism, the repressions of
Puritanism, with its doctrine of original sin, its heavy concept of
preordained guilt, that had seeped from North to South; or was
it the sense of decay and dissolution cast up on the shores of the
New World within a period of two hundred years; or the con-
science-ridden demonology of the old Spanish conquistadores,
transmuted in some undefined way, that implanted this surprising strain in American fiction? It is impossible to say, but the
evidence is unmistakable that we have had the results of such an
ominous heritage expressed in the apocalyptic visions of Brown,
Poe, Hawthorne, Melville, Bierce, Hearn, and in our own time,
Faulkner and Wolfe. Yet it may be that this strain is not peculiarly American at all, but largely a universal manifestation of
the human subconscious. We may perhaps have observed in these
writers only a preoccupation with an omnipresent tendency,
brought to greater artistic development and thus to a sharper
realization.

HERMAN MELVILLE
The Seeker

AMERICAN PROSE assumed a richness of texture that even Poe had
not given it, in the work of a man who was only ten years Poe's
junior but who lived into the last decade of the nineteenth century. Herman Melville developed the most verdant and luxurious
prose instrument of his time, but it derived essentially from a
source that had provided Brown and Poe with their less prodigal
styles. Brown's, though often turgid and nearly always high-
flown, was a style lavish and tending to run away with itself.
Poe's style, while often thought to be spare and severe, is actually
rich not only in imagery and the resources of poetic manner but
in esoteric adjectives, long conjunctive sentences and sonorous

periods. Called upon as Poe and Brown were by the exigencies of their subject matter to explore strange deeps and forbidden areas of the psyche, they were compelled to write an "imaginative" prose, to build up and elaborate with allusiveness and oblique attack the medium through which to convey their apocalyptic vision of life. Melville's vision, being deeper and more subtle than theirs, as well as more robust, required an instrument of even greater power, register and prodigality. He found this style, or, more properly, developed it out of a necessary compulsion, and bequeathed to our fiction a new dimension, a new intensity in language that was not equaled until the advent of Faulkner and Wolfe.

Poe was a boy of ten when Melville was born; Poe had published some of his greatest work by the time Melville began to contribute juvenile pieces to the Lansingburgh (N. Y.) *Advertiser* in 1839. Poe died in the year *Mardi* appeared. In the period, 1839 to 1849, during which the two writers were mutually active, there must have been occasions when each noticed the work of the other; but it is doubtful if either of them recognized their spiritual kinship. It is quite impossible to trace in Melville any direct influence of Poe, but it may not be too fanciful to see in the almost passionate relationship of Melville to Hawthorne a secondary influence of considerable importance. Poe was one of the first to detect those elements in Hawthorne which had counterparts in his own work; and it was to these same dark and shadowy depths to which Melville responded with such forthright and happy abandon. The austere remoteness in Hawthorne, on the other hand, the abnegating Puritan in him, was the element which later rebuked and disappointed Melville, as it would have alienated Poe. Worlds apart as Poe, the "exquisite," and Melville, the man-of-war's man, might seem to be, Poe, the convivial, enterprising editor or the prober of the soul, and Melville, the hearty traveler or the accuser of the universe, are spirits easily reconcilable. They are, in fact, so patently of lineal relationship that the absence of superficial "influences" seems wholly irrelevant. It is with the deeper parallels and identities that we are concerned, and these are abundant.

Melville's literary beginnings were certainly inauspicious and gave no indication whatsoever of the mighty genius later to be poured forth in *Moby-Dick*. The first extant writings were the "Fragments from a Writing Desk," newspaper squibs of the type fashionable in the 1820's and '30's, in which the youthful author emulated Irving's whimsy and concocted a literary style of highfalutin prettiness. "By my halidome, sir, this same village of Lansingburgh contains within its pretty limits as fair a set of blushing damsels as one would wish to look upon on a dreamy summer day." In his adolescent egotism, he wishes himself beautiful as Apollo and "dressed in a style which would extort admiration from a Brummel, belted round with self-esteem, and sallying in dizzy triumph among the ladies—complimenting one, exchanging repartee with another, tapping this one under the chin, and clasping this one around the waist; and finally, winding up the operation by kissing around the circle." In another place he apostrophizes his mistress in the approved fashion, picturing her as a voluptuous houri, in the manner of Poe at his worst. The style is similar to Poe's when most high-flown and literary, and the entire performance is negligible, undistinguishable from hundreds of like effusions in the press of the time. However, it is interesting to find Melville acknowledging even in these early efforts his admiration of and indebtedness to such preceptors as Coleridge, Burton, Milton, Shakespeare, Scott, Byron and Lord Chesterfield, as well as Cooper. A long step forward is the prose of *Typee*, showing that Melville had either written much and discarded it all, or that he had matured so greatly in the intervening years that a stronger prose was the natural expression of his growing up. For a man of twenty, the "Fragments" are almost discreditable; for a man of thirty, *Moby-Dick* is a mighty performance; these ten years witnessed in Melville a spiritual and intellectual progress of prodigious extent; the wonder is how it was achieved.

We have no intermediate examples of his writing between the "Fragments" and *Typee;* but we have the record of Melville's physical adventures which go far to explain the development. On January 3, 1841, he took passage on the *Acushnet* from New

Bedford for a whaling cruise, the embarkation upon a voyage not alone of great significance for his outward life but for his spiritual growth. Not altogether a raw youth, and not unfamiliar with the sea (he had made a trip to Liverpool before the mast at seventeen), he still was essentially provincial and of course adolescent in his view of life and his experience of the world. But as he said, the cruise of the *Acushnet* was his university; out of it came material not only for *Typee, Omoo* and *Mardi,* but for *Moby-Dick* and all his most significant work. When the ship touched Nukuheva, Melville took French leave, unable to abide the conditions on shipboard, and escaped to the interior where he, and his companion Toby, lived four months among the savage Typees, literally, "maneaters." Later he knocked about the South Seas for another year, and at Honolulu signed as a man-of-war's man aboard the frigate *United States,* sailed around the Horn, and arrived in Boston in October of 1844. This itinerary served to furnish him with all the essentials for outward event upon which to base his austere reckoning of man's fate.

Whatever the immediate urge that set him to work on his first book, the next year found him with *Typee* already on the press and soon to make a reputation for him in both America and England. Whether he had written much or nothing between the "Fragments" and *Typee,* he had evolved a fresh, clean style worlds removed from the cloying prose of the early work, and in his first romance had stuck to a plain unembroidered prose admirably suited to his subject matter. It is unquestionably the sanest, happiest of his books—a story of adventure pure and simple, with some sociological overtones for the times that were indeed forthright; in fact, the first edition was amended by certain elisions regarding the deleterious effects of the Christian missionaries' work upon the Nukuhevan civilization. Told straightforwardly, *Typee* is an almost literal transcript of Melville's personal experiences in the islands. Little creative imagination was needed, but a world of authentic talent was required to organize the material and present it with the effectuality he achieved. Strictly eschewing all moralist commentary, with an eye closely on physical movement and dramatic values in the old picaresque tradition, Melville was able to write one of the healthiest of all adventure romances, almost entirely free of the philosophical content and symbolical significance of his later work. In one respect only it foreshadowed that uncompromising truth-seeker its author was later to become. The honest accounts of sexual freedom of the natives were not only upsetting to the contemporary public, they also reported that Melville was a man who would write of the truth as he knew it; and though he allowed his original version of *Typee* to be bowdlerized, he grimaced at the emasculation. The Mrs. Grundys of his day were powerful, and Melville was a struggling young author seeking a hearing. Therefore no wonder he allowed the following to be revised out of his text: "Look at Honolulu, the metropolis of the Sandwich Islands!—a community of disinterested merchants, and devoted self-exiled heralds of the Cross, located on the very spot that twenty years ago was defiled by the presence of idolatry. What a subject for an eloquent Bible-meeting orator! . . . But when these philanthropists send us such glowing accounts of one-half of their labors, why does modesty restrain them from publishing the other half of the good they have wrought?—Not until I visited Honolulu was I aware of the fact that the small remnant of the natives had been civilized into draught horses and evangelized into beasts of burden. But so it is. They have been literally broken into the traces and are harnessed to the vehicles of their spiritual instructors like so many dumb brutes."[1]

Melville was persuaded of the desirability of bending to the public's limitations; but perhaps this concession only strengthened him later in his refusal to concede anything to the tastes and weakness of his audience. Apart from this anticipated intransigeance in the matter of speaking his mind, there is very little in *Typee* that would give a clue to Melville's development; for all that he had displayed in this book, he might very easily have become another R. H. Dana or G. P. R. James. The apoca-

---

[1] Melville wrote to his editor and literary advisor, Evert Duyckinck, "The *Revised* (Expurgated?—odious word!) Edition of 'Typee' ought to be duly announced—and as the matter (in one respect) is a little delicate, I am happy that the literary tact of Mr. Duyckinck will be exerted on this occasion."

lyptic vision of his mature years was only being prepared here by
a clear-eyed realism and a manly honesty as bluff and hearty as
a sou'westerly in the *Acushnet's* topgallants.

Almost the same might be said of *Omoo*, which appeared in
1847. It continued the account of Melville's wanderings after
escaping from the island of the Typees, and it has the same fresh,
briny savor. It marks, however, a very definite advance over the
first book, in literary value, in characterization and in variety.
This is not the work of an apprentice, but of a seasoned work-
man who thoroughly understands his craft. Less picturesque
(there is no counterpart of Fayaway's story, the idyllic love affair of *Typee*), *Omoo* is packed with variations on the picaresque
theme; it rambles and has no proper plot, or need of one. The
sharpness of eye, the wealth of detail, the honesty of characterization, all testify to a deepening and accelerating of ability in
Melville, and must have shown him, if he had had doubts before,
that he was indeed meant to be a writer. Direct and vigorous,
the language of *Omoo* becomes an accurate instrument; but once
again it gives little indication of the prodigious vitality and richness of diction which became the keynote of the Melvillian
prose. It might appear almost that Melville was divesting himself
on purpose of the enormous resources, that he was trying his
hand at clarity and leanness for exercise, against the time when
his style in all its riot and splendor could be employed upon a
theme worthy of it.

Omoo is a travel book, but it is also much more. *Typee* contained some living characters; Kory-Kory, Mehevi, Toby and
Fayaway are believable, but there was no primary intent to
create living beings; Melville plainly had set out to tell a tale of
adventure. In *Omoo*, however, we find a score of perfectly
realized individuals often hit off in a paragraph or two, frequently brought to life by the difficult means of dialogue.

An old scalawag shore doctor on one of the islands, determining to make money on the beached crew of the *Julia*, Melville's
ship, is one part shrewdness, and two parts gullibility. Here is
how Melville manages to establish this difficult combination of
characteristics:

"Very bland and amiable, Doctor Johnson advanced, and, resting his cane on the stocks, glanced to right and left, as we lay before him. 'Well, my lads,'—he began—'how do you find yourselves today?'

"Looking very demure, the men made some rejoinder; and he went on.

" 'Those poor fellows I saw the other day—the sick, I mean—how are they?' and he scrutinized the company. At last, he singled out one who was assuming a most unearthly appearance, and remarked that he looked as if he were extremely ill. 'Yes,' said the sailor dolefully, 'I'm afraid, doctor, I'll soon be losing the number of my mess!' (a sea phrase, for departing this life) and he closed his eyes, and moaned.

" '*What* does he say?' said Johnson, turning round eagerly.

" 'Why,' exclaimed Flash Jack, who volunteered as interpreter, 'he means he's going to *croak*.' (die).

" 'Croak! and what does that mean, applied to a patient?'

" 'Oh! I understand,' said he, when the word was explained. . . . 'Men,' said he, 'if any more of you are ailing, speak up, and let me know. By order of the consul, I'm to call every day; so if any of you are at all sick, it's my duty to prescribe for you. This sudden change from ship fare to shore living plays the deuce with you sailors, so be cautious about eating fruit. Goodday! I'll send you the medicines the first thing in the morning.'

"Now, I am inclined to suspect that with all his want of understanding, Johnson must have had some idea that we were quizzing him. Still, that was nothing, so long as it answered his purpose; and therefore, if he *did* see through us, he never showed it."

Or, for vigorous evocation of a scene, consider the vignette in which a pathetic native couple is perfectly realized. Melville and his friend, Doctor Long Ghost, have been walking along the beach, when they encounter a Kanaka's hut. "The hut proved to be a low, rude erection, very recently thrown up; for the bamboos were still green as grass, and the thatching fresh and fragrant as meadow hay. It was open upon three sides; so that, upon drawing near, the domestic arrangements within were in plain sight. No one was stirring; and nothing was to be seen but a clumsy old chest of native workmanship, a few calabashes, and bundles of tappa hanging against a post; and a heap of something, we knew not what, in a dark corner. Upon closer inspection, the doctor discovered it to be a loving old couple, locked in each other's arms, and rolled together in a tappa mantle.

" 'Halloa! Darby!' he cried, shaking the one with a beard. But Darby heeded him not; though Joan, a wrinkled old body, started up in affright, and yelled aloud. Neither of us attempting to gag her, she presently became quiet; and, after staring hard and asking some unintelligible questions, she proceeded to rouse her still slumbering mate.

"What ailed him we could not tell; but there was no waking him. Equally in vain were all his dear spouse's cuffs, pinches, and other endearments; he lay like a log, face up, snoring away like a cavalry trumpeter.

" 'Here, my good woman,' said Long Ghost, 'just let me try'; and taking the patient right by his nose, he so lifted him bodily into a sitting position, and held him there until his eyes opened. When this event came to pass, Darby looked round like one stupefied; and then, springing to his feet, backed away into a corner, from which place we became the objects of his earnest and respectful attention.

" 'Permit me, my dear Darby, to introduce to you my esteemed friend and comrade, Paul,' said the doctor, gallanting me up with all the grimace and flourish imaginable. Upon this, Darby began to recover his faculties, and surprised us not a little by talking a few words of English. So far as could be understood, they were expressive of his having been aware that there were two 'Karhowrees' in the neighborhood; that he was glad to see us, and would have something for us to eat in no time.''

After *Omoo* there was an interval of two years before another Melville volume was placed before the public. In 1849, the year of Poe's death, a strange, unclassifiable book made its appearance under the title *Mardi*. Followers of the successful young author who had lived among cannibals[2] might with justification have expected another vigorous account of somatotomic activity, and

[2] During a trip to England in 1849, Melville half wryly noted in a diary that he was well known as the celebrated author of *Peedee, Hullaballoo* and *Pog-Dog*, and would go down to posterity as the man who lived among the cannibals.

doubtless did. They were in for a distinct disappointment, for once Melville had launched his crew and got them shipwrecked, he forsook the travelogue and record of curious customs. Instead he plunged into the first great satire-fantasy in our literature, the precursor of his own greater allegory, *Moby-Dick*, but to be compared only with that book for size, breadth, depth and a certain Rabelaisian gusto. Internal evidence leads one to believe that *Mardi* was begun not as a new and more humanistic Gulliver but merely as a tale of adventure at sea. But the simple relating of objective adventure no longer satisfied Melville, who had grown immeasurably in the few years since *Typee*, and before he had gone a third through the book it was evident that his mind, freighted and voluminous, must disgorge some of its wisdom, must write out some of its poetry, and announce some of its doubts concerning the world and mankind, good and evil. *Mardi* was the receptacle into which with an all too prodigal hand he poured this new-found intellectual euphoria, to the detriment of the tale's unity, but certainly to our enrichment.

Even if he had never written *Moby-Dick*, Melville's essential centrality in the apocalyptic stream would be indubitable, for *Mardi's* theme is the pursuit of the unknowable, the seeking of spiritual grace, the unending quest for the meaning of the universe with its "chronic malady" evil. Time as an abstraction becomes for him a concept upon which to lavish pages. In brief, *Mardi* was a trial effort for the great ambitious pursuit of the white whale, but on its own merits it remains a landmark in fiction of this strain.

We begin to see the Melvillian prose, rich and varied in texture, assume that warp and woof that approximates the sonorous periods and the deep organ tones with all stops out, of the mature Melville. Nowhere in *Typee* or *Omoo* can such a passage as this be found (and in few books anywhere, outside of Melville's later works, or Thomas Browne): "Oh, men! fellowmen! we are only what we are; not what we would be; nor every thing we hope for. We are but a step in a scale, that reaches further above us than below. We breathe but oxygen. Who in Arcturus hath heard of us? They know us not in the Milky Way. We prate of faculties divine; and know not how sprouteth a spear of grass; we go about shrugging our shoulders; when the firmament-arch is over us; we rant of etherealities; and long tarry over our banquet; we demand Eternity for a life-time; when our mortal half-hours too often prove tedious. We know not of what we talk. The Bird of Paradise outflies our flutterings. What it is to be immortal, has not yet entered into our thoughts. At will, we build our futurities; tier above tier; all galleries full of laureates; resounding with everlasting oratorios! Pater-nosters for ever, or eternal Misereres! forgetting that in Mardi, our breviaries oft fall from our hands. But divans there are, some say, whereon we shall recline, basking in effulgent suns, knowing neither Orient or Occident. Is it not so? Fellow men! our mortal lives have an end; but that end is no goal; no place of repose. Whatever it may be, it will prove but as the beginning of another race. . . ."

The internal evidence mentioned above that Melville had no original intention of writing a philosophical novel is that, for more than a third of the book, we have only a superlative narrative on the plane of physical adventure, in which the narrator and his chum Jarl escape from a whaler, drift about in an open boat for a space of days, finally board a two-master adrift with its tiller lashed and two natives, Samoa and Anatoo, man and wife, clinging to the maintop. Anatoo, particularly, is fully characterized, a shrill native termagant neatly parceled and keenly comic. The voyagers eventually board another whaler, with a motley crew, bound on an allegorical quest. Here the adventure qua adventure ends. *Mardi* becomes henceforth a novel of ideas, a fantasy, a satire, something wholly new to Melville.

The voyage is a profane Pilgrim's Progress, the search through the world (Mardi) for Yillah, a semi-divinity from the Island of Delight, Oroolia. Melville took occasion to satirize most of the nations of earth (Dominora: Great Britain; Vivenza: the United States, etc.) and deals not only with politics, history and sociology, but with anthropology, manners and economics. Babbalanja, the philosopher, and Yoomy, the poet, hold long discourse on all imaginable subjects, and often report is had of Yillah, though she is never found. Yet the searchers even go so far as

Serenia, Christ's Kingdom, and to the misty realms of metaphysics in their quest for her. One would say that Melville's point is simply to say that it is vain to hope for truth, or beauty, or delight, or wisdom, in any ultimate sense, though man may meet with many enjoyable and, in their way, worthwhile adventures along his path. So seemingly trite a moral is after all the best that can be salvaged from *Mardi*, which is the reason one cannot assign a very high place to this book; but at least it was an endeavor, and a milestone. Moreover, *Mardi*, in its geniality and general good humor, misses the real depths which a more significant probing of its theme might have revealed. In all respects, it was only a rehearsal for the real performance. The vigorous adventurer had not become the seer, but he was entering a period of metamorphosis.

While this sea change was transpiring, two more romances of the sea came from Melville's now regularly plied pen (he had married just previous to the writing of *Mardi* and had found domestic bliss needed to be paid for), *Redburn* (1849) and *White-Jacket* (1850). *Redburn* was turned out hurriedly, regarded by its author as a potboiler, but it is a fresh, able story of Melville's own youth and first expedition to sea; while *White-Jacket* is, in every respect, a first-rate novel of life aboard a man-of-war, and probably the best-constructed of all Melville's longer works. Its story resumes the chronology of Melville's life where *Omoo* had left off, with his signing aboard the U. S. frigate at Honolulu, and its narrative covers the trip back home around the Horn.

A sober tale, *White-Jacket* might almost be said to have anticipated the realism of Howells, and it stands clearly outside the characteristic tenor of Melville's work. Full of remarkably accurate portraits, each of them admirable for its probity and three-dimensional veracity, the novel is as circumstantial as *Madame Bovary*. Surgeon Cuticle, Jack Chase, Jermin and Mr. Pert are drawn to the life. And the swarming life of a ship of the line, the little world bounded by the ship's scuppers, becomes a fully realized universe on a strictly factual plane. The fact that *White-Jacket's* picture of flogging, as an established practice in the Navy, caused reforms is evidence of the novel's real power and circumstantial truth. A sane, distinguished record of a voyage, seen through the eyes of a superior individual whose insignia of difference in intellectual rank was his white canvas jacket (in contradistinction to the blue jackets worn by the regular crew), this book stands out from all the other great works of Melville's prime for its undeviating matter-of-fact report of life. The over- tones which gave Melville his peculiar distinction in fiction, the Orphic pronouncements, the inspired allegory, and the apocalyp- tic vision are all foreign to the spirit and the letter of *White- Jacket*. However, it is plain to see that this novel was the culmi- nation of its author's art in one of its manifestations: it was the masterpiece of the series begun with *Typee*, as *Moby-Dick* was of the other order of Melville's genius, announced with *Mardi*.

When we approach *Moby-Dick* (1851) we come to the sum- mit of the American novel in the nineteenth century, if not of all time. It is impossible to speak in the same breath of any other long fiction by an American of that century, for no other native writer even attempted the task that Melville here set himself. We cannot think of anyone else who was equipped to handle so formidable a theme, and Hawthorne alone came to grips with similar problems on any extended scale. Poe and Brockden Brown, working in more circumscribed areas, sometimes seemed to be probing the dark recesses of the soul and often made ef- forts to sound the universe (Poe particularly, in *Eureka*), but their approach was radically different. In one gigantic stride Mel- ville outstripped all, and poured into one vast book the white- hot torrent of his burning vision, literally pitching the stuff out in sheaf after sheaf, through one summer and fall. Tumultuously the book sprang from his overcharged brain. "Give me a condor's quill!" he cries. "Give me Vesuvius' crater for an inkstand. Friends! hold my arms! For in the mere act of penning my thoughts of this Leviathan, they weary me, and make me faint with the outreaching comprehensiveness of sweep, as if to include the whole circle of the sciences, and all the generations of whales, and men, and mastodons, past, present and to come, with all the revolving panoramas of empire on earth, and throughout the whole universe, not excluding its suburbs."

Whether one considers *Moby-Dick* the greatest American

novel depends, of course, on whether one accepts the Orphic style, the rich, often inexact apostrophes, the lush and lyrical prose, the sheer bulk and weight of the subject and the torrential flood of the manner. There is little of the technician about Melville; there is hardly any of the traditionally required observation of manners, and even, perhaps, a minimum of character building in *Moby-Dick;* but its overwhelming importance derives from the serious nature of its intention, from the various strata of its symbolism, from its deep and steady concern with the ultimate questions that have baffled men during long centuries: the problem of evil, the nature of man's existence on earth, interpreted through the majestic view that recalls Aeschylus and Sophocles in the great literature of the past. But to the extent that *Moby-Dick* is an improvisation, it is a masterly one; and like the great Victorians and the greater Russians, this novelist wrote out of a superfluity of genius rather than of virtuosity.

"To produce a mighty volume you must choose a mighty theme," Melville declared; and when he set down the portentous opening sentence, "Call me Ishmael," he knew that he had launched his great work, the story for which he had been preparing, that he had saved up until he was ready for it—the story of the White Whale.

Captain Ahab, with the whalebone attachment to the stump of leg left him by a previous encounter with Moby-Dick, represents Mankind and man's continuing battle with the inscrutable forces of the universe. Ahab, sometimes a frenzied fanatic, sometimes an austere and noble humanitarian, is hardly a fully rounded character, but he is certainly much more than a type; Stubb, Starbuck, Flask, and the motley cannibals and Fee-geeans, Queequeg, Daggoo, Tashtego, and little Pip, are figures capable of interpretation only as allegorical and representative types. Chief Mate Starbuck, a Quaker, typifies the imaginative man restrained by prudence; Stubb is the naturalist, whose horizon is bounded by what his senses can tell him; and Flask is of the earth earthy, a wholly circumscribed individual, happy in his ignorance, and willingly the tool of his superiors. A crew of separate individuals, each seemingly living in isolation from the rest, but all subservient to the will of Ahab, and comprising in their totality a microcosm of the human race, are the set pieces for this vast allegory of our common contest with the unknown.

The quest of Moby-Dick is a long one, but it is accomplished in three ultimate encounters, and the Whale emerges as victor, breaking the *Pequod* asunder, drowning all hands save the narrator himself, who like the motto from Job can say, "And I only am escaped alone to tell thee." The ship goes out of sight, "But as the last whelmings intermixingly poured themselves over the sunken head of the Indian at the mainmast, leaving a few inches of the erect spar yet visible, together with long streaming yards of the flag, which calmly undulated, with ironical coincidings, over the destroying billows they almost touched;—at that instant, a red arm and a hammer hovered backwardly uplifted in the open air, in the act of nailing the flag faster and yet faster to the subsiding spar. A sky-hawk that tauntingly had followed the main-truck downwards from its natural home among the stars, pecking at the flag and incommoding Tashtego there; this bird now chanced to intercept its broad fluttering wing between the hammer and the wood; and simultaneously feeling that ethereal thrill, the submerged savage beneath, in his death-gasp, kept his hammer frozen there; and so the bird of heaven, with archangelic shrieks, and his imperial beak thrust upwards, and his whole captive form folded in the flag of Ahab, went down with his ship, which, like Satan, would not sink to hell till she had dragged a living part of heaven along with her, and helmeted herself with it.

"Now small fowls flew screaming over the yet yawning gulf; a sullen white surf beat against its steep sides; then all collapsed, and the great shroud of the sea rolled on as it rolled five thousand years ago."

Along the way, *Moby-Dick* manages to contain an incredible amount of poetry, of pure cadenced prose, of the richest imagery. It contains allusions not only to the whaling industry but to so many conterminous subjects that critics have drawn attention to its similarity to the work of Rabelais. Catalogues and quotations, rambling essays (which, however, are artistically defensible in that they add to, not detract from, the sense of unification) and wild rhetoric establish Melville's place in the apocalyptical tradition. The "Whiteness of the Whale", a chapter of eerie power, is an instance in point. This "whiteness" of evil, or of the indefinable strangeness of man's view of the universe, has a definite relationship to the haunting melancholy and abstract dark intimations in the work of Poe. There is more than a little of the Poesque about this "whiteness": "Is it that by its indefiniteness it shadows forth the heartless voids and immensities of the universe; and thus stabs us from behind with the thought of annihilation, when beholding the white depths of the Milky Way? Or is it, that as in essence whiteness is not so much a color as the visible absence of color; and at the same time the concrete of all colors; is it for these reasons that there is such a dumb blankness, full of meaning, in a wide landscape of snows—a colorless, all-color of atheism from which we shrink? And when we consider that other theory of the natural philosophers, that all other earthy hues—every stately or lovely emblazoning—the sweet tinges of sunset skies, and woods; yea, and the gilded velvets of butterflies, and the butterfly cheeks of young girls; all these are but subtile deceits, not actually inherent in substances, but only laid on from without; so that all deified Nature absolutely paints like the harlot, whose allurements cover nothing but the charnel-house within; and when we proceed further, and consider that the mystical cosmetic which produces every one of her hues, the great principle of light, for ever remains white or colorless in itself, and if operating without medium upon matter, would touch all objects, even tulips and roses, with its own blank tinge—pondering all this, the palsied universe lies before us a leper; and like wilful travellers in Lapland, who refuse to wear colored and coloring glasses upon their eyes, so the wretched infidel gazes himself blind at the monumental white shroud that wraps all the prospect around him. And of all these things the Albino whale was the symbol."

The poetry of *Moby-Dick* is not sustained; it is as if Melville subscribed to Poe's dictum that poetry, if it is to be effective, must be brief. And certainly relief is had from the vaulting leaps and singing rhetoric by long passages of terse, clean prose like that in which Melville describes the meeting at sea of the *Pequod* and the *Delight*.

Tangible bodying-forth of an abstract notion, this is the fundamental intention and the successful aim of *Moby-Dick*. Poe was adept at this difficult, perhaps most difficult of all, artistic intention. Poe's term, "ideality," is applicable with fullest force to *Moby-Dick*, a novel that exists solely by and for its idea. But there is also wrought into the fabric of this book a fierce and consuming power of reality; and the combination of "ideality and reality" is, by Poe's measurement, the final artistic achievement. *William Wilson* was Poe's nearest comparable success in this field; but compared with *Moby-Dick* it was a simpler effort. Far richer because far more complex, holding stratum after stratum of symbolic meaning, *Moby-Dick* represents a tremendous advance not only over *William Wilson* and the shorter pieces of Poe, but over the novels of Hawthorne. The one is a richly orchestrated, multiple-themed structure comparable to a symphony; the others sonatas for solo instruments.

After *Moby-Dick* there was hardly any further road for Melville to take in the apocalyptic direction; at least, it is difficult for us to imagine what trend he could have taken. Actually this strange, passionate yet somehow laced and restrained genius, burst out in another quarter. He wrote the searing autobiographical novel, *Pierre*, which continues to baffle criticism. Compounded as it is of some of the finest Melvillian touches, yet sinking at intervals to the worst melodrama and highfalutin preciousness, *Pierre* is ambiguous in other ways than its author intended. Lacking unity, sprawling, often wordy and extravagant, it is probably the most poorly organized novel by Melville; but in spite of all this, it is probably the most crucially important from the viewpoint of the biographer and of anyone who wishes to understand this wayward writer.

It may be little more than coincidental that Poe lived all his life in the shadow of a consuming mother-image, and that his relationship with all women was frustrated and immature; while similarly Melville was harassed and truncated by a reticence and withdrawal from sex that seem very nearly morbid. Both men married, but Poe in his marriage was certainly skirting the edge of abnormality; and Melville in his was not only wretched but apparently, so far as the sexual element is concerned, insufficient. Both seem to have regarded a surrender to animal passion as immoral. Poe's fiction, and especially his poetry, are not lacking in either women or love, but it is always a suspect and unnatural delineation. Melville's work sidesteps both, with but few exceptions. *Pierre*, alone of his major writings, contains female characters, and what use is made of them? We find Marie Glendinning, patently Melville's mother, Maria Gansevoort, portrayed as a paragon beside whom all other women are insignificant; we find Lucy, the intended wife of Pierre, a cold, unapproachable yet somehow deified young woman, and Isabel, whom Pierre after discovering that she is his half-sister falls in love with, an even more worshipful object, though with something of the mistress about her. Pierre's relations with these women are abnormal in every respect; the mother receives an unnatural amount of adoration and subservience, the potential bride a strange uxorious regard, the sister a more than brotherly interest. Incest is hinted, and society brands Pierre with it. Motivated by the most altruistic intentions, Pierre is hunted to earth and hounded to death; and this is the ostensible pattern of the novel. But its real interest lies in what it discloses of Melville's tortured and divided attitude toward sex, the subject that, apart from the treatment of it here, was taboo in all his work.

A blight falls upon Melville after *Pierre*, but it was already implicit long before. For all the robustious spirits, depth of feeling and impetuous power in Melville, one senses an incompleteness, a lack, that is almost paradoxical. There are provinces of the body and spirit which Melville does not enter: sex in most of its manifestations is one of them. He attempted to storm it in *Pierre*, and failing, seemed to withdraw. Of course, concomitant barriers had risen to discourage him; the books from *Mardi* on met with little popular success; but Melville must have known that he was written out. He could have gone on repeating himself, but he was not that sort of artist or man. The best he had to offer had been spurned, and he chose to remain silent. The famous forty-year hiatus between *Pierre* and *Billy Budd*, with the exception of a few minor works, seems now to have been the result not of wounded ego but of emptiness. In a letter to Hawthorne, during the composition of *Moby-Dick*, he had prophesied his decline: "I am like one of those seeds taken out of the Egyptian pyramids which, after being three thousand years a seed, and nothing but a seed, being planted in English soil, it developed itself, grew to greenness, and then fell to mould. So I . . . I feel that I am now come to the utmost leaf of the bulb, and that shortly the flower must fall to the mould."

In the posthumous *Billy Budd* he once more came to grips with the problem of innocence versus the evil of things-as-they-are; and the youthful Budd, surely innocent though he has killed a man, is condemned to death by the inexorable logic of moral necessity. A strong and beautifully executed work, this brief novel fittingly climaxes the dark career of Melville.

It is evident that, preoccupied almost to the point of obsession with the riddle of man's relationship to God, Melville traced in his books a course that ran the gamut of a temperate hedonism (*Typee, Omoo*) through a skeptical Christianity (*Mardi*) to a bleak pessimism (*Moby-Dick, Pierre*) and a final near-reconciliation (*Benito Cereno, Billy Budd*). In the early books we saw the essentially lighthearted Melville in youth, exulting in the freshness of an exotic world; in *Mardi*, at one giant stride, the tormented philosopher appeared and began sounding for "truth." In *Moby-Dick* Melville accused the Deity and announced his glimpse of the "mortally intolerable truth," i. e., the cold white silence which greets all our most passionate questionings. *Pierre* confirmed those glimpses, and bitterness was never so eloquently expressed: "It is not for man to follow the trail of truth too far, since by so doing he entirely loses the directing compass of his mind; for arrived at the Pole, to whose barrenness only it points, there, the needle indifferently respects all points of the horizon alike." *Billy Budd*, at the close of his life, showed however that Melville had desperately accepted our mortal status quo and courageously faced it. Yet even in this recognition of human

limitations, the sum of his comfortless message lies in his acknowledging that the question, "What is truth?" is "still more final
than any answer." The apocalyptic visions had failed to render
any more easy verdict; and the realist in Melville had spoken the
final word.

BIERCE AND HEARN
Poe Redivivus

IT CAN have been only the factor of temperament (enormously
complex as that is) which induced Brockden Brown, Poe and
Melville to work in the shadowy depths of human experience, or
in what Poe called the "outré." Factors of environment, social,
economic and geographical status, do not seem to have particularly influenced their work; but all of these men were Eastern
seaboard dwellers. The next two American writers of any stature
to develop in a lineal relationship with them lived in the West.
Ambrose Bierce was born in Ohio but spent his most active days
in San Francisco; Lafcadio Hearn, a world citizen, came to literary maturity in Ohio and Louisiana. Evidently if any generalization can be made concerning these apocalyptics it is that a
majority of them lived in the South; but a case could hardly be
made for the determining power of that fact.

Temperamentally, however, these writers had much in common; and an examination of the work Bierce did, and the scarcely
larger body of writing left by Hearn, shows how central their
position was in the Brown tradition. Neither figure is of great
importance; compared even to Brown, they are seen to be in-
substantial; but both men wrote fiction that will live; and Bierce
particularly had a quality of imagination that few artists in any
age possess. Hearn's rich and exotic style and his remarkable ability to portray the ghostly and bizarre assure him a secure minor
position in our literature.

Born in 1842, eight years before Hearn, Bierce outlived him
by ten, disappearing somewhere in Mexico in 1914. So far as can
be determined their paths never crossed, though there are many

curious parallels in their lives and works. Bierce gave up his native land at the end; Hearn left the United States to become as Japanese as possible in the final phase of his life. Both spent their best energies in the prime of life on journalism. Each enjoyed a regional fame but hardly achieved national recognition while alive. The similarity of their interests in fiction is demonstrable. In temperament they bore resemblances; each was hotheaded, idealistic, hence cynical and inclined to doubt the value of human life. A strong sense of idealism is, in fact, one of the striking characteristics of the apocalyptics from Brown on; these men looked at life with great expectations and discovered with surprise and hurt that life was not so noble and good as they had expected (and still secretly hoped); whereupon the black, evil heart of life became the only part they were capable of seeing and showing. The inversion only proved how deep-seated the malady was.

After Bierce had served his time as soldier in the Civil War, he went west on a topographical mission, and finding himself in San Francisco, stayed there to become the local Samuel Johnson. This was in the days of the Gold Coast's literary youth but considerably beyond the period of its adolescence. Bret Harte had already packed up and set out to storm the East; the way was clear for a forceful young writer to make his weight felt, and Bierce soon did just that. His earliest contributions were verses in imitation of Poe, published in the San Francisco *News-Letter* and the *Alta Californian;* and a little later he took over the "Town Crier" page of the former journal. Forthright and bristling with dogma, Bierce's column was read with delight by the rough and ready Californians of the time; such diatribe and malediction had seldom been seen before, even in the San Francisco that had nurtured Lynch Law and Vigilance Committees. In 1872, however, Bierce left California for a four-year sojourn in London, which made of him a confirmed Anglophile, and served on his return to gild him with the imprimatur of British acceptance. He became more solidly entrenched as the West Coast literary dictator, and having published while abroad such books as the *Fiend's Delight, Nuggets and Dust* and *Cobwebs*

from an Empty Skull, he was now little less than a phenomenon
on our rocky Pacific shore. The approaching *fin de siècle* period
in France (gravely influenced by Poe) had thus by round-about
means had a double effect on Bierce. He was always a Poe disciple; and to have found the English wits imitating their French
colleagues, who in turn were taking their cue from his own earlier
countryman, was enough to confirm Bierce in his loyalty to the
apocalyptic mood. And now, for the next twenty-five years, he
settled down to the exercise of his mordant wit and venomous
satire in the column "Prattle" which appeared regularly until the
turn of the century consecutively in the San Francisco *Argonaut,*
Wasp and Hearst's *Examiner.* Although much of this journalism
has been preserved in Bierce's *Collected Works,* little of it has
permanent value. The historian of the '80's and '90's in western
America will always find it useful, but the verbal pyrotechnics
expended on forgotten personalities, the sometimes tawdry bom-
bast, have lost their savor and become mere museum curiosa.

In 1891 Bierce published *Tales of Soldiers and Civilians;* and
in 1893, *Can Such Things Be?* His claim to a position in American literature rests wholly on these two books, a slender enough
chain upon which to hang a reputation; but, as it happens, a
strong one from the standpoint of the apocalyptic tradition.
Bierce wrote fiction exclusively and solely in this vein; he modeled his form and his subject matter directly upon Poe, and
while he never achieved the artistry or the psychological overtones of his master, he exhibited some aspects of the imagination
never seen before. Irked as he was by contemporary jibes at his
Poe-idolatry, it is nevertheless perfectly apparent that Poe was
his inspiration and exemplar, and hardly any other influence can
be detected in his work.

If it be objected that Poe's characters seldom seem lifelike, what
must be our objection to Bierce's? They have absolutely no relevant characteristics that strike us as human, save their outward
description; it is never for the character's sake but always for
the plot's sake that a Bierce story exists. Bierce was interested,
even more than Brown, Poe or Melville, in the *idea* of the story—
seldom in the human significance of it. In fact, some of the

stories exist essentially for the whiplash ending, which in Bierce's handling antedated O. Henry. But the Bierce story can be reread with some profit, for there is real evidence of a technician's hand. The element of atmosphere contributes a good deal to the effectiveness of these stories, which in all cases deal with the bleak, gloomy or horrible aspects of life. Madness induced by fright, terror of the supernatural, death in battle, these are the Biercean themes. There is no humor in any line of Bierce's creative work; in fact, Bierce never wrote a humorous sentence in his life, though there is plenty of death's-head grinning throughout the *Collected Works*. It is doubtful if any of the apocalyptic writers from Brown to Faulkner have perceived what humor is, or been able to write it; they have excluded it from the categories of human behavior; their definition of life rules out the possibility of real levity. In its place we find a savage and bitter gibing at human frailty, the more savage because the more heartbreaking to the shattered idealist who has found humanity is frail. The best these writers can do is show us a caricature of comedy, and from Poe to Faulkner we find them offering as "humorous" what is merely grotesque.

However, of Bierce we can say that he never tried to be funny in his fiction; he did try most desperately for shocking effects, and he succeeded greatly in such well-anthologized stories as "A Horseman in the Sky," "An Occurrence at Owl Creek Bridge," "The Man and the Snake," and "The Damned Thing." In the first two of these stories, from the *Tales*, we have exigent pictures of "occurrences"—action in highly unusual circumstances by lay figures who are manipulated by the author so that, regardless of plausibility, their dispositions will have maximum dramatic effect. The soldier in "A Horseman in the Sky" reveals in the penultimate sentence that he has shot his father; and we feel the shock. We can go through the story backwards, pick up the threads that led us to this denouement, and find that Bierce had made a nice puzzle for us and untangled it skillfully. We react to the story as we might to a cleverly demonstrated mathematical problem; but we do not feel the human sympathy or identity which serious fiction ought to arouse. The man in "An Occurrence at Owl Creek Bridge" through whose brain is flashing a long sequence of remembered action, holds nothing of our sympathy; but we are startled and possibly amazed, and we shiver slightly in the realization that perhaps this is the way death can come. We read through these and other stories of war, and toward carnage an attitude emerges which is entirely realistic and quite modern. Bierce wrote from the viewpoint of the individual sufferer in war; he never attempted to glorify any aspect of killing; and on the reportorial level, the *Tales* are the best minor pictures of modern warfare up to their time. No doubt Crane's *Red Badge of Courage* owed much to Bierce.

"The Damned Thing" and "The Man and the Snake" from *Can Such Things Be?* are typical of the supernatural tales; again it is the frame that becomes of first importance; the actors are pawns but what they do is calculated to induce that thrill of fear which is one of the lesser functions of fictional art but surely still a function. Diabolism seldom reached such heights as in this collection; and if read properly, accepting the limitations Bierce imposed upon himself, these tales are worth considering; they compare favorably with many of Poe's similar stories.

A great tenet in Bierce's creed was the primacy of the short story. It was derived from Poe; as was his attitude toward the novel, which he called "a short story padded." His notions of the novel give a fair picture of his critical thinking. The novel (a form in which he never wrote, though he "collaborated" with a Dr. Danziger on a "romance"), he held to be "a species of composition bearing the same relation to literature that the panorama bears to art. As it is too long to be read at a sitting the impressions made by its successive parts are successively effaced, as in the panorama. Unity, totality of effect, is impossible; for besides the few pages last read all that is carried in mind is the mere plot of what has gone before. To the romance the novel is what photography is to painting. Its distinguishing principle, probability, corresponds to the literal actuality of the photograph and puts it distinctly into the category of reporting; whereas the free wing of the romancer enables him to mount to such altitudes of imagination as he may be fitted to attain; and the first three essentials of the literary art are imagination, imagination and imagination. The art of writing novels, such as it was, is long dead everywhere except in Russia, where it is new. Peace to its ashes—some of which have a large sale." [1]

The handful of short stories, and a score of witty "definitions" in his *Devil's Dictionary* are about all that Bierce left us, and Hearn left hardly more; Hearn's contribution to the apocalyptic province was probably more important than Bierce's; at least he introduced a note of Continental exoticism and gave to his work a meticulous polish. Bierce's prose, while often clear and forceful, is marred by wooden phrasing and journalese; Hearn's errs on the side of preciousness and overelaboration. Hearn, however, was unquestionably the more reflective and the larger mind; lacking Bierce's intensity, he easily outclassed him in breadth of interests and fundamental humanity. What was violent in Bierce became gently mysterious in Hearn. The ghostly, queer and inexplicable fascinated both writers to an almost equal degree; but Bierce took these misty grounds by storm, flung his characters into horror, shook them by the throat and paraded the ghoulish with gusto. Hearn made use of identical material, and in his hands it became quiet enigma, eerie but subdued and wondering strangeness. Exoticism for its own sake, and exploration of all that was curious and rare, all forms of alienated experience and hardly explicable manners and customs—these were Hearn's passions, quietly and continuously pursued through his entire career.

That career became one of the strangest in American literature, climaxed by self-exile. Hearn was the curious child of an exotic marriage. He was born on the island of Leucadia in the Ionian Sea, of a Greek mother and an Irish father, both of whom abandoned him to the care of an Irish aunt who sent him to Roman Catholic seminaries in France and England, but he early ran away to London, and in 1869 arrived penniless in America. His peregrinations took him first to Cincinnati, where he began

---

[1] From *The Cynic's Word Book* by Ambrose Bierce. © 1906 by Albert & Charles Boni., Inc.

his long term of journalistic slavery, then to New Orleans. Small, nervous, physically ill-favored, with large myopic eyes that caused him great anguish though he read literally nine-tenths of the time, he became second only to George W. Cable as interpreter of the South to itself. He was hardly known at all in the North until *Chita* (1888), and by the time his name began to mean something in America he had turned his back on the Occident.

But the early days in New Orleans were the period of his real growth as well as accomplishment. He greatly admired Baudelaire, Gautier, Loti and the French exquisites, some of whom he translated admirably. As a youth at Cincinnati he even imitated Baudelaire's predilections in women, and lived with a young Negress; later in New Orleans he was fascinated by the Creole argot and tradition. Toward love he had the true romantic attitude, and because it bears upon his literary theory it is worth noting. In a lecture to his Japanese students late in life he said, "Consider again the place and the meaning of the passion of love in any human life. It is essentially a period of idealism, of imagining better things and conditions than are possible in this world. For everybody who has been in love has imagined something higher than the possible and the present. Any idealism is a proper subject for art. It is not at all the same in the case of realism. Grant that all this passion, imagination, and fine sentiment is based upon a very simple animal impulse. That does not make the least difference in the value of the highest results of that passion. We might say the very same thing about any human emotion; every emotion can be evolutionarily traced back to simple and selfish impulses shared by man with the lower animals. But because an apple tree or a pear tree happens to have its roots in the ground, does that mean that its fruits are not beautiful and wholesome? Most assuredly we must not judge the fruit of the tree from the unseen roots; but what about turning up the ground to look at the roots? What becomes of the beauty of the tree when you do that? The realist—at least the French realist—likes to do that. He likes to bring back the attention of his reader to the lowest rather than to the highest, to that which should be kept hidden, for the very same reason that the roots of a tree should be kept underground if the tree is to live."[2]

Now, this is not only the way we would expect a romantic to think about love, but it is soundly consonant literary theory. Compare Poe's similar dictum: "In my view, if an artist must paint decayed cheeses, his merit will lie in their looking as little like decayed cheeses as possible." Seemingly a paradox, since Poe and Hearn and their like lost no opportunity to write of gruesome subjects, there is still good reason for this dictum. The dreary face of reality held no charms for them; and while they dared to picture subjects less pleasing even than "decayed cheeses" or "unseen roots" they would have recoiled from any photographic description of the unpleasant facts of everyday existence. It was legitimate to paint horrifically in the interests of the imagination, but since it took little imagination to reproduce the manifold misery of real life, that was taboo. Imagination, fancy, "ideality"—these essentially "spiritual" categories seemed the only defensible ones for the romantic artist.

For Poe, Hearn felt something like reverence, and he was almost as greatly influenced by him as was Bierce. "Poe," he wrote,[3] "was a writer who understood the color-power of words and the most delicate subtleties of language as very few English or American writers have ever done." He paid tribute to Baudelaire for the famous translations, doubting "whether any other French author could have succeeded in rendering Poe with one half the success," but at the same time criticized with some evidence of jealousy certain aspects of the work. "No really capable critic who compares the English of the *Tales* with the French version can deny that they have lost a great part of their literary value through the process of transmutation." Hearn was qualified as a translator and had intimate knowledge of the translator's problems; he could hardly have helped knowing that Poe's foreign presentation was in capable hands with Baudelaire, but still he would say the last word for his hero.

---

[2] From *Books and Habits* by Lafcadio Hearn. © 1921 by Mitchell McDonald.
[3] From "A French Translation of Edgar Poe," in the New Orleans *Item*, October 22, 1879.

It is in his work, of course, that Hearn exemplifies the Poesque attitudes; and from *Some Chinese Ghosts* to his last tales of Japanese mystery he adhered to an announced pledge of "worship of the Odd, the Queer, the Strange, the Exotic, the Monstrous." Examine the description of the hurricane in *Chita*, and the powerful aftermath of the storm in which the "Spoilers of the dead" plunder the vast wash of corpses: "There are silks, satins, laces, and fine linen to be stripped from the bodies of the drowned,— and necklaces, bracelets, watches, finger-rings and fine chains, brooches and trinkets. . . . 'What a beauty!—Oh, what a beautiful woman! Look at the beauty!' That ball-dress was made in Paris by—But you never heard of him, Sicilian Vicenzu. . . . 'What a lovely little bride!' Her betrothal ring will not come off, Guiseppe; but the delicate bone snaps easily; your oyster-knife can sever the tendon. . . . 'Look! What a beautiful girl!' Over her heart you will find it, Valentino—the locket held by that fine Swiss chain of woven hair—'The wealth!' And it is not your quadroon bondsmaid, sweet lady, who now disrobes you so roughly; those Malay hands are less deft than hers,—but she slumbers very far away from you, and may not be aroused from her sleep. 'Have you seen it, lady? Have you seen the beauty?' . . . Juan, the fastenings of those diamond ear-drops are much too complicated for your peon fingers: tear them out!— 'Excuse me, my love!' "[4]

This is ghoulish enough and in some ways does not square with the sentiments quoted previously regarding realism; however, what here interests Hearn is not the gruesome, but the queer and monstrous. The storm has been dwelt upon at such length and so broodingly, and its violence has been so well described, that to avoid anticlimax Hearn relied upon a shocking aftermath. The tenor of *Chita* is romantic; its several climacteric levels depend somewhat for effect on a realist portrayal of horrors. Poe's method was similar, but the demonic vigor and vivid impressions in Poe are the result of a much more intense imagination. Hearn softens, wraps in sable the tenuous figurations of his fancy; the impressions they leave are seldom strong, but something does carry over, and that is a sense of the word colors and a feeling

[4] From *Chita* by Lafcadio Hearn. © 1907 by Harper & Brothers.

of quality that lifts Hearn above the ruck of writers of his time. Bierce makes a powerful immediate impression, but the shock over, there is little to detain one. Hearn never makes a strong claim upon the attention, but he can be reexamined with pleasure and not to the detriment of the impression he first creates.

One would hesitate to contend strongly for a claim that, in Hearn and Bierce, Poe lived again. With whatever baleful gleam their work carried on his tradition, it was a fainter light. The tortured, unresting spirit of the visionary who can never reconcile the beast-in-man with the man-God—that spirit had mounted to mighty intensity in Melville, and has not since been as fully expressed. Bierce, living into the opening year of the first World War, fell far short of his predecessors' vision or eloquence. The next American to rise in this haunted realm, with imaginative power and technical equipment far exceeding those of all his elders save Poe and Melville, began his career upon the close of that war, and a final assessment of his position is still to be made. I am speaking of William Faulkner, gifted beyond his contemporaries in sheer verbal ability and word splendor, with technical virtuosity and imagination of a high order.

Taking a backward glance, it is interesting to conjecture what Brockden Brown would make of *Absalom, Absalom!* I think he would revel in it. If he had had the fortune to be born a century and a quarter later than he was he might even have written it, so little has the basic attitude of the apocalyptic mind shifted, despite the advances in insight and technique represented in the work of Poe, Melville, Hearn and Bierce.

The Fury of
WILLIAM FAULKNER

NOT SINCE Poe's time has the South enjoyed the distinction of harboring a writer of the first rank—not, that is, until the advent of William Faulkner, who, it is said, rests uneasily upon the conscience of that South; and it, certainly, rests uneasily upon the conscience of William Faulkner. A fierce critic of the South,

Faulkner is still one of its staunchest defenders. Like the southern colonel of romantic fiction, he may abuse and condemn the land of his nativity as much as he wishes, but no one else may indulge the same sentiments aloud in his presence. For a long while it was thought that Faulkner, like Poe, was merely writing in the irresponsible mood of any moment in which to envisage and embody terror, horror, gloom—the black night of the soul. The Faulkner novels were, for a long time, considered *tours de force*, without external referents, or only with such as were indivisible from any writing that used the modern South for background. But with the consecutive appearance of the novels, it became increasingly clear that Faulkner had been building a vast, savage, demonic *Tragedie Humaine* of the American South, or more specifically, of that section of Mississippi in and about what he calls Jefferson, which is Oxford, his home town. Inside this amazing, convolute and inimitable saga is everything that Poe was able to suggest in his macabre tales, much that Brown and Melville and Hawthorne foreshadowed, plus not only Faulkner's own incredibly fecund conjurations of the terrible and phantasmal, but also a very definite and real world of social significances and broad slapstick humor, which is outside the domain of any apocalyptic writer, any Gothic novelist of any time or place.

Because it has become clear that Faulkner is a critic of the multiform inequities of Southern society, and that he is concerned to the point of obsession with that degeneration he finds in Southern culture, the South apparently is none too sure it relishes having again a first-rank writer; the South (and the rest of the country too, for that matter) seems to treat Faulkner with the same lack of appreciation that was meted out to Poe. With the exception of *Sanctuary*, no Faulkner novel has sold over a few thousand copies. Critical acclaim has been widespread and hearty; but Poe also had his admirers. Faulkner can sell a short story now and then to slick magazines, but only at the expense of his art. Yet Faulkner has himself largely to blame for his comparatively meager audience. The faults in spite of which he has become a considerable novelist have obscured his supreme qualities from a public which will buy equally serious work by Hemingway, Dos Passos or Steinbeck. Those faults are perhaps the expense of his virtues and so indivisible from them; but if so, the paradox is nearly incredible, and Faulkner, an amazing craftsman, could erase them if he wished to. The cast of mind which I have named apocalyptic is an ineradicable attribute of its possessor; and I believe Faulkner can no more help writing as he does, or alter his fundamental method, than he can move to Maine and write of cod fishing.

This writer is an artist of integrity. He shuns publishers' cocktail parties and teas. He has not allowed himself to be lionized and feted; and he will not seek or curry favor. However, this unwillingness to play the ignoble game of expediency seems not to be the major factor in Faulkner's comparative obscurity. He is invariably well reviewed, and even coteries and cliques among critics and other writers regard him seriously. What bookstore salespeople in general say about his books is impossible to judge; but in some instances known to me, they lay great stress upon his (1) "morbidity," (2) moral unreliability and (3) unintelligibility. Such allegations undoubtedly discourage thousands of readers, and put off a great many who presumably would appreciate Faulkner. The unacknowledged censor of our literature is the ignorant bookstore clerk; and he is also far more powerful in shaping popular literary opinion than any Samuel Johnson.

The three aspects of Faulkner which an average unsophisticated reader would note, and which would tend to alienate him are, in order of importance: his recondite narrative method; his pessimistic, nihilistic philosophy with its attendant emphasis on the abnormal and subnormal in human behavior; and lastly, his ornate, involved prose style. These three factors unquestionably have acted to discourage a wider appreciation of Faulkner's merits that coexist with the three fundamental drawbacks. Whether these "drawbacks" are actually to be considered as such, though I believe they are, is a question quite apart from the consideration of Faulkner's unpopularity.

On the other hand, Faulkner's proficiency in the short story is an acknowledged fact; he is one of the masters of the short story, and yet his methods in this form are no different from those in the novel. There just isn't as much of them. That is not illogical; Faulkner's narrative generalship, his brilliant evasions and suspended illuminations, his gorgeous, hot and rank prose can best be savored in small doses. They are of overpowering effect. But when delivered in three hundred pages they are sometimes less than overpowering and merely tedious and ridiculous. The idiot Snopes's love affair with the neighbors' cow is alternately touching and funny in the first confrontation, and would have been memorable if it had been the last; but as the boy makes love through whole sections of *The Hamlet,* our sense of proportion ridicules our sympathy, and we end in dubiety if not boredom or disgust. We are genuinely moved to horror and a profound unease when Emily is disclosed to have kept her lover's corpse in bed for forty years; but the book-long cortège that carries Addie Bundren's dead body in and out of horrendous or merely fantastic and low-comedy situations is finally dreary and exhausting, alike to our sense of probability and our interest. Any of Faulkner's novels contains almost unbelievably brilliant sections, tremendously effective in themselves; but no Faulkner novel (unless, perhaps, *The Sound and the Fury*) ever adds up to the excellence of its parts. I think the disappointing factor in the novels lies in just that prodigality of talent and virtuosity of knowingness which finally defeats itself through excess. There is too much of Faulkner in any of his novels.

It is this quality of excess which is Faulkner's chief defect; in every novel we feel the strain and stress of a prodigious talent overexerting itself. After *Sartoris* (1929), the most self-possessed of his books, each novel seems to surpass its predecessor in this evident struggle for force, strangeness, difference. If it were not for the power of Faulkner's imagination, which is quite unequaled by any of his contemporaries, these violently laboring novels would have failed entirely. But it is the vividness with which Faulkner can bring to bear his and our concentration upon his characters and their background that saves him, that gives even his halting, disjointed, technically quixotic novels a kind of demonic energy and urgency which carries us along in spite of ourselves.

The best of them is *The Sound and the Fury*, a work of his most fruitful and satisfactory period, *circa* 1929. In that year and the two years preceding and the two following it he wrote and published *Sartoris*, *As I Lay Dying* and *These Thirteen* (a collection of his best stories), as well as some of his least successful efforts, *Sanctuary*, *Mosquitoes* and *Light in August*. The later novels are increasingly garrulous in a crabbed, involved fashion, and read like the product of a collaboration by Henry James in his last phase and Poe. *Absalom, Absalom!* and *The Hamlet*, and even some of the long stories in *Go Down, Moses*, are gossipy and tedious. Once the old magic of the Faulkner methods is unveiled, it is too easy to see what a bare fabric lies underneath. The shocks in *Absalom, Absalom!* are deftly withheld until the proper time, meted out with the same nice and fastidious hand, but when they come we have already expected them. We have felt them before in Faulkner, and they were better the first time. It is true that new values begin to emerge. We discover that a Southern saga of degeneration and recrudescence begins to unfold, in the downfall of such families as the Sutpens, and in the emergence of such families as the verminous Snopeses. But this is poor compensation for what we have lost. In another order of novelist, in novels of social history or of manners, it would be acceptable; but in a writer whose metier is the imponderable dark recesses of the spirit, the shadowy deeps of the soul, the abnormal and bizarre, it seems somewhat irrelevant.

There is another characteristic, it must be added, in these later novels and stories (and one which was present to a lesser extent in the earlier novels); namely, humor. It is the kind of sardonic, abrasive humor that one finds in Melville and Brockden Brown, and which almost directly gave Erskine Caldwell his method, though there is more of human sympathy in Caldwell than can ever be found in Faulkner. This factor, the existence of a comic sense cropping up in an apocalyptic writer, is an anomaly difficult to reconcile. But it is the hard laughter of cruelty and satire, and not the true rough-and-ready yet indulgent humor of a Mark Twain. It is the obverse medal of that saturnine melancholy which underlies all of Faulkner, yet which cannot always control his abounding imaginative vitality. It is one expression of the enormous force, breaking out in every direction, possessed by Faulkner. The humor of *As I Lay Dying* is the broadest and most characteristic, and the most memorable; that of *The Hamlet* is equally Faulknerian but seems less remarkable because we have seen it before.

Excessive as are these books, overburdened with rhetoric and laden with dubious narrative dodges, the best of them make their points as effectively as such points have ever been made in the novel. They are saved from the spurious melodrama and fustian "horror" of the traditional Gothic novel because they have a foundation in realism. The South is in these books in a form recognizable if distorted; we cannot doubt the authenticity of such characters as Mrs. Compson, Caddy, or even Temple Drake. They ring true, as do the Varners, the Snopeses, and even the Bundrens. It is the macabre, the horrific and abnormally degenerate in action and character that place the books in the category of fantasy; and it is the excess of these things, the superabundance of every quondam desirable quality, as intensity of feeling, verbal virtuosity and extreme technical competence, which cause Faulkner's novels, one and all, to seem unequal. In their parts they are magnificent; in sum they tend to seem overdone.

This criticism applies least to *The Sound and the Fury*, which does have a real consistency and cumulativeness of effect. When Luster drives Benjy around the square and turns left at the monument, one has an instant and incredible sense of revelation, as if all that had gone before was preparation for this moment of tremendous light and knowledge; and as one has untied, skein by skein, the knotted circumstances of the Compson family's disintegration, one feels that immense and steady piling up of detail and intimacy which only the great novels give. On the other hand, it is true that Benjy's soliloquy, and equally that of Quentin, sustain themselves only at the expense of our patience. It is a story told obliquely through the minds of three persons: Benjy, the idiot; Quentin, the sympathetic brother; and Jason, the scoundrelly brother; and the final chapter is, in the older tradition, told by the omniscient but rigorously Flaubertian author.

The last chapter is the best, the more human, understanding, and effective; but this may be only an appearance, since it is based wholly on the strengths of the preceding three sections.

The real story of *The Sound and the Fury* is put succinctly into the mouth of old Dilsey, the Negro mammy of the Compson household. "I've seed de first en de last." It is the dissolution of a Southern family, the end-product of a line which has approached decay and now falls into dust. This is the absolute burden of every Faulkner novel except *Pylon* (1935) and perhaps *The Wild Palms* (1939), though it may be discovered referentially in both of them. *The Sound and the Fury* includes as essential elements of its partial disclosures and baits those conceivable degenerate tendencies, incest, and idiocy and murder, dipsomania, fornication and theft. The Compsons are decaying before our eyes; Caddy, after succumbing to the physical love of her brother Quentin, goes "bad"; Quentin himself, we learn later, commits suicide; their father drinks himself to death; Benjy is a congenital idiot; their mother is one of the gallery of self-pitying, ineffective Southern gentlewomen Faulkner has written of; and of all the people in the book, only the Negroes emerge with remnants of human decency about them. Dilsey has all the character, and without her it is doubtful if the Compson clan would have cohered long enough for its horrendous story to have been played out.

Once more, *The Sound and the Fury* is a technical triumph, beautifully economical of its means, better written than any of Faulkner's succeeding novels (less drunk upon words), and startlingly bold in its use of point of view. The Benjy section is believable; and encouraged by his success with it, Faulkner repeated in the St. Elmo Snopes passages of *The Hamlet*, but without approaching the earlier attempt in power or convincingness. In this connection, another of the novels, *As I Lay Dying*, using a similar method, i. e., achieving its narrative progression through revelations of a varied set of points of view, is less successful because, unlike *The Sound and the Fury*, in which the method is to deal with one character's revelations at a time, and once only, it deals with them piecemeal and alternately among all the characters throughout the book. The method, at best, is artificial and tends to destroy verisimilitude; in *As I Lay Dying* there is no sense of reality whatever, because we cannot even for the moment believe in the revelations of the characters. That is, we are not sufficiently prepared, hence incredulous, and we are unable to suspend disbelief as we are able to do in continuous narrative. It is a good game, though; and that is what the Faulkner novels reduce themselves to: fascinating exercises of the detective sense, as we ferret out the meanings and solve the puzzles so ingeniously set in them.

One has the sense of stress and strain in any Faulkner novel, as if the writer had made a private bargain with himself to assign no traditional cause to any behavior, and to have all behavior, so far as remains within human limits, quite as distinct from what might be called normal as is conceivable. There is the boy Vardaman in *As I Lay Dying* who, bringing home a fish at the precise time when his mother dies, persists in identifying his mother as the fish. "It was not her because it was laying right yonder in the dirt. And now it's all chopped up. I chopped it up. It's laying in the kitchen in the bleeding pan, waiting to be cooked and et. Then it wasn't and she was, and now it is and she wasn't. And tomorrow it will be cooked and et and she will be him and pa and Cash and Dewey Dell and there wont be anything in the box and so she can breathe. It was laying right yonder on the ground. I can get Vernon. He was there and he seen it, and with both of us it will be and then it will not be." That is the beginning of his confusion, mounting to the certainty announced in a chapter only one sentence long: "My mother is a fish."[1]

These novels have been highly praised by many critics, but they need not detain one too long, nor need such praise be underestimated. If we had only the novels to judge Faulkner's stature by, we would still be right in calling him one of the great romantic writers of our time. However, we have the short stories with which to compare the novels, and that comparison sets up a standard which the long narratives fall very far short of. In value,

---

[1] From *As I Lay Dying* by William Faulkner. © 1930 by Harrison Smith. © 1932 by William Faulkner.

after *The Sound and the Fury*, the hierarchy of the novels may well be: *Sartoris*, probably the most traditional narrative Faulkner ever wrote; *As I Lay Dying*; and in increasing negligibility, *Light in August*, *Absalom, Absalom!*, *Sanctuary*, *Pylon*, *The Hamlet*, *The Wild Palms*; and at the bottom, the early efforts, *Mosquitoes* and *Soldier's Pay*.

The least happy of Faulkner's numerous technical experiments has been his dabbling in a sort of pseudo-Jamesian prose. *Absalom, Absalom!* is the chief exhibit in this vein, together with some of his long stories in *Go Down, Moses*. At best writing a richly overburdened prose, with frequent archaic and stilted touches, and more frequent bad rhetoric, Faulkner evolved a style for these works which resembles in some sense the dream-language of H. C. Earwicker. One has the feeling that Faulkner simply let his typewriter rattle and took no trouble to prune, revise or rewrite. If a first essay failed to get across the meaning, he simply added another brace of phrases, so that finally the meaning not only would not get across but reversed itself several times. This mystification, legitimate in an orderly work of art, becomes finally a test for Faulkner of his own ingenuity, for he must and finally does always unravel his snarled skeins in a miraculous way. He seems to throw intentional obstacles in his way in order to show the virtuosity he is capable of in eventually dislodging them. This is a far cry from the modest and completely rational involutions of an Arsene Dupin story; but it is somehow, one feels, the same obscure psychological necessity driving the spinner of the web along. For that matter, *Sanctuary's* value, such as it is, inheres almost solely in its qualities of mystery thriller. But as an example of the perfervid prose style in which Faulkner descends to a near caricature of himself, observe almost any passage in *Absalom, Absalom!*[2] This is entirely typical:

"I don't think she ever suspected, until that afternoon four years later when she saw them again, when they brought Bon's body into the house and she found in his coat the photograph which was not her face, not her child; she just waked the next morning and they were gone and only the letter, the note, re-

---

[2] From *Absalom, Absalom* by William Faulkner. © 1936 by Random House.

maining, the note written by Henry since doubtless he refused to allow Bon to write—this announcement of the armistice, the probation, and Judith acquiescing up to that point, who would have refused as quickly to obey any injunction of her father as Henry had been to defy him yet who did obey Henry in this matter—not the male relative, the brother, but because of that relationship between them—that single personality with two bodies both of which had been seduced almost simultaneously by a man whom at the time Judith had never even seen—she and Henry both knowing that she would observe the probation, give him (Henry) the benefit of that interval, only up to that mutually recognized though unstated and undefined point and both doubtless aware that when that point was reached she would, and with the same calm, the same refusal to accept or give because of any traditional weakness of sex, recall the armistice and face him as a foe, not requiring or even wishing that Bon be present to support her, doubtless even refusing to allow him to intervene if he were, fighting the matter out with Henry like a man first, before consenting to revert to the woman, the loved, the bride."

It is quite probable that Faulkner's reputation will rest largely upon his great short stories, and that *These Thirteen* (1931), *Doctor Martino* (1934), *The Unvanquished* (1938) and *Go Down, Moses* (1942), together with a body of still uncollected tales, are the books by which his name will be remembered. A score of these stories are among the finest written in America; two or three are unquestionably on a par with those of Hemingway and hence the best short stories written in the world in the twentieth century. An examination of them will provide the best key to Faulkner's genius, when it is operating at its optimum.

Among the earlier stories "A Rose for Emily" and "That Evening Sun Go Down" are the masterpieces, while "The Bear" may be taken as an excellent example of his later style. Not since Poe has an American produced a horror tale to match "A Rose for Emily," which is a perfect story from the technical point of view, and one of the most effective and violent stories even Faulkner himself has written. Its gradual unfolding of the character of Miss Emily, its fully acquiescent gifts of revelation, the carefully sown clues and the well-prepared yet shocking climax and denouement, are among the marvels of the Faulkner virtuosity. Let us recount the incidents in their narrative (not chronological) order. We learn, at the outset, that Miss Emily had died, that she was somehow queer and a recluse, "a fallen monument," and the object of the townspeople's curiosity. Then we begin to get the touched-in canvas; we see that Emily Grierson was of the Southern aristocracy, that she had fallen upon lean days, and yet had eked out her decadent respectability with that force of character and will which is sometimes the alleged attribute of Southern aristocracy. When called upon by a committee of aldermen seeking to force her to pay taxes, she turned them out of her house with quiet authority. Faulkner describes the scene, and we are given our first and only portrait of Emily —"a small, fat woman in black, with a thin gold chain descending to her waist and vanishing into her belt, leaning on an ebony cane with a tarnished gold head. Her skeleton was small and spare; perhaps that was why what would have been merely plumpness in another was obesity in her. She looked bloated, like a body long submerged in motionless water, and of that pallid hue." The words "skeleton" and "body long submerged" begin at once to arouse our attention and, in retrospect, are seen to have had a definite intention as setting tone for the climax.

Smells, too, are recorded early in the story—that of the dank, close odor within Miss Emily's barricaded home—that of the more pungent and pressing smell which exuded from the house "a short time after her sweetheart—the one we believed would marry her—had deserted her." [3] And certainly, in as broad an adumbration of the story's hingeing point as might have been given, Faulkner mentions the death of Miss Emily's father, at which time she met callers at the door "dressed as usual and with no trace of grief on her face. She told them that her father was not dead. She did that for three days, with the ministers calling

[3] From "A Rose for Emily" in *These Thirteen* by William Faulkner. © 1931 by Harrison Smith. © 1931 by William Faulkner.

on her, and the doctors, trying to persuade her to let them dispose of the body." [3]

After they had "buried her father quickly" Miss Emily went through a period of sickness, rescued from it at length by the appearance of a Yankee who began to take her for afternoon rides in a yellow-wheeled buggy and matched team of bays from the livery stable. For a Grierson to stoop thus was evidence that Miss Emily, like old lady Wyatt, a distant kinswoman, must be losing her mind. And during this apparent courtship, Miss Emily had occasion to buy some rat poison, or at any rate poison, though she would not say for what purpose she was buying it. The Yankee did not propose, however, and still Miss Emily was seen with him, until the ladies of the town wrote to her distant cousins, who came at once, and during their stay the Yankee was not seen. But they did not stay long, and within three days a neighbor saw Miss Emily's Negro let the Yankee in "at the kitchen door at dusk one evening. And that was the last we saw of Homer Barron." [3]

The years passed, Miss Emily's hair turned pepper-and-salt iron-gray which was the way it stayed until her death at seventy-four. And upon her death, the townspeople crowded into that house like vultures. One room "in that region abovestairs which no one had seen in forty years" was forced open—and now come to life all the well-sown hints and foreshadowings, in swift succession, as in four astounding paragraphs (one of them one sentence of seven words) Miss Emily's "rose" is bequeathed and discovered and becomes a charnelhouse flower all in a breath. The room, "decked and furnished as for a bridal" is covered by an acrid pall of tomblike dust; a man's clothing lies draped upon a chair; and we are struck like a blow between the eyes by that seven-word sentence: "The man himself lay in the bed." Dead forty years, on his face there is a "profound and fleshless grin," a lover cuckolded by "the long sleep that outlasts love, that conquers even the grimace of love." [3]

This is the climax, but there is a penultimate and incredibly more devastating revelation, that ties up every vagrant thread and makes the horror of Miss Emily final and absolute: in the pillow next the murdered man is the indentation of a head. "One of us lifted something from it, and leaning forward, that faint and invisible dust dry and acrid in the nostrils, we saw a long strand of iron-gray hair."

Subtle, fiendishly brilliant, "A Rose for Emily" surpasses anything of its kind in the short story done so far in America. It is the logical development of Poe, but brought to a higher degree of force since its action takes place not in some "misty mid region" but exactly and circumstantially in a recognizable South, with all the appurtenances and criticisms of a society which Faulkner knows and simultaneously hates and loves. (We recall the closing words of *Absalom, Absalom!* when Quentin responds to Shreve's question, why does he hate the South? " 'I don't hate it,' Quentin said quickly, at once, immediately: 'I don't hate it,' he said. *I don't hate it* he thought, panting in the cold air, the iron New England dark; *I don't. I don't! I don't hate it! I don't hate it!*"[4] One would say that "A Rose for Emily" shows how little Faulkner has been restrained by the conventions of Southern life which have dictated to many Southern writers how little of reality they could deal with, and at the same time shows his ineluctable kinship with Poe, as technician and as master of the morbid and bizarre.

"That Evening Sun Go Down" is a yet more subtle and original story, which provides us with an almost perfect demonstration of the fact that Faulkner as short-story artist is superior to Faulkner as novelist. This wonderfully made story happens to employ techniques very similar to those of *The Sound and the Fury*, as it happens also to concern some of the same characters. And while the novel itself marks the zenith of Faulkner's performance as novelist, the story succeeds so greatly in outdistancing the novel, that we are forced to conclude Faulkner's gifts place him most logically as a writer of short fiction. It is, briefly, an exigent study of terror—the terror felt by a nearly inarticulate Negro woman induced by knowledge that her husband is going to kill her. None of this is ever said by Faulkner. Nobody says anything overtly in the story, because the story is told through the eyes and consciousness of a little boy (the Quentin

---

[4] From *Absalom, Absalom!* by William Faulkner. © 1936 by Random House.

of *The Sound and the Fury* and other novels—and one suspects his prototype was Faulkner himself) who does not understand anything of what is going on. The reader gets it all, and in a manner at once urgent, dynamic and forceful—a feat of writing for which Faulkner cannot be given too high praise. Nancy, the Negress, does the washing for Quentin's family; and she has a husband, Jubah, a short black man with a razor scar down his face and apparently a violent character. Nancy is not a good Negress, but we know why. She sleeps, for pay, with white men, including Mr. Stovall, a cashier in the bank and a deacon in the Baptist church, who will not pay her for her services. Eventually Nancy becomes pregnant (in the narrator's words "we could see her apron swelling out" and Jubah told the boy and his little sister, Candace, that it was a watermelon under her dress), but the deed was not Jubah's. Nancy is not a good Negress, but "I ain't nothing but a nigger," she says. "It ain't none of my fault." And that is Faulkner's comment on the mores in his native South which have given the white man leave to use the black woman without hindrance. As for Jubah, he has some excuse for violence; and he is a haunted man, hounded alike by his hatred of the whites who have debauched his wife, and his hatred of her for having permitted it. "I can't hang around white man's kitchen," Jubah said. "But white man can hang around mine. White man can come in my house, but I can't stop him. When white man want to come in my house, I ain't got no house."[5]

Nancy lives just down the lane from the big house where the children live, and she is afraid to stay in her house, so she coaxes the children, Caddy, Jason and Quentin, to stay with her while she pops popcorn and tells stories—all the while with her mind divided and her eyes at the windows; another time she begs Dilsey, the Negro housekeeper who lives in the big white house, to let her sleep there; but ever more exigently the knowledge that Jubah, who had been ordered off the property by the children's father, is coming back, is back, is lying in a ditch with his knife open, impinges upon the Negro woman, and we know as, terror-stricken, she says, "When even your own kitchen wouldn't do no good. When even if I was sleeping on the floor in the room with your own children, and the next morning there I am, and blood all—",[5] that terror, if not Jubah's knife, will end her life. The social criticism as substructure holds up this excellent tale of fear. Through the narrative the children make comments (the story is told largely in dialogue) which, in their apposite irony, become a sort of Greek chorus upon the action. Caddy chides the youngest, Jason, by telling him he is "scairder than a nigger." "Who will do our washing now?" Quentin asks—putting the quietus forever on Nancy. But it is Nancy's own last words, and her high keening which was not crying and not singing but something more terrible, under the circumstances, than either, which leave the chief impress. "I just done got tired. I just a nigger. It ain't no fault of mine."[5]

Caddy, the most knowing of the children, foreshadowing her development elsewhere as a woman of wild hot ways and tragic tendency, asks the questions which searchlight the story and point up what might otherwise be its ambiguities. "Why is Nancy scared of Jubah? What is Jubah going to do to her?" and so on. Caddy is most observant; she notes when Nancy takes hold of the hot globe of a lamp and cannot feel it; when she talks louder than usual in an attempt to disavow fear; when she suddenly breaks into cold sweat at a sound in the darkness outdoors. So it is the terror of the unspeaking Negress, and its ramified causes, which make "That Evening Sun Go Down" a compelling and intricately wrought story. There is no denouement, no final climactic moment; it is a gradual unfolding and a final pervading impression which was the author's point, a more necessary and austere sort of story-telling than that of "A Rose for Emily," where the progression of events and their logical disclosures provide the interest, and the turn of the knife occurs inevitably at the end. Faulkner's stories fall largely into the two groupings: the well-plotted traditional type ("Turn About" is a good example); and the Chekovian, sometimes discursive but always tightly written sketch. The furious imagination and the con-

5 From "That Evening Sun Go Down" in *These Thirteen* by William Faulkner. © 1931 by Harrison Smith. © 1931 by William Faulkner.

trolled technique give both types a power that lifts them to a new level of intensity in our fiction.

"The Bear," a story of 1942, seems to announce an entirely new note in the Faulkner ethos. So far as anyone could tell, the philosophy underlying Faulkner's work heretofore has been a kind of furious nihilism or a hard-bitten aristocratic contempt for existence or a despair without fear or even hope. The values that have been considered abiding from time to time by men, have not, by and large, appeared to mean much to him. But "The Bear" may just possibly foreshadow a different attitude in which the high-sounding words, honor, pity, justice, courage and love, again have a validity and an acceptance. In fact, the story is about just those qualities which, Faulkner says now, in sum equal truth, which is changeless.

Technically, "The Bear" falls somewhere between the advanced work of *The Sound and the Fury* period, and the better devices of the "well-plotted" stories. This story, printed in the *Saturday Evening Post*, is not one of Faulkner's more original technical achievements. Its prose is unfortunately the weighted, rambling instrument of *Absalom, Absalom!* and, in general, of all his later work. Despite all this, "The Bear" is one of the great Faulkner stories and gives one hope that a new orientation toward experience on the part of this author may bring about a new burgeoning of his genius comparable to that of the years when he was writing *These Thirteen*.

Specifically, one would say that Faulkner shows an affirmative attitude in "The Bear," and a new, deeper, more human approach which may constitute a sounder base for the claims to significance of his art. The boy in this story emerges with clear and tender immediacy—like the Jody of Steinbeck's *Red Pony*. Of what other character in the whole range of Faulkner's work can as much be said? And it is because Faulkner has permitted himself to say "yes" to some principles of human conduct which hitherto he has scorned or avoided. The boy ("he was ten") goes into the woods to hunt bear, and under the tutelage of an old man, half-Negro and half-Indian, Sam Fathers, and the example of a mongrel dog, Nip, comes to a consciousness of the values of compassion, courage, and even love, through the stalking and confronting but never the killing of Old Ben, a bear his father has been hunting for years. It takes the boy four years to undergo these alterations of spirit attendant upon his growing up; and in the end he has learned lessons that, it seems, Faulkner has taken two decades to learn. The boy's father explains the significance of what happened when the bear, Old Ben, "with the fierce pride of liberty and freedom . . . at times even seemed deliberately to put that freedom and liberty in jeopardy in order to savor them." He explains how the old half-breed Sam knew humility through suffering (he was the son of a Negro slave) and yet has saved in himself the pride of a wild and invincible race (Chickasaw Indian). He illumines the bravery of Nip, the little dog, which "can't be fierce, because they would call it just noise," but which can be brave. He explains it in words "as quiet as the twilight, too, not loud, because they did not need to be because they would last. 'Courage, and honor, and pride,' his father said, 'and pity, and love of justice and of liberty. They all touch the heart, and what the heart holds to becomes truth, as far as we know truth. Do you see now?'

"Sam, and Old Ben, and Nip, he thought. And himself too. He had been all right too. His father had said so. 'Yes sir,' he said."[6]

Whatever may be the line taken in Faulkner's unwritten fiction, the chances are that on the larger canvas which he is evidently working toward, we shall continue to be treated to a compelling delineation of Southern idealism gone to seed, with the rampant parvenu class, represented by the termite Snopeses, constantly ascendant. If there is to appear a strain of moralism in the Faulknerian universe, it will probably belong to the losing side.

I doubt that Faulkner, in this phase, could write another story like "A Rose for Emily," and that may mean that, for once, we have seen an American writer emerge from the wild miasmal depths where Brown and Poe and Melville were at home, into

[6] From "The Bear" in *Go Down Moses* by William Faulkner. © 1942 by Random House,

freer altitudes where a view of humanity in its workaday aspects is possible. But I think it would be a foolhardy observer who would make any such claims for William Faulkner. Because the mores he has observed, the milieu that claims him, his fundamental methods and his ultimate philosophy are probably subject only to superficial change. That vast, savage and demonic tragedy which he sees life in the South to be is after all the fundamental fructifying principle of his art.

TEMPERAMENTISTS

WASHINGTON IRVING
A Revaluation

IT IS A curious truth that one of the great American literary reputations of the early nineteenth century was founded largely upon a single work, and a flimsy one at that. Washington Irving's *Sketch Book* earned an international reputation; but, as Poe remarked in 1838, "Irving is much overrated, and a nice distinction might be drawn between his just and his surreptitious and adventitious reputation—between what is due to the pioneer solely, and what to the writer." We can agree to that; but the truth remains that Irving exerted a marked influence on other American writers of his time, some of whom, greater than himself, in turn handed on the peculiar qualities first prefigured in his writing. For this reason it is quite possible to say that Irving unconsciously shaped a principal current in American fiction, whatever may be the relative unimportance of his own work.

Irving's own derivations are fairly explicit. That he was a passionate Anglophile has been repeatedly pointed out, and indeed he admitted it. After paying brief tribute to the charms of his own land, "The Author's Account of Himself" in the *Sketch Book* continues, "But Europe held forth the charms of storied and poetical association. There were to be seen the masterpieces of art, the refinements of highly cultivated society, the quaint peculiarities of ancient and local custom. My native country was full of youthful promise; Europe was rich in the accumulated treasures of age. . . . I longed to wander over the scenes of renowned achievement—to tread, as it were, in the footsteps of antiquity—to loiter about the ruined castle—to meditate on the falling tower—to escape, in short, from the commonplace realities of the present, and lose myself among the shadowy grandeurs of the past." The tone is sufficiently like that of the youthful Henry James to be remarkable; but Irving ends with a characteristic humorous twist: "I will visit this land of wonders, thought I, and see the gigantic race from which I have degenerated."

For Irving the appeal of the "old home" was entirely romantic. He sought that established traditionalism which, he thought, alone provided the requisite backdrop for true literature. Henry James, we feel, reacted similarly in part, but James was reacting also to a stifled unrest in the arid commercialism of America, a dissatisfaction Irving never acutely felt. But however romantic Irving may have been in his original aspirations toward Europe, he managed to set down a not unrealistic picture of it. Some of the best pages of the *Sketch Book* and *Bracebridge Hall* are precisely those in which romantic predisposition dissipates and he tells of things as he actually saw them. If he had done so oftener, the books would have been better; but it is impossible to doubt that his intention was realistic, if his disposition was incorrigibly romantic.

In mere point of time, Irving is of course the best-known progenitor of all American fiction; and it is a fact that though Joseph Dennie, Brockden Brown and other Americans had essayed to produce "literature," Irving alone among these pioneers succeeded in gaining the ear of the world and keeping it. When the *History of New York* appeared in 1809 it was evident that this "savage from barbarous America" could write; even his English compeers conceded that. The famous felicity of style (the result of a rigorous apprenticeship in his earlier years) immediately invited comparison with Addison and Goldsmith. But the temper of the writing was not classical or neo-classical, but romantic. If Irving's prose read like Cowper's or Crabbe's, its content conjured up Byron, Scott and Moore. Diedrich Knickerbocker's whimsy and his strictly American themes gave the *History of New York* a strange new savor; but the voice was always familiar; it had the well-tempered, quietly paced, above all urbane rhythm of the eighteenth century masters and could not fail to charm the ears of Britons. Their delight was infectious: it took only that imprimatur to persuade Americans they had at last produced a man of letters.

But between the publication of Knickerbocker's *History* and the *Sketch Book* lay an interval of ten years. It was as a man of thirty-six that Irving set out to prove whether he was capable of earning a reputation and a living as a writer. Shortly after the *History of New York* appeared, he made his second and formative pilgrimage to the land of his forebears, and he stayed there seventeen years. The immediate excuse for setting sail was not to become a writer, but to assist in his brothers' business enterprises. When those failed he stayed on, disclosing his real ambition; but the excuse had been an acceptable one. "Thus Irving," says his biographer, "unlike Henry James, who saw this type of conflict so clearly, escaped lasting animus from Americans. Nor was he thwarted by Philistia, as was his greater countryman Poe —and, perhaps, Whitman and Mark Twain."[1] If there was any feeling against the youthful author of the *Salmagundi Papers* (which had had only a local New York reputation) and the *History of New York*, it was quickly dispelled in the blaze of glory that soon surrounded the writer of the *Sketch Book*. Appearing in 1819, this collection of essays and short stories made an instant and favorable impression. Reading them today, it is difficult to account for the almost hysterical enthusiasm that greeted them; but they are almost the sole basis for Irving's fame. An examination of them, therefore, will be helpful as a guide in understanding the great influence they exerted upon American writers who followed Irving.

II

It is generally thought that the *Sketch Book* is the ultimate expression of Irving's romanticism; but actually this book shows how far Irving had gone along the road to a quasi-realism, an attenuated realism that found more artistic expression in the work of Hawthorne. What he was attempting, he says, was a sketch

[1] *The Life of Washington Irving*, by Stanley T. Williams. © 1935 by Oxford University Press.

of scenes and manners similar to the work in a different medium by his friend Leslie, whose closely worked Dutch miniatures were so popular. Geoffrey Crayon was to paint his times in words, mixing his colors as assiduously and working in details with the indefatigable patience of a water colorist painting a baroque interior.

Geoffrey Crayon's *feeling* toward his subject was unmitigatedly romantic. He was often deluded by surface appearances; he stood in awe of many commonplaces in English life; he venerated customs that, to an American and presumably a democrat, ought to have occasioned his censure. But Geoffrey Crayon *approached* his material with only a half-hearted romanticism. His eyes were on the central object, and he described what he saw, though his vision was impaired by the aura of supposed romance which surrounded all he saw. This pilgrim was more reverent than passionate. The interpretative faculty was usually absent, but when present, missed the logical interpretation. Such essays as "The Wife," "The Broken Heart" and "The Pride of the Village" are weakly inapposite because vitiated by this veneration for what was "England" simply because it *was* English. But those stories which hark back to the American scene, such as "Rip Van Winkle" and "The Legend of Sleepy Hollow," have their moments of vigor and memorability, and are of course the most perdurable stuff in the *Sketch Book*. On the other hand, when he was able to find a theme consonant with the nostalgic reverence informing all the English portions of the book (and drenching *Bracebridge Hall* to the drowning point), he rose to adequate expression. "Stratford-on-Avon," "The Stage Coach" and "Westminster Abbey" are quite acceptable in the vein of the English village school, and if they have not the magic of Lamb or the majesty of Addison, they are remarkably agreeable and somewhat astonishing as productions of a mere visitor.

It is, however, with the American stories that we are principally concerned, since they represent Irving at his best. He actually spent much time among the country people of New York state; and when he drew upon his observation, and not upon romantic preconceptions or upon his reading, he was most successful both in delineating character and approaching that romantic realism which became a broad stream in American fiction after him. What he says of Diedrich Knickerbocker is, of course, self-revelation: "His historical researches, however, did not lie so much among books as among men; for the former are lamentably scanty on his favorite topics; whereas he found the old burghers, and still more their wives, rich in that legendary lore, so invaluable to true history. Whenever, therefore, he happened upon a genuine Dutch family, snugly shut up in its low-roofed farmhouse, under a spreading sycamore, he looked upon it as a little clasped volume of black-letter, and studied it with the zeal of a book-worm."

It must be admitted though that his studies yielded little in the way of psychological insight. They did produce a gallery of striking types seen exteriorly: Rip Van Winkle, his wife, Ichabod Crane, Brom Bones, Farmer Van Tassel and old Baron Katzenellenbogen. Ichabod Crane is the trusty forerunner of a myriad scapegraces in our literature; and not so much because we know anything about what went on in the poor pedagogue's psyche as because we know for a fact what he looked like and what happened to him. Irving saw clearly the external lineaments; but the mind's labyrinth and the heart's paradoxes were a closed book to him. Geoffrey Crayon painted what he saw; like the Dutch miniature colorists, he wished to portray nothing more. And it would be difficult to find, even in the work of those who succeeded Irving and widely extended his tendencies, more striking caricatures than those of Rip and Ichabod. The hand of the colorist worked cunningly in such a deft paragraph as this: "He rode with short stirrups, which brought his knees nearly up to the pommel of the saddle; his sharp elbows stuck out like grasshoppers'; he carried his whip perpendicularly in his hand, like a sceptre, and, as his horse jogged on, the motion of his arms was not unlike the flapping of a pair of wings. A small wool hat rested on the top of his nose, for so his scanty strip of forehead might be called; and the skirts of his black coat fluttered out almost to the horse's tail. Such was the appearance of Ichabod and his steed, as they shambled out of the gate of Hans Van

Ripper, and it was altogether such an apparition as is seldom to
be met with in broad daylight." Could Leslie have done better
with his craftiest brush?

In Irving's happiest work he made the most of the juxtaposition of solid realism and tenuous myth. The telling effect of
"Sleepy Hollow," "Rip Van Winkle" and "The Spectre Bridegroom" arises from the fact that the legendary is so firmly inter-
woven with earthy realism. Here again we see the foreshadowing of what might be better done by the hand of a Hawthorne.
Acting on this principle, Irving soundly conceived his system of
inducing a suspension of disbelief. "Sleepy Hollow" is firmly
grounded in the everyday, and when the supernatural appears,
it gains our whole acceptance. Whether this was Irving's conscious intention is questionable; but it was a wholly successful
rule. Doubtless his ill-defined inclination toward realism tended
to bring about the happy result; and, in fact, there is a nice correspondence between the technique of the Irving short story
and the general philosophy of his composition which tempts one
to emphasize it unduly.

Balzac enumerating the furnishings of a room, or Zola describing the death of a harlot, was not more circumspectly naturalistic
than Irving when he set about to paint a scene. Farmer Van Tassel's broad domain is all there before us: "His stronghold was
situated on the banks of the Hudson, in one of those green, sheltered, fertile nooks, in which the Dutch farmers are so fond of
nestling. A great elm-tree spread its broad branches over it; at
the foot of which bubbled up a spring of the softest and sweet-
est water in a little well formed of a barrel; and then stole
sparkling away through the grass, to a neighboring brook, that
babbled along among alders and dwarf willows. Hard by the
farmhouse was a vast barn, that might have served for a church;
every window and crevice of which seemed bursting forth with
the treasures of the farm; the flail was busily resounding within
it from morning to night; swallows and martins skimmed twitter-
ing about the eaves; and rows of pigeons, some with one eye
turned up, as if watching the weather, some with their heads
under their wings, or buried in their bosoms, and others swelling,

and cooing, and bowing about their dames, were enjoying the
sunshine on the roof. Sleek, unwieldy porkers were grunting in
the repose and abundance of their pens; whence sallied forth,
now and then, troops of sucking pigs, as if to snuff the air. A
stately squadron of snowy geese were riding in an adjoining
pond, convoying whole fleets of ducks; regiments of turkeys
were gobbling through the farmyard, and guinea fowls fretting
about it, like ill-tempered housewives, with their peevish dis-
contented cry. Before the door strutted the gallant cock, that
pattern of a husband, a warrior, and a fine gentleman, clapping
his burnished wings and crowing in the pride and gladness of his
heart—sometimes tearing up the earth with his feet, and then gen-
erously calling his ever-hungry family of wives and children to
enjoy the rich morsel which he had discovered." And the interior of the farmhouse is as thoroughly itemized: "It was one
of those spacious farmhouses, with high-ridged, but lowly-slop-
ing roofs, built in the style handed down from the first Dutch
settlers; the low projecting eaves forming a piazza along the
front, capable of being closed up in bad weather. Under this
there were hung flails, harness, various utensils of husbandry, and
nets for fishing in the neighboring river. Benches were built along
the sides for summer use; and a great spinning-wheel at one
end, and a churn at the other, showed the various uses to which
this important porch might be devoted. From his piazza the
wondering Ichabod entered the hall, which formed the centre
of the mansion and the place of usual residence. Here, rows of
resplendent pewter, ranged on a long dresser, dazzled his eyes.
In one corner stood a huge bag of wool ready to be spun; in another a quantity of linsey-woolsey just from the loom; ears of
Indian corn, and strings of dried apples and peaches, hung in
gay festoons along the walls, mingled with the gaud of red pep-
pers; and a door left ajar gave him a peep into the best parlor,
where the claw-footed chairs, and dark mahogany tables, shone
like mirrors; and irons, with their accompanying shovel and
tongs, glistened from their covert of asparagus tops; mock-
oranges and conch-shells decorated the mantel-piece; strings of
various colored birds' eggs were suspended above it; a great

ostrich egg was hung from the centre of the room, and a corner cupboard, knowingly left open, displayed immense treasures of old silver and well-mended china."

And for sheer gustatory exuberance it would be difficult to find a more enthusiastic catalogue of the trencherman's delight than Irving's depiction of "the ample charms of a genuine Dutch country tea-table, in the sumptuous time of autumn. Such heaped-up platters of cakes of various and almost indescribable kinds, known only to experienced Dutch housewives. There was the doughty doughnut, the tenderer oly koek, and the crisp and crunchy cruller; sweet cakes and short cakes, ginger cakes and honey cakes, and the whole family of cakes. And then there were apple-pies and peach-pies and pumpkin-pies; besides slices of ham and smoked beef; and moreover delectable dishes of pre-served plums, and peaches, and pears, and quinces; not to men-tion broiled shad and roasted chickens; together with bowls of milk and cream, all mingled higgledy-piggledy, pretty much as I have enumerated them, with the motherly tea-pot sending up its clouds of vapor from the midst—Heaven bless the mark!" Dickens himself never did better justice to the dinner table.

Undoubtedly the third most durable story in the *Sketch Book* is "The Spectre Bridegroom," which, although probably sug-gested to Irving by his readings in the German romantics, mem-orably synthesizes those elements of the legendary and the real. The old aunts who flutter about the little baroness; Baron Katz-enellenbogen; his horde of poor relatives; the personality of the castle itself—these are struck off with very fine effect. Sagacity and sly wit characterize many passages. Pungently Irving says that the old women, "having been great flirts and coquettes in their younger days, were admirably calculated to be vigilant guardians and strict censors of the conduct of their niece; for there is no duenna so rigidly prudent, and inexorably decorous, as a superannuated coquette." After the specter of the baroness' lover has made its appearance below the bedroom window, and the girl has secured her aunt's agreement not to tell of it, Irving whimsically remarks, "How long the good old lady would have observed this promise is uncertain, for she dearly loved to talk of the marvellous, and there is a triumph in being the first to tell a frightful story; it is, however, still quoted in the neighborhood, as a memorable instance of female secrecy, that she kept it to herself for a whole week." And this will do for an example of the epigrammatical quality of Irving's wit: "The baron, it is true, like most great men, was too dignified to utter any joke but a dull one," and that horde of hangers-on who "one and all, possessed the affectionate disposition common to humble relatives, were wonderfully attached to the baron, and took every possible occasion to come in swarms and enliven the castle." They found that his jokes were "always enforced, however, by a bumper of excellent Hockheimer; and even a dull joke, at one's own table, served up with jolly old wine, is irresistible."

On the whole, the *Sketch Book* proved to be enspiriting for diverse American writers. The effect was not immediately apparent, and it was probably a diffuse stimulation, arising more from Irving's manner than from his content. The gentlemanly essay, the Christmas book, the modest homily, were still to be popular for many years; but the *Sketch Book's* chief influence upon the imagination of other writers was its style. Whittier, as a young aspirant in letters, wrote to Mrs. Sigourney in 1832, "The style I have adopted is about halfway between the abruptness of Laurence Sterne and the smooth gracefulness of W. Irving. I may fail,—indeed, I suspect I shall,—but I have more philosophy than poetry in my composition"; and Lowell, in one of his last public addresses, recalled that when he "was beginning life, as it is called, . . . the question 'Who reads an American book?' still roused in the not too numerous cultivated class among us a feeling of resentment and helpless anger . . . (yet) we had Irving, who after humorously satirising the poverty of our annals in his 'Knickerbocker,' forced to feel the pensive beauty of what is ancient by the painful absence of it, first tried to create an artificial antiquity as a substitute, and then sought in the old world a kindlier atmosphere and themes more sympathetic with the dainty and carefully shaded phrase he loved. He first taught us the everliving charm of style, most invaluable and most difficult of lessons. Almost wholly English, he is yet our earliest classic. . . ." Poe, Hawthorne, Prescott, Longfellow and Holmes deferentially remarked the debt American literature owed to Irving, though Hawthorne alone according to internal evidence inherited to any striking degree his method and matter. As a young man shut up in his dark Salem chamber, Hawthorne studiously emulated the Irving style, and it is incredible that the peculiar charm of the mythlike and legendary in "Rip Van Winkle" and "The Spectre Bridegroom" did not enormously stimulate the author of "The Great Stone Face" and "Young Goodman Brown." Frequently overt allusions to Irving occur in Hawthorne's writings; and there is the letter accompanying a presentation copy of *The Blithedale Romance*, an occasion which, the greater writer gracefully says, "affords me—and I ask no more—an opportunity of expressing the affectionate admiration which I have felt so long; a feeling, by the way, common to all our countrymen, in reference to Washington Irving, and which, I think, you can hardly appreciate, because there is no writer with the qualities to awaken in yourself precisely the same intellectual and heart-felt recognition." (We shall see through comparative analysis in a later chapter to what extent Hawthorne actually was in Irving's debt.)

The most notable and directly tendentious effect of the *Sketch Book* upon a succeeding American work is observable in Longfellow's *Outre Mer*, where unmistakable correspondences occur which suggest that more than a few of Poe's famous allegations concerning Longfellow's plagiarism are not wholly unfounded. *Outre Mer* is, of course, forgotten today, but it had a vogue almost as great in its time as that of the *Sketch Book*.

III

Three years after the *Sketch Book* appeared, Irving brought out a further collection in similar vein, *Bracebridge Hall*. This book, however, was only a pale imitation of its predecessor; and while it in turn stimulated a number of imitations (principally J. P. Kennedy's *Swallow Barn*), it added nothing to his reputation. In fact, the high-water mark of Irving's career had already been reached; nothing he did afterward measured up to the relatively low standard of the *Sketch Book*. The worst aspects of that work were multiplied and enlarged upon in *Bracebridge Hall;* and even worsened, because in it Irving forsook almost wholly his former reliance on observation and personal experience, and went to books for inspiration. *Bracebridge Hall* is indeed what Samuel Rogers said (though he applied it even to the *Sketch Book*) "Addison and water."

On the heels of *Bracebridge Hall* came *Tales of a Traveller*, a compound of Germanic legends rewritten and embellished, but scarcely improved. Even the critics who had been most enthusiastic about the *Sketch Book* were disappointed. Yet Irving managed to retrieve his dwindling reputation by going to Spain, a country just then exciting the curiosity of England and America, and purloining from the historian Navarrete a life of Columbus. Irving's plagiarism of this work has been a scandal among literary historians for many years; but of course his contemporaries were largely unaware of the real authorship of the *Life and Voyages of Columbus*, and it reestablished Irving for the time as a writer, though some deplored his forsaking fantasy and fiction for the sober role of historian. Today we are not impressed by this aspect of Irving's work; the *Columbus, Granada, Tour on the Prairies, Astoria, Adventures of Captain Bonneville* and *Life of George Washington* all betraying the hand of the slipshod craftsman, relying upon second-hand sources or lifting material of others. It may be said with justice that after the *Sketch Book* the only works worth consideration are the *Tales of the Alhambra* and the *Life of Goldsmith*, with perhaps a glance at *Wolfert's Roost*, which was actually a product of Irving's earlier period, being a collection of Crayon essays originally published in magazines and reissued as a volume in 1855.

We can assign as the reason for the quality of the *Alhambra* Irving's return to his practice of combining that measure of realism found in the best parts of the *Sketch Book* with the romantic interest in the legendary. A revealing letter to the critic Allibone (written in 1857) reinforces the internal evidence of the book: "The account of my midnight rambles about the old palace is literally true. . . . Every thing in the work relating to

myself and to the actual inhabitants of the Alhambra is unex-
aggerated fact: it was only in the legends that I indulged in *ro-
mancing.*" (Irving's italics.) However, the legends themselves
were buttressed by settings with a sound basis in reality and contain vignettes of Spanish life equally as truthful as those pre-
tending to represent the "actual inhabitants of the Alhambra."
"The Legend of the Moor's Legacy" and "The Legend of the
Rose of the Alhambra" are in the vein of Irving's best tales, a re-
working of the same mine that produced his other and more
famous stories. The *Alhambra* has a sort of unity that even the
Sketch Book lacked, achieved by the simple device of encompassing all the fantasy and observation within the walls of the great
palace. On the other hand, there is a monotony, an unrelieved
evenness of tone which, apart from the frequent sentimentalism,
vitiates our interest in the work, as it lies outside the taste of our
time. This latter criticism, the matter of temper, can of course
be levied against the whole of Irving's work; but once we concede the conventions of his time and accept the limitations of
early nineteenth-century American taste, it is quite possible to
appreciate the excellences that first elevated Irving in critical
esteem.

The last of Irving's writings with any claim upon our attention is his *Life of Goldsmith,* a superficial work as biography,
but one which exhibits in all their bloom his felicities of language
and softness of tone. Largely compounded of excerpts from
Boswell, and built upon the researches of two earlier biographers,
Pryor and Forster, it was by no means as ambitious a project as
the *Life of George Washington* with which Irving closed his
career; but its simplicity and a certain eighteenth-century charm
keep it alive.

Almost the only productions that have currency today, however, are the essays and stories in the *Sketch Book,* but if they
did nothing more than bring to a higher degree of development
the tale of the miraculous and adumbrate that successful turning toward England, the spiritual home of such an orphan of
tradition as Henry James, they performed a vital service to our
literature. It is not so much to them that we owe respect but to

what they pioneered: indicating pathways that might be followed by more highly endowed successors.

NATHANIEL HAWTHORNE
Bystander

WHEN HAWTHORNE shut himself up in the famous Salem bedroom for his long apprenticeship, he was charting a new course for serious creative writers of his time in America and laying a good foundation for a great, if truncated, American career in fiction. Irving and Cooper were already famous; but they were writing books very inferior indeed to the ones this somber, lonely man was preparing himself to produce. In time he would be as famous as they, and his books were destined for a more enduring and honored niche in our literature. His plan of sequestering himself in chambers for a long period of practice, learning his craft, was not wholly premeditated, probably; but as events proved, it was a sound method. It was to become time-honored in other lands; and Zola, Balzac, Gissing and many English and Continental writers followed a like system, starving in garrets while shaping their art to viable ends. Hawthorne evidently selected the method by a natural inclination toward solitude; and no doubt the fictitious creatures of his imagination were more than adequate substitutes for the companionship of live persons, in this period and throughout his life.

Hawthorne was a morbidly shy and unsociable man. All his life he thwarted attempts of others to become intimate; he discouraged or rebuffed all friendships, and only some of the ties formed in schooldays ever held firmly for him in his adult life. Bridge, Pierce and, to a much lesser extent, Longfellow, alone seemed to have the keys to his friendship in any substantial degree. The solitude and enforced sequestration of his apprenticeship were thus not by any means uncongenial to him; and it was quite certain that when he began to write his earliest sketches and *Fanshawe*, he found a real pleasure in holding at arm's length the world and its denizens of whom he was both afraid and scornful, while his real need for companionship and human intercourse found satisfaction in the figures of dream and invention.

Our first great psychological novelist, Hawthorne was simultaneously Poe's only serious competitor in the short story. After the juvenile attempt at a novel, Hawthorne devoted himself exclusively for many years to the production of tales and sketches, until he had nearly a hundred of them to show; and in many of them the same qualities which were later to be welded in his long works had been foreshadowed, tested and explored. Taking for his province the conscience of Puritanism, and the decay of old families, he began to fashion out of legends and his own fancy the sort of half-dreamlike, half-real fantasies that had earlier occupied Irving. Instead of the legends of New York, he unearthed those of New England. But after he had found his materials, he looked far more deeply beneath the surface than ever Irving had been able to do. There was little of the sunny inconsequentiality of the New Yorker in this sober descendant of William Hathorne, Puritan scourge and witch-hunter of old Salem. The reading of life in his stories was to be far more serious, and his judgments far more severe. His art, too, much less spontaneous, was to be by long odds the more subtle and refined. His vision encompassed the shadowy depths of existence, and out of that shade he wrought the greatest books of any American up to his time. That there was much of life he left out of account in them cannot be denied; his contemporary and erstwhile friend, Melville, was to probe even deeper into the shadows; but in Hawthorne's books, on the whole, we find the largest body of considerable art produced up to his day in America. The sporadic bursts of power and insight, as in Melville's *Moby-Dick*, did not outweigh the impressive totality of Hawthorne's output.

Nevertheless Hawthorne's early attempts were inauspicious and they were patently modeled upon Irving's familiar essays in the *Sketch Book, Bracebridge Hall*, etc. This was recognized by contemporary critics, and Park Benjamin, writing in the *New England Magazine* for October, 1835, remarked that the young author was "the most pleasing writer of fanciful prose, except

Irving, in the country." Such youthful pieces as "The Old Apple Dealer," painting a faithful and humble picture of a rustic character, or the innocuous "A Rill from the Town Pump" and "A Village Uncle," setting forth the homely virtues of simple lives and provincial scenes, are quite specifically in the Irving vein. When, however, the Salem recluse produced a sketch like "Sights from a Steeple," he was beginning to discover his own voice, although its mannerisms and accents were still those of Irving. Geoffrey Crayon never worked .with more Dutch faithfulness of detail than Hawthorne showed in "Main Street," "Snowflakes," and the numerous other slight pieces. Strangely enough, there was never any great advance in artistry or any increase in depth and significance, though Hawthorne continued to write such sketches up almost to the time of *The Scarlet Letter*, or, in other words, as long as he continued to write short pieces at all.[1] It was as if Hawthorne's powers, while expanding in scope, remained essentially what they had been after the first period of journeyman work in his solitary chamber.

"Sights from a Steeple" (1831), of the very least perdurable stuff, has some claim to importance because it displays Hawthorne, for the first time, in his lifelong role as bystander. In it he had suggested that perhaps the best mode of existence for a man was that of a Paul Pry, one who merely observed life without ever becoming involved. This fanciful pronouncement he doubtless uttered in jest, but it became all too accurate a prescription for his own life, and in all of his years he was marked most by his passivity. As was said of the typical character in the stories of Hemingway, he became a man to (and for) whom things were done. There can be little question but that he later regretted that he had become a bystander, and that he realized, like the man in Henry James's story, "The Beast in the Jungle," that he had missed much of human experience in his refusal (which fixed itself into inability) to participate in the business of living as most men live. It gave to his work a tone of low vital-

---

[1] Matthiessen remarks a similar stasis with regard to the stories proper. He finds "no progress in essentials" observable in "Ethan Brand," one of the last stories, over "The Gentle Boy," one of the earliest.—*American Renaissance*.

ity, and it sent him to the Puritan legends and the stuff of history for his subjects. He himself admitted to Longfellow, "I have . . . great difficulty in the lack of materials; for I have seen so little of the world that I have nothing but thin air to concoct my stories of, and it is not easy to give a lifelike semblance to such shadowy stuff. Sometimes through a peep-hole I have caught a glimpse of the real world, and the two or three articles in which I have portrayed these glimpses please me better than the others."

Yet it is precisely Hawthorne's shy, retiring personality and his brooding interest in the spiritual reality which, he believed, lay behind the "unreal" surface of things, that give his slight sketches their interest. Similarly, it was the personality of Irving, humorous, whimsical, detached, which made something more than newspaper prattle of his little essays. Felicitous prose and pseudo-classical cadences mark the essays of both writers. Reinforcing Benjamin's opinion, Poe was later to remark that *Twice-Told Tales* was the only work produced in America, except Irving's *Tales of a Traveller*, possessing "real merit."

For it cannot be doubted that the tales which Hawthorne began to publish in Christmas books and magazines spoke definitively of a new voice in our literature; the sketches seemed to be of Irving, but the stories were new-minted. A technical debt to Scott, and an occasional flavor of Brockden Brown, are all that can be detected in the way of extraneous influence in them. The legends of the Dutch, as exploited by Irving, had become the legends of the Puritans, in the hands of Hawthorne. "Sleepy Hollow" had been exchanged for the Essex Woods where Young Goodman Brown witnessed the witches' Sabbath; "Rip Van Winkle" had been expanded and metamorphosed into "Wakefield." Just as Hawthorne concerned himself with the inexplicable evidences of the supernatural, and sometimes with what was weird and evil, Henry James later found in *The Turn of the Screw* a method of developing the Hawthorne interests even further. In fact, James saw much in Hawthorne that must have given him guidance and aid throughout his career; and it was symptomatic that he proclaimed "the fine thing in Hawthorne is that he cared for the deeper psychology, and that, in his way, he tried to become familiar with it." Moreover, Hawthorne's insistence upon the reality of spirit and the unreality of matter, equally impressed James; in Hawthorne's stories there were to be observed "glimpses of a great field, of the whole deep mystery of man's soul and conscience. They are moral, and their interest is moral; they deal with something more than the mere accidents and conventionalities, the surface occurrences of life." [2]

It is this more serious concern with man's inner life that so sets Hawthorne apart from all the American writers of fiction who preceded him. Neither Cooper, Irving, Brown nor Poe entertained this concern for the psychological and moral issues which were to be the great focus of fiction until the realists arrived on the scene. The romancers were content to depict those surface occurrences which James reprehended; the apocalyptics were concerned, it is true, with madness, horror and various agonies of the psyche, but it was a largely external concern, an interest held for the sensational, pictorial and melodramatic effects that could be gained by it. Moral issues seldom invaded the domain of Brown and Poe; and it was not until the advent of Melville that a real seriousness of intention found expression through the apocalyptic vision. Hawthorne's great distinction was in taking seriously what had been neglected or overlooked by all his predecessors, and making great art of the inner drama of conscience which his own Puritan New England inheritance dictated. This is the justification for the use of allegory which, in some cases, became a juggernaut and destroyed the framework of the story it was intended to vivify. Through allegory Hawthorne was able to retain the "surface occurrences of life" and yet invest them with a meaning transcending their mundane aspects. When he succeeded, it was greatly; when he failed, the results were lamentable. A "Young Goodman Brown" or an "Ethan Brand" explored regions hitherto untouched; while a "Celestial Railroad" or a "Bosom Serpent" seemed only to stand like stiff caricatures of John Bunyan. Even Pearl in *The Scarlet*

---

[2] *Nathaniel Hawthorne*, by Henry James.

Letter often strikes one as a fantastic lapse of Hawthorne's art, she is so thoroughly and immitigably allegorized.

The great stories of Hawthorne are not so numerous as might be supposed; they stand out clearly from the highly competent ones, and most of them have been well anthologized: "Young Goodman Brown," "The Birthmark," "Ethan Brand," "Rappacini's Daughter" and "The Artist of the Beautiful." In these, as in many others of his tales, there is a curious thing to note: they all deal, in one way and another, with the theme of solitude—of removal from society, or of isolation. The novel which was to have crowned all Hawthorne's efforts, *The Ancestral Footstep*, also deals with this theme, and one recognizes again the absolute primacy of this factor in Hawthorne's genius. Secrecy of the heart, stories locked within the bosoms of men, unrecognized impulses which spring from the inner life, these are the themes of the short stories; their characters are solitary men and women, and they are seen set apart from others, they are put into action against a backdrop of solitude; it is as if only against such a background could Hawthorne's imagination begin to function greatly. True reality and ultimate importance are always envisioned by him as springing from the realizable conditions of character divorced from society. This was the factor central to the imagining of the stories; but when, near the close of his life, he planned his last romance, the theme was to be treated by means of a vast double-allegory, of the search for an elixir of life, in which the elixir was to be, not merely youth and terrestrial immortality, but a release from that irksome and crippling isolation that had been the final, cramping horror of Hawthorne's own existence. *The Ancestral Footstep*, in its unfinished state, and the other abortive attempts at bodying forth this obsessive theme, *The Dolliver Romance, Septimius Felton* and *Dr. Grimshawe's Secret*, are attempts to come to grips with the problem that Hawthorne could not solve in his life or in his art.

Meanwhile, before he made the great assault upon his lifelong dilemma, he managed to expand into novel length the same sort of interpretation of the secret life that had been variously dealt with in his stories. As originally conceived, *The Scarlet Letter* (1850) was to have been a short tale. As it now stands, it is still little more than an elaborated short story, and Hawthorne himself never applied the term "novel" to it. This allegory of the irreparability of adultery as sin, and of the hypocrisy which it engenders—this pioneer study of the so-called New England conscience was unquestionably, for its time, a tremendous forward stride in fiction. While Stendhal and Balzac had already advanced the frontier of the novel very far indeed beyond what Hawthorne would ever be capable of doing, still, for the English language, and especially for America, this book seemed a deeply probing and courageous interpretation of moral issues. The inexorable judgment passed upon Hester and Dimmesdale was negated by the indulgent sympathy of their presentation; and it is the degeneration of character, the cowardice and hypocrisy which the minister exhibits, the ever-increasing inner pain that Hester suffers from the irresistible development of the child Pearl, the symbol of sin,—it is in this that the tragedy consists, and not so specifically in the sin that was originally committed. Hawthorne's inquiries into the processes of mind and heart which occupy Dimmesdale, Hollingsworth and Hester are the significant sections of the book; but when we compare them with what Hawthorne's French contemporaries in the developing "psychological novel" were able to do, we see how elementary his treatment is. But if, on the other hand, we place it beside *The Deerslayer*, or the *Narrative of Arthur Gordon Pym*, or *Bracebridge Hall*, or *Ormond*, we cannot help feeling that a masterpiece had been wrought in American fiction; and no book except *Moby-Dick*, to appear by the middle of the century in America, could bear comparison with *The Scarlet Letter*.

The House of the Seven Gables (1851), *The Blithedale Romance* (1852) and *The Marble Faun* (1860) all contain essentials of Hawthorne's genius, and this is particularly true of the latter; but none of them measures up to *The Scarlet Letter*. Probably the *Seven Gables* is the nearest thing to a novel that Hawthorne ever wrote; and its pictures of family decay are indeed compelling; both this book and *The Marble Faun* clearly had germinative influence upon Henry James, and their importance might be taken to lie strongly in that effect.

Far more interesting to any student of the artistic temperament and the development of literary genius, with reference to Hawthorne's time and place in our literature, is the unfinished work of his last years. As early as 1855, Hawthorne had entertained the idea of writing a romance to be called *The Ancestral Footstep*, but after going to Italy he became interested in the legend of Donatello, and evolved *The Marble Faun*. However, while still in that country and before *The Marble Faun* was written, he began to work on the book which was alternately to have as its allegorical center the quest of an elixir of life, or of a sense of roots in the past and an identification with the race, the two themes being interchangeably introduced in the four existent versions of the unfinished romance. He wrote only sketches of his intended book, as if his inability to solve the condition of isolation in his life served correspondingly to frustrate his solution in the book. He could not dispel the alienation which always had held him aloof from life; he could not make a positive identification with any part of life, although he seemingly desired this more than anything else. His "power to act as a man among men" was so nearly paralyzed that the several attempts to resuscitate it were unsuccessful, and only put him more completely off from active participation. The Brook Farm sojourn was always an unhappy memory; in fact, it seemed unreal to him as he looked back upon it; his sojourn in the custom house at Salem was a vexatious period, and while he occasionally complimented himself upon his apparently growing ability to mingle with men, it was in reality an enormous relief for him to quit his duties there. In Liverpool as consul he avoided all contact with persons who might conceivably have been his intellectual equals, and he declined opportunities to meet the literary great of the day in England. He shunned the company of humankind, and he thwarted efforts of every sort from everyone to come into intimacy with him. He realized this deficiency and he desired to correct it; but the only steps he took were these last faltering ones, in an art that likewise failed him.

He wrote in his notebook in 1843: "A cloudy veil stretches over the abyss of my nature. I have, however, no love of secrecy and darkness. I am glad to think that God sees through my heart, and if any angel has power to penetrate into it, he is welcome to know everything that is there. Yes, and so may any mortal who is capable of full sympathy, and therefore worthy to come into my depths. But he must find his own way there. I can neither guide nor enlighten him. It is this involuntary reserve, I suppose, that has given the objectivity to my writings; and when people think that I am pouring myself out in a tale or an essay, I am merely telling what is common to human nature, not what is peculiar to myself. I sympathize with them, not they with me. . . ." This passage is particularly revealing, inasmuch as it shows the haughty reserve with which Hawthorne held the world at arm's length. He actively resisted confidences, and we remember the story of Herman Melville's passionate advances and Hawthorne's cool rebuffs as exigent examples of the "unconquerable reserve" that was such a powerful determinant in the type of work which Hawthorne did. Toward life and humanity he exhibited a wonderful detachment, and the only occasions when his reserve seems to have broken down, or a little warmth to kindle in him, were in the privacy of his home, among his children.[8]

In the notebooks it is announced that plans were made to write a romance whose plot was to hinge upon the secret, in the possession of a descendant of an English family, who had emigrated to America, which would have the power of destroying the branch of the family still in England. In some way this theme was connected in Hawthorne's imagination with a "bloody footstep" he had heard of—a legend current at Smithell's Hall, a country estate in England. The figure of the footstep seemed to possess him with preternatural fascination; perhaps he dreamed of making it as symbolical of ancestral sin as the scarlet letter had been of moral obloquy in New England. At all events, the story that began to take shape on paper during his stay in Italy

---

[8] In a letter of 1844, Hawthorne wrote that a friend "spoke with immitigable resolution of the necessity of my going to dine with Longfellow before returning to Concord; but I have an almost miraculous power of escaping from necessities of this kind. Destiny itself has often been worsted in the attempt to get me out to dinner."

was obsessively concerned with the notion of a primal fault and its effects upon a double line of descendants in England and America.

On April 1, 1858, Hawthorne began to place on paper his notes and jottings for the ambitious work. As the story now appears, it is written in scenes (a favorite method with Hawthorne), but it is by no means consecutive, and its plan alters as it progresses. Middleton, the last and contemporary American remnant of the family, has returned to England, bent upon piecing together the strands of his family legend which, he thinks, may have some sensible interpretation if only the English side of it can be discovered; on the other hand, he fancies that the English Middletons will be happy to have their own mystery unraveled by the revelations he may be able to give them, through the part of the legend that has come down by his branch. Middleton's interest in "our old home" was not the sort that prompted Henry James to forsake these shores; but his thoughts turned in that direction; Middleton is no Lambert Strether, but he is an ambassador of a kind. The immediate occurrence that sets him off on his English quest is the discovery of a paper showing that somewhere back in the Middleton genealogy one of his ancestors changed his name from Eldredge to Middleton. This, and the legend that had come down by word of mouth concerning some ancient trouble, crime, even murder, and of riches and a palatial home now vanished,—all this had persuaded Middleton to the journey. In the words of Hawthorne's notes: "His imagination has dwelt much, in his boyhood, on the legendary story of his family; and the discovery of the document has revived these dreams. He determines to search out the family mansion; and thus he arrives, bringing half of a story, being the only part known in America, to join it on to the other half, which is the only part known in England. In an introduction I must do the best I can to state his side of the matter to the reader. . . . Middleton finds a commonplace old English country gentleman in possession of the estate, where his forefathers have lived in peace for many generations; but there must be circumstances contrived which shall cause Middleton's conduct to be attended by no end of turmoil and trouble. . . . The more serious question, what shall be the nature of this tragic trouble, and how can it be brought about?"

The commonplace old English gentleman metamorphosed considerably a few days later, thus: "Eldredge, bred, and perhaps born, in Italy, and a Catholic, with views to the church before he inherited the estate, has not the English moral sense and simple honor; can scarcely be called an Englishman at all. Dark suspicions of past crime, and of the possibility of future crime, may be thrown around him; an atmosphere of doubt shall envelop him, though, as regards manners, he may be highly refined. Middleton shall find in the house a priest; and at his first visit he shall have seen a small chapel, adorned with the richness, as to marbles, pictures, and frescoes, of those that we see in the churches at Rome; and here the Catholic forms of worship shall be kept up. Eldredge shall have had an Italian mother, and shall have the personal characteristics of an Italian. There shall be something sinister about him, the more apparent when Middleton's visit draws to a conclusion; and the latter shall feel convinced that they part in enmity, so far as Eldredge is concerned."

Writing on, from day to day, and dating each day's stint, Hawthorne built the narrative, changed its course, sketched brief scenes, left gaps, inserted synopses of the intended action, and in general seemed uncertain of the course of the work. Hitherto his novels had been written at white heat, and with little revising went directly to the publisher. *The Ancestral Footstep* and its three variants were differently done. What is more, all this preliminary warming-up seems to have exhausted Hawthorne, and he was never satisfied with what he had done.

He saw, apparently, that his symbol of the bloody footstep, by itself, was not strong enough to carry the weight of the fable he had to tell. As a pictorial figure the footstep was good, but it had none of the significance he needed. Still he could not relinquish it, and so in other trials, *Dr. Grimshawe's Secret* and *Septimius Felton,* he superadded the visionary element—the search for earthly immortality. Here he was coming closer to the successful embodiment of the drama of his own life and its search for that larger life which from Salem days to Liverpool had existed beyond a wall he could not breach.

It might have been of himself and not of Colcord, a shadowy character in *Dr. Grimshawe's Secret*, that he was writing when he set these words down: "He was capable only of gentle and mild regard,—that was his warmest affection; and the warmest, too, that he was capable of exciting in others. So that he was doomed . . . to be a lonely creature, without any very deep companionship in the world, though not incapable, when he, by some rare chance, met a soul distantly akin, of holding a certain high spiritual communion." Significantly, those rare characters in Hawthorne destined for happiness and good fortune are invariably bequeathed with at least a mild share of extroversion, as the youthful Edward Redclyffe in the same novel: a little boy who "had too quick a spirit of life to be in danger of becoming a bookworm himself. He had this side of the intellect, but his impulse would be to mix with men, and catch something from their intercourse fresher than books could give him. . . ." It is as if Hawthorne, picturing to himself the fuller life enjoyed by those who were able to take it with open arms, peered out upon these lives with a sort of envy. He did not succeed in making such happy characters come to life; it is the demon-ridden Hester Prynnes, Dimmesdales, Miriams and Ethan Brands who have the shadowy verisimilitude which passes for existence in the Hawthorne gallery.

The final abortive romance in its several forms is, with the exception of *The Ancestral Footstep* fragment, a faked and hopelessly Godwinian phantasmagoria; it reads far more like Brockden Brown than Henry James, and hence is in a very real sense atavistic. While *The Ancestral Footstep* itself looks to the future and actually foreshadows James, *The Dolliver Romance, Dr. Grimshawe's Secret* and *Septimius Felton* creak along on the most preposterous Radcliffean hinges.[4] It is a pity that Haw-

---

[4] It is probably no accident that the young hero of *Dr. Grimshawe's Secret* bears the astonishingly similar name, Redclyffe . . . as if Hawthorne's subconscious received no check from his sense of propriety; or perhaps it was a conscious attempt to pay respects to his prompter in this tale.

thorne's imagination and circumstances did not conspire to complete the first casting of his romance of the bloody footstep, for *The Ancestral Footstep*, the briefest and roughest version, is by long odds the most likely and promising. If he had been able to breathe life into that outline, he would have cast American fiction ahead by several decades; or at the very least, he would have given Henry James a springboard from which the younger man might have made his vaulting leaps much sooner and farther.

The truncation of Hawthorne's career—the frustration attendant upon his two great psychological handicaps—is a loss to our literature that is beyond calculation. If, in the first place, he had been able to solve the problem of his isolation and passivity; and second, if he had sought and found roots more green than the grim, brittle ones of New England Puritanism, his art might have encompassed the completion of his last romance, and crowned the career of the most genuinely artistic sensibility of his time. And yet when one contemplates the solitary Hawthorne's place in the stream of "romantic realism," a kind of poetic suitability appears in the fact that his bones are buried in Sleepy Hollow—immortalized by Irving, his predecessor—and the finest monument to his memory yet written is the biography by James, his great successor.

HENRY JAMES
Life Refracted by Temperament

"OUR OLD HOME," in Hawthorne's phrase, exerted an irresistible lure upon many American writers, the greatest of whom was Henry James. Like Irving and Hawthorne before him, James responded with an almost religious feeling to England and the Continent. As a young man, Irving had often fingered Newberry's picture books, and admired prints of the Thames and London Bridge. Irving grew up so familiar with such scenes and so thoroughly imbued with the English "idea" that he even looked like an Englishman. As a child Henry James caught a glimpse of this famous visitor who looked so English; and the similarity of their interests was foreshadowed in James's own childish preoccupation with the same delightful books, collections of travels called "The World Displayed." [1]

Henry James's childhood and youth were hardly normal. The elder James characterized himself as one who could never remain long in one place; when he was in Boston, his thoughts were always in London or Paris; when overseas, everything back home called imperiously; and thus the James household was forever shuttling back and forth. Young Henry had little opportunity to grow roots. By the time he had cast off the family towline, he regarded himself as a cosmopolitan, a dweller in the world of art whose allegiance was not to any country but to the world. But he was faced, nevertheless, with the necessity of selecting backgrounds for his fiction; and his acquaintance with the international scene suggested a viable field. For ten years he produced stories and novels that gave small indication of the stature his work was later to attain. We may pass them over, not because they are inconsiderable when compared to any of the work of Irving or Brown or Cooper, but because they fall so far short of his own mature work. *Roderick Hudson*, which probably can stand comparison with *The House of the Seven Gables*, is a youthful book. But in *The American* (1887), published a year later, Henry James in his first period reached maturity.

The conception of Newman, the American who travels to Europe and attempts to marry the daughter of an aristocratic French family, gives the novel its stature. As in all the following works of his first period, James is concerned to create character; and Newman's is a full-bodied, forceful figure upon which the excellence of the novel certainly depends. Newman does not succeed in carrying out the marriage, because the family so strenuously objects. The daughter enters a convent, renouncing her world if it cannot contain the man she loves. In his anger at the family, Newman accidentally comes upon a family scandal, when he learns that the mother had killed the father, hitherto thought to have died of natural causes. He is tempted to publish

[1] See *The Life of Washington Irving*, by Stanley T. Williams.

the fearful secret but an innate nobility restrains him. He burns the evidence and sails for America.

Newman clearly comes out best in this first strong conjunction of the "international" cultures. Although he is shown up as a "barbarian," and recognizes himself as such, he is still a lively, wholesome and meaningful individual. By contrast, the aristocrats of Europe are corrupt, and James's American is on the side of the angels. In his later books the tables often are turned; and for all his belated conversion, Strether of *The Ambassadors* remains a barbarian limned against the subtle graces of an older culture which excludes him.

The American was a departure for James, but it does not prefigure entirely the basic theme which was subsequently to underlie many James novels. That theme, succinctly stated, is: the good life is the inner life; but those who live it cannot compete with the "animal" people, before whom they eventually go down in defeat. This amounts to the tragic view in James, and it may be traced immediately to Hawthorne. *The Blithedale Romance*, for example, has all the characters and situations of a conceivable James novel, in which the plot hinges upon the betrayal of a sensitive character who lives the inner life, by two other characters, one of whom is usually the lover of the first. In *The Blithedale Romance* Priscilla is the character worth saving, while Zenobia and Hollingsworth between them plot her destruction. And then there is the fourth character absolutely essential to a James novel: the bystander who wishes to protect and assist the hero or heroine, but who is constitutionally unable to take an active part in life. Hawthorne did full justice to this type in Coverdale.

In *The Portrait of a Lady* it is Isabel Archer, of course, who ought to be saved; and her betrayers are Osmond and Madame Merle; while Ralph Touchett is the ineffectual bystander, and, one suspects, a character for whom Hawthorne and James themselves were prototypes. In *The Golden Bowl* it is Maggie who fights a losing battle against the predacious Prince and Charlotte. Milly Theale is done in by the machinations of Densher and Kate Croy. Always the spiritual vessel is broken in the hands of the healthy, unscrupulous animals.

James's novels are concerned to show the death not only of what is beautiful in the spirit but in objective society, which had once been able to find that sense of beauty. The society which he at first so much admired and yearned so to become a part of and to possess, he at last concluded was moribund. And the novels give ample evidence that the aristocracy of late nineteenth-century Europe was in its death throes. To make this discovery must have cost James dear, for he once revered that same society to a degree approaching idolatry. It is difficult to determine the reasons James assigns for the decay of the culture he once admired; it could not be the encroachments of the barbarians, who finally vanquished the bearers of the holy fire. Is it simply that in this society, desire to live the good life had never been strong enough; or is it that James finally learned he had never penetrated to the heart of that revered and incomprehensible beauty, imbibed like mother's milk by the descendants of European tradition, and so foreign to an American that he could never digest it? He wrote in 1886, "The position of that body [the English upper class] seems to me to be in many ways very much the same rotten and *collapsible* one as that of the French aristocracy before the revolution—minus cleverness and conversation; or perhaps it's more like the heavy, congested and depraved Roman world upon which the barbarians came down." [2] From that time on he never revised his opinion, although he became reconciled to the decadence and used it as the great fundamental theme of his work.

There is a further sense in which James straitly continues the tradition of Hawthorne—a result of the intimate similarity of temperament in the two writers. Hawthorne, we have observed, was always at a remove not only from his creations but from life itself. His conception of the ideal type of the artist, and man, a sort of Paul Pry, must have fascinated James. Throughout James's books we have the feeling that their author stands aside and views the configurations of raw life with alarm, or at best, with curiosity. We seldom feel that he, too, is involved in the terrible business of living. One great type among his characters

---

[2] From *Letters* by Henry James. © 1886 by Charles Scribner's Sons.

is the passive man and woman; almost without exception they talk, observe, comment, and do not plunge into life's maelstrom. Maria Gostrey in *The Ambassadors*, or Mrs. Assingham in *The Golden Bowl*, Ralph Touchett in *The Portrait of a Lady*—they all are fascinated spectators; they do not participate. It is as if James has in him a strong element of the feminine principle. Life without action interests him inordinately. Even his major characters are acted upon; they are caught in snares of circumstance set by the vulgar and exuberant. We are meant to sympathize with their predicament—as who should say, these are the people who count—these lovely, ineffectual ones who were meant to shine, sheltered like tapers, and not to be set out in the gusty wind of life. Milly, Maggie, Isabel, and to some extent even Lambert Strether, are flotsam sucked down into the whirlpool. They ought to be saved, but reality will not permit it. Strether, in his role of bystander, has let life slip by him; when he awakens to that realization, it is far too late for him to recover. The man whose story is told in "The Beast in the Jungle" has waited all his life for something to happen. In "The Altar of the Dead" the two people look only toward the ultimate quiescence of death, since the action they watch led finally to temporal dissolution. In James's own life there was a minimum of struggle. He was always comfortably off, and his only conflicts were concerned with his literary labors. A biography of James that took no account of his mental life would be a very bare recital of dates and journeys, and singularly undramatic. He lived in an isolation from the ordinary affairs of men that was almost complete. He had no love affair even; and of course the mysterious accident that is supposed to have robbed him of virility may account not only for his removal from the event supposedly central to our life, but also from a vigorous concern in his fiction for the average tensions and conflicts that beset men and women. Action of the kind the word ordinarily connotes interested him not at all; but action on the moral level was his tremendous concern, and gives his work its ultimate importance. The three last novels, *The Ambassadors, The Golden Bowl* and *The Wings of the Dove*, move triumphantly in this high realm. In spite of their vast fault, their near-unreadability, they are among the great contributions to our literature.

The Ambassadors (1903) marks James's final return to his "international" theme, but it explores relationships far more subtly and, on the whole, meaningfully than did the earlier novels on the same subject—*The American,* for example. Lambert Strether, the aging "ambassador," has come to Paris to rescue Chad Newsome from the toils of Europe and a questionable woman. Strether has been sent by Chad's widowed mother, the patroness of a green-covered magazine that Strether edits in the town of Woollett, Massachusetts. If he succeeds, it is assumed he will also have won the hand, and fortune, of Mrs. Newsome. Chad is the more urgently needed at home, to manage the factory in which some vaguely disreputable household article is made. At the outset it is clear that Strether believes quite wholeheartedly in the benevolence of his mission. But imperceptibly it is borne in upon him that all the values of Mrs. Newsome and Woollett have undergone a transmutation, and that it is Chad who stands on surer ground. In fact, before long he has become the positive champion of the life of ease and "culture" that has seduced Chad. He not only condones the "sin" in which Chad and his mistress, Madame de Vionnet, are living; but he becomes an ardent admirer of the woman. She has civilized Chad, he believes. She has given him a personality and stature that, if he had remained in Woollett, he would never have achieved. Yet before Strether is quite won over, he presents Mrs. Newsome's plea with all the eloquence he can muster, and lets it ferment in Chad's mind.

Once Lambert Strether turns traitor to his benefactor, he lets himself go. The life of Paris utterly charms him, and he begins to sense the wonder of a life that has passed him by. Perhaps it is not too late for him to start again; certainly it would be a crime to uproot Chad. Through Chad he can somehow enjoy a vicarious realization of his own blasted chances of really living. The fact that a son of his own had died young brings Chad all the closer to him.

But Mrs. Newsome discovers his defection and promptly dispatches another set of ambassadors, the pushing Pococks. They bring what pressure they can to bear on Chad, and before long

Strether senses that Chad is being won back to the crass views of Woollett. He even discloses that he hasn't the high regard for Madame de Vionnet with which Strether credited him. And so the tables have been deftly turned, and it is Lambert Strether who has received the education, has once and for all seen the paltriness of American life, is won to the ideals and conventions of an older culture. Although this is the fact, Strether is not presented as having been taken in by what is false and merely on the surface in that culture. He accepts the principle that there may be a life divorced from business and material goods, and that it is the good life.

In *The Golden Bowl* and *The Wings of the Dove* James returned to the *Blithedale Romance* type of situation he had formerly developed in *The Portrait of a Lady*. Through suffering, innocence triumphs in *The Golden Bowl*, but at the expense of many human values. Maggie Verver's is a costly victory; and only her prodigious capacity for love makes it possible. There are but four major characters in this novel, and the plot hinges upon various combinations of their relationships. Maggie and her father, Mr. Verver, are offered at the outset in a more than usually close relationship; they live together and are tied by bonds that suggest an almost matrimonial connection. At the same time the Prince, Amerigo, and Maggie's friend, Charlotte, who are destined to become respectively husband and wife of the Ververs, are engaged in a romantic affair of their own. The recombining of the four characters at last presents Maggie and Amerigo linked in marriage, while Mr. Verver weds Charlotte. However, the new combination works to the disadvantage of each union; Maggie, still platonically attached to her father, is not equal to the ravenous sensuality of the Italian prince; and Charlotte does not find in the aging Mr. Verver the virility which can satisfy her. And so the old combination reappears; and Charlotte and the Prince resume their extramarital relationship. Maggie, loving Amerigo with a fullness he cannot at first comprehend, is aware of the betrayal committed by her husband and her best friend. But she endures the situation. Her passivity actually saves her marriage and that of her father.

The symbol of the golden bowl itself holds the crux of the

novel: when the Prince and Charlotte first see the bowl in a shop window, and notice its flaw, and when Mrs. Assingham breaks the bowl upon the floor, we yet have the sense that Maggie will heal the breech through her embracing love, and her patience. She knows that Charlotte and Amerigo were engaged in the deepest intimacy (just as were Gilbert Osmond and Madame Merle before Isabel Archer came into their lives) and her discovery of what it all means becomes a part of the nobility of her character, the alembic, so to speak, through which she passed to become greater than either of them.

Even the Prince and Charlotte have the grace to suffer from their betrayals. And while they are not beyond the deepest of deceptions, that of deceiving themselves, they at least have the possibility of redemption. But they do deceive themselves even when they have vowed to each other the sanctity of their trust in the marriages which they entered into with deceit aforethought.

" 'It's sacred,' " Amerigo says of their trust.

" 'It's sacred,' " Charlotte echoes. "They vowed it, gave it out and took it in, drawn, by their intensity, more closely together. Then of a sudden, through this tightened circle, as at the issue of a narrow strait into the sea beyond, everything broke up, broke down, gave way, melted and mingled. Their lips sought their lips, their pressure their response and their response their pressure; with a violence that had sighed itself the next moment to the longest and deepest of stillnesses they passionately sealed their pledge." [8]

Significantly it is the Prince who belatedly recognizes the purity of Maggie's love. He is saved by the attentions of that love, and Charlotte is left to drift upon a false belief in her success, which in reality is the hollowest failure. Prepared to be confronted with Maggie's knowledge of his intrigue, the Prince finds that Maggie has known all the while and will not demand his acknowledgment of it. From the moment he makes this tremendous discovery, he begins to re-align himself on her side.

[8] From *The Golden Bowl* by Henry James. © 1904 by Charles Scribner's Sons.

Charlotte never makes this discovery, and she is left to swim in her own bright deception. In fact, Maggie is instrumental in maintaining Charlotte's misconception, for she denies that there has been any infidelity.

It is quite evident that in these last novels James's concern is almost exclusively with the subtle nuances of human behavior, and that moral action quite alone interested him. Hawthorne was concerned to set his characters in motion against a more or less recognizable and traditional backdrop; but James left out all that was not apposite to his purpose, with the consequence that the emphasis is always upon the inner life, and the surface is left to suggest itself as best it may. The gain in intensity is of course obvious; and yet much of that is dissipated by the recondite and involved manner of the prose itself. Incidentally, in this respect *The Ambassadors* is clearly the most readable of the major novels.

Like *The Golden Bowl* and *The Portrait of a Lady*, *The Wings of the Dove* develops the situation in which a young woman is deceived by two friends who are in love with each other. Milly Theale, the millionairess, is the innocent in this novel; Martin Densher and Kate Croy are the lovers who choose to make use of her. Since Milly is in frail health, and it is the opinion of her doctor that her health will improve if she becomes interested again in life, and since "life" and "love" are in a sense identical, she sets out to marry Densher. But Densher is in love with Kate, and between them they decide to use Milly, principally so that they may have a trysting place in her rooms. As Densher prolongs his pretended lovemaking to Milly, her health becomes progressively worse until she is on the point of dying. Kate suggests that he actually marry her, thus obtaining her money, and after her death they can live very well on the proceeds. Kate can sway Martin to her will because she will not as yet sleep with him, and dangles that consummation before him.

Martin becomes insensibly aware of the true beauty of Milly's character, and cannot bring himself to propose. Meanwhile Milly accidentally learns of his infatuation with Kate, and this kills her.

She leaves a large bequest to Martin so that it is now possible for him and Kate to marry. But once more the catalytic, Milly's understanding, has had its intended effect upon the relationship of the conspirators. Martin knows at last that Milly's was the greater character, and he can no longer feel the same toward Kate. His love for her has undergone a reversal: the predatory pair have been defeated by their own victim.

James's demands upon his reader are exacting. First, he requires a closeness of scrutiny and a sustained attention. The amount of communication in his last novels depends wholly upon one's willingness to study and ferret out his meanings. In Brownell's words, James "follows his thought with the most intimate exactness—no doubt—in its subtle sinuosities, into its complicated connotations, unto its utmost attenuations; but it is often so elusive, so *insaisissable*—by others than himself—that he may perfectly express without in the least communicating it." This is perhaps an exaggeration, but it indicates the degree to which critics of his time felt reluctance to assimilate his content. To them "the great mass of his later writing is of a difficulty to conquer which requires an amount of effort disproportionate to the sense of assured reward."[4] What, one wonders, would they have made of *Finnegans Wake?* It is true that James, in constructing his art, indicated the direction taken by Joyce. There are not a few correspondences in the technical ingenuities and discoveries of James and those of the post-Freudian school. The single-minded concentration upon the thought and point of view of the characters in all of these final novels showed the way for the so-called interior monologue. James's use of point of view is one of his most interesting innovations; frequently we are led along the mazes of his novels solely through the eye and mind of their chief protagonists.

James demands, second, a willingness on his reader's part to sublimate ordinary interest of story progression in a whole new set of interests. What in the average novel is the interest of basic and boldly described human conflicts becomes in James's

---

[4] From *American Prose Masters*, by W. C. Brownell. © 1923 by Charles Scribner's Sons.

novels that growing out of the most tenuous gradations of action and response. The way a character flutters an eyelid may be the springboard for a chapter. One is treated to a ten-thousand-word dissertation upon the likelihood of acceptance or refusal of an invitation to tea. The labyrinth in these novels through which it is necessary to find one's way, to disentangle some seemingly unimportant point of etiquette, can doubtless excuse the impatience of the Brownells. But they miss the whole point of James. These Brobdingnagian excursions into social minutiae have an immense relevance. It is in the subtle nuances of a culture grown complex that the Jamesian drama consists. It is the fine-spun web of intellectual play and interplay that gives the novels their incredibly well-wrought distinction. Probably a sick culture cannot be analyzed in any other way. Fielding's brusque delineations of a robust culture are apposite for his age; James's complexity, like that of Proust and Joyce, alone is equal to the real interpretation of a cultural and social *malaise* like that of *fin de siècle* Europe.

The temperament of Henry James was the factor that made his work what it is. The same might be said of any writer; but in James's case it has a special significance. It is also the temperament of humanity that held his primary interest. For him, the degree to which men are conscious is the measure of their value. Temperaments fully developed, he seems to say, are the indication of social and individual maturity. The dilemma in which James and his characters find themselves is that they possess a fully developed consciousness that is out of synchrony with any received moral tradition. In this sense James forecasts the dilemma of the artist in the twentieth century, who must attempt a reconciliation of the values of a liberal social and political economy with those of a conservative theology. In James the conflict is best seen when we observe the contradictions of *The Princess Casamassima*, where the liberal ideology of the novel collides with the irreducible Jamesian moral conservatism. The surface of this "first period" novel is the most traditionally realistic of any that he wrote, and it describes most faithfully the death of a social and moral order; but it succeeds least as a depiction of moral decay; and the last novels, overtly not concerned with such problems, leave a far more definite and devastating impression of the collapse of both social and moral standards.

After James the novel could never be the same. A "novelists' novelist" in truth, James influenced the twentieth-century novel more than any preceding writer. Joyce, Proust, Hemingway, and all subsequent writers whose worlds are strangely refracted through a temperament, can best be understood by looking back to James and the revelations in his great, difficult, and prodigiously contrived art.

EDITH WHARTON and WILLA CATHER
The James Influence

ALTHOUGH the art of fiction writing attracted several women early in the history of the American novel, curiously none of them achieved eminence, and it was not until the close of the nineteenth century that any woman practitioner of imaginative prose writing attained to real excellence. Until Sarah Orne Jewett and Mary E. Wilkins began to write, in the 1870's and '80's, we had, to speak accurately, no fiction of stature from a woman's hand. Their work was best in the field of the short story, and it was largely localized and narrow in interest. With the appearance, however, of Edith Wharton, Willa Cather, Susan Glaspell and Ellen Glasgow, all of whom began to publish early in the twentieth century, the distaff side made strong bids for an important role in American fiction.

In American literature, until the present century, women have made far greater contributions in poetry than in prose, greater in quantity as well as quality. They continue to be preeminent in verse, though there are now literally scores of competent writers of prose in their ranks for every poet of note. In the nineteenth century we had Emily Dickinson and Lizette Reese, and early in the twentieth century Lola Ridge, Sara Teasdale, Marianne Moore and a host of excellent younger women. The more private and intricate speech of verse seems to have been the congenial medium for the American woman writer's expression.

In the whole range of American fiction, then, it seems apparent that only Edith Wharton and Willa Cather have contributed a sizable body of work that to our present sight may last. That work itself is hemmed in with faults, and even the masterpieces of these two writers do not measure up with the great productions of Hawthorne, James or Hemingway. It seems, however, to stem out of the same tradition, and even quite consciously so. Mrs. Wharton was an avowed disciple of James; and Miss Cather, in her earlier works at least, was apparently influenced by Edith Wharton. Such "influences" mean very little, of course; but there is a quality of imagination exhibited by these writers which seems to have points of marked similarity. They see the world through a finely refracting sensibility and wrest from that vision shapes of relevant and recognizable truth. The world of Edith Wharton is in many respects a superficial and heartless world; the people who live in it are seldom seen through and through; we are given all their surface seemings, but we hardly probe them to the uttermost. The world of Miss Cather is likewise a plane of immediate appearances; but we are oftener made to feel the underlying realities, because she is less interested in the ironies of a social stratum and more concerned with what may be taken to be the eternal constants of life. For this reason Willa Cather is probably the greater writer of the two.

Edith Wharton was one of those apparently "rare" writers actually born in New York City; moreover, she was born into that genteel set which comprised the upper brackets of society, the well-to-do who, while not extremely rich, were so well-off that money was a commodity taken for granted, especially by the women whose privilege and even duty it was to spend it. She married a Bostonian and spent a good part of her life traveling, acquainting herself with upper middle-class family life in England and France. Like Henry James, she cultivated a taste for the works of French literature, and particularly of novels and short stories. For James himself she entertained the highest regard, and was thought to be in some ways his protégé. Her admiration for his work shows through all of her own. This, then, was the background against which she worked, and it greatly influenced her choice of subject matter and her manner of treatment.

Yet she was always critical of the society in which she moved, and the fine edge of her best novels was sharpened by precisely that detachment she maintained from her environment. *The House of Mirth* (1905) contains an excellent genre picture of the Fifth Avenue "smart set" seen by knowing eyes, evaluated by a sensitive intelligence, and set forth without rancor but condemned all the more certainly in a restrained irony. Its heroine, Lily Bart, may be taken to reflect in her attitudes many of her creator's viewpoints, and Lily is assuredly anything but a protagonist of her own social milieu. While the husbands in this wealthy set are spending their days grubbing for money on Wall Street, the wives lavishly distribute the earnings on Fifth Avenue. The women, without definite goals and possessed of little cultural attainment, assuage their boredom in flirtations and affairs with unattached young men, and with the husbands of their friends. They exist in a world of expensive shops, concern themselves endlessly with fripperies and fashions, and eke out what satisfaction there may be in gossip about their neighbors' indiscretions.

Lily Bart, though she has reached the age of twenty-nine, is still unmarried, and there seems little prospect that she will get a mate, because she cannot find a man of intellectual attainments and sensibility to match her own. She is attracted, however, to one male in this circle of money-grubbers, Lawrence Selden, a bachelor whose wealth is hardly sufficient to enable him to move with complete freedom in Fifth Avenue society. In spite of that, Lily is powerfully attracted to him; but she is enough of a snob, or at least is restrained to such an extent by the mores of her tribe, that she never gives final consent to Selden. And she is, we are left in little doubt, definitely a cut above the women of her circle. Lawrence Selden sees her so. As Mrs. Wharton shows us, through Selden's eyes, Lily is a person of real worth:

"Everything about her was at once vigorous and exquisite,

at once strong and fine. He had a confused sense that she must have cost a great deal to make, that a great many dull and ugly people must, in some mysterious way, have been sacrificed to produce her. He was aware that the qualities distinguishing her from the herd of her sex were chiefly external: as though a fine glaze of beauty and fastidiousness had been applied to vulgar clay. Yet the analogy left him unsatisfied, for a coarse texture will not take a high finish; and was it not possible that the material was fine, but that circumstances had fashioned it into a futile shape?" [1]

This doubt, fostered early in Selden's mind, is the crux of the novel, and the reason for its existence. We are given an opportunity to learn, through several hundred pages, whether Lily is indeed of fine material, whether its shape is futile, whether the gloss is real or imaginary. For at any rate Lily gets deeply into debt and turns for assistance to a wealthy friend. The flaw in Lily, fostered by the society in which she cannot help having been born, was her inability to escape the inexorable demands of position. Squandering money, enmeshed in a web of compromise, her wealthy savior demanding the kind of payment she considers dishonorable, Lily is indeed a miserable heroine. To elude her friend and his importunities, she goes to Europe, where Mrs. Wharton is able to evoke, in somewhat Jamesian terms, a contrast between the traditional grace of an older society, and the garish and hateful necessities of her own. But fate is treading hard upon Lily's heels; when she returns to America she is penniless, or nearly so, cannot make a living, and just before taking an overdose of chloral, pays back, out of a small legacy, the sum she had borrowed from her importunate savior. After Lily's death, of course, Lawrence Selden, but not the reader (who has known it all along), discovers her honorable solution to her problem. He sees now that she is not the parasite he had sometimes thought, that the vulgar clay was in fact fine material and indeed had been cast into a futile shape by circumstance.

The House of Mirth shows many faults of an early novel; it

---

[1] From *The House of Mirth* by Edith Wharton. © 1905 by Charles Scribner's Sons.

is derivative and never wholly satisfying, and its structure would have been enormously improved had we not found out until Selden did, Lily's essential nobility. Still it is a highly competent work; its ironies are subtle and well wrought, and the portrait of Fifth Avenue worthies is a merciless one.

It was perhaps with surprise that her readers picked up Mrs. Wharton's next novel, the mood and setting of which were quite foreign to the life about which she might be supposed to know most. In 1911 she published *Ethan Frome*, which remains without doubt her best work. It is, however, a *tour de force*, and gives one the impression of having been concocted, manufactured. This impression, it must be admitted, is always an afterthought; the story is so well told, so perfectly constructed, so convincing on its surface, that at first blush it seems completely successful. It is only when one compares it with the greater achievements of Hawthorne and James that one sees the thinness of its texture. *Ethan Frome* is, after all, a very fine story, a tribute to the skill of an accomplished craftsman.

Within the brief confines of this novel, which is in fact more accurately to be described as a novelette, we are given another of those astringent examples of New England insular life, which had been done before with considerable artistry by Mary E. Wilkins and Sarah Orne Jewett; but in Mrs. Wharton's story there is a new and larger reference of significance. Ethan Frome himself is hardly realized so well as Mrs. Frome; her existence is absolute, her reality unquestionable. Seldom in our fiction has the embittered, unloved, shrewish wife been better portrayed. Mrs. Frome, with her thin, "high-boned face under its ring of crimping-pins," stares at us out of her tragic isolation as one of the unmistakably durable character creations of American literature. The third party forming the triangle in this old situation is Mattie, Mrs. Frome's poor relative; she provides the contrast of beauty and gentleness, and of course, the fulcrum for tragedy. In Mattie, Ethan finds everything that his wife cannot give him; the code of conduct, inherited from a Puritan legacy, demands that he shall not accept the happiness he has stumbled upon. And yet Ethan cannot bring himself to disavow his love for Mattie.

He takes, with her, the way out of a dilemna which is in consonance with his morality; he attempts suicide with her. The sleigh ride which was to have resulted in death for the lovers became instead the crippling seal set upon their love, binding them forever to Mrs. Frome in the cruelest of conceivable bondages. For the rest of their lives these three spiritually and even (two of them) physically deformed creatures exist in a hell of corrosive hatred. From this situation Mrs. Wharton has wrung the utmost of drama and pain; we are led to the knowledge of it in a devious way, so that when its full import strikes we are all the more horrified and filled with pity.

Essentially, of course, the situation is melodramatic, and reflection shows that only the very deftest manipulation could have gained our credibility with reference to Ethan's attempted solution. The sleigh ride itself is remarkably meretricious; but within its frame it is effective, and there is undeniably more than a trace of grim Hawthornesque sense of inevitability in the tale. Unacceptable as may be the morality of *Ethan Frome* to the modern sense, there is no doubt but that it veraciously reflects a historic attitude peculiar to the early New England mind. One has the feeling, however, that the author "worked up" her material, that she had read her Hawthorne, her Sarah Orne Jewett, and that the story grew out of an imposed will rather than a felt knowledge. Where *The Scarlet Letter* convinces despite its often labored imagery, *Ethan Frome* persuades because of its straightforward exposition; but there is not, in the latter novel, a sense of completely created belief; it does not bear up under an ultimate reconsideration. Even so, it transcends as a work of the imagination any other novel of similar scope dealing with the New England scene since Hawthorne. It is a minor masterpiece of artful construction, a *tour de force* among its author's many perhaps more authentic but less adequately executed novels.

Such a one is *The Custom of the Country* (1913), where again Mrs. Wharton created a thoroughly unpleasant leading character in the person of Undine Spragg, a heartless and evil woman who is yet presented as a typical product of her time and society. The "custom of the country" is its condoning of divorce, its assumption of the virtues of wealth, its actual poverty of respectable and socially useful traditions. The "country," it might be said, is something of a misnomer, since Mrs. Wharton's acquaintance with the United States was quite a narrow one, confined largely to New York, and especially its exclusive moneyed set. However, that set was sufficiently representative in its time, and it is difficult to quarrel with Mrs. Wharton's criticism of a culture that was, in great measure, typical of a whole society.

To follow the unenviable career of Undine Spragg is to delve into a quagmire of immorality, but as far as her society is concerned, she moves through it with few deterrents and is even to be considered a respectable integer in the social microcosm. Mrs. Wharton's objectivity helps to point up the disparity between her real worth and that estimation of it held by her milieu. This stamps all the more indelibly the seal of dishonor upon her society, which can give sanction to so distorted a moral estimate. Undine's rise in the world is accomplished by the simple expedient of successive marriages. As a girl she ran off with Elmer Moffatt, who, she imagined, was wealthy. When he lost his money she promptly divorced him, remarried and again found she had backed the wrong horse. She left that husband and became involved in an affair with a married man who she expected would divorce his wife and marry her; but this he did not do. On the rebound she married a French noble; and in this chapter of her life she displays the vulgarity which is at bottom her chief characteristic. Meanwhile she has been blackmailing her second husband, willing for him to retain custody of their child if he will pay her a sufficient sum of money. In attempting to meet her demands, he impoverishes himself and commits suicide. In the meantime the French marriage has of course failed, and Undine, still in quest of the wealth that is to insure her happiness and social position, comes full circle by remarrying Elmer Moffatt, who has now become a great capitalist. He would also have gained honor by being appointed an American ambassador; and this would have crowned Undine's ambitions. But, as the novel ends, Undine learns that Moffatt cannot be appointed since it is one of the rules that no ambassador may have a wife who had previously been divorced.

Upon this minor note of frustration, Undine's history ends. On the whole she had lived a successful life, according to the code of society. But we are left in no doubt as to the corruption of the woman and her society; with great restraint and a clear irony Mrs. Wharton gives us to understand the measure by which she has failed, the extent of her worthlessness, the waste and depravity of her life. *The Custom of the Country* is a black and bitter novel, for all its apparent serenity of surface.

If Undine Spragg lost her chance for happiness through a pervading vulgarity, a lack of moral values, another product of this society, Newland Archer, hero of *The Age of Innocence* (1920), lost his through a lack of force. Archer is one of those Jamesian Americans who realize the shoddiness of the commercial culture in which they have been raised but who cannot break the ties it has knotted around them. New York in the 1870's has its complement of conservative families, among whom Archer moves. His marriage, like his other relationships, has its elements of dissatisfaction. When Archer meets the beautiful Ellen Olenska, estranged wife of a Polish nobleman, he at last finds the woman who can offer him sensitivity, a perception of beauty, a realization of the things that matter to him. They admit their love but neither can do anything to legalize it; Ellen's parents will not allow her to divorce her Polish husband, and Archer is unable to contemplate separation from his family. Ellen leaves the country, and Newland Archer is resigned to a half-life. Much later he learns that his wife had known of his attraction to Ellen, and after his wife's death he make a pilgrimage, in company of his son, to Paris, where Ellen lives. Twenty years have passed, and it is merely an act of obeisance to the past which Archer acknowledges; but as the result of it we are given the revelation that lifts the whole series of relationships into a Jamesian realm.

As Archer and his son are speaking of Madame Olenska, the boy says:

" 'But mother said—'

" 'Your mother?'

" 'Yes: the day before she died. She said she knew we were safe with you, and always would be, because once, when she asked you to, you'd given up the thing you most wanted.'

"Archer received this strange communication in silence. . . . At length he said in a low voice: 'She never asked me.'

" 'No. I forgot. You never did ask each other anything, did you? And you never told each other anything. You just sat and watched each other, and guessed at what was going on underneath. A deaf-and-dumb asylum, in fact! Well, I back your generation for knowing more about each other's private thoughts than we ever have time to find out about our own.' " [2]

And again in typical James fashion, Archer shuns the completion of his own story. Later, when his son goes to see Ellen, Archer sits outside. " 'It's more real to me than if I went up,' he suddenly heard himself say; and the fear lest that last shadow of reality should lose its edge kept him rooted to his seat as the moments succeeded each other.

"He sat for a long time. . . . At length a light shone through the windows, and a moment later a man-servant came out on the balcony, drew up the awnings, and closed the shutters. At that, as if it had been the signal he waited for, Newland Archer got up slowly and walked back alone to his hotel." [2]

Mrs. Wharton's subjects are for the most part part exactly these dramas of marriage intrigue and unhappiness, but they always manage to reflect the sickness of a society and thus transcend the immediate references. In her other considerable novelette, *The Old Maid*, she again attacks the problem of an unconsummated relationship between man and woman, and the effects of bringing an illegitimate child into the closed circle of "respectable" society. In many of the novels these same fundamental issues are dealt with through various typical examples; but in the four major works the possibilities of her subject matter were largely exhausted.

Always a knowing craftsman, Mrs. Wharton published one work of criticism that reflects her own methods and the models which she consciously studied. *The Writing of Fiction* (1925) pays tribute especially to the masters of French nineteenth-cen-

---

[2] From *The Age of Innocence* by Edith Wharton. © 1920 by Charles Scribner's Sons.

tury realism, and to the English and Russian novelists who were also the object of Henry James's admiration. James himself was quite naturally of deepest interest to Mrs. Wharton, and while her concern with the subtle nuances of social intercourse was perhaps as intense as James's, her rendering of them never reached such heights of passionate thoroughness. Furthermore, she was content to remain in her native land. While she certainly felt the lack of an American tradition and the absence of respected historical custom, she never disavowed her roots or attempted a transplanting which would have been disastrous in a writer of her comparatively slight capabilities. But for James she retained a regard approaching idolatry. She had studied his methods with great profit to her own art, as a passage from *The Writing of Fiction* will show:

"James sought the effect of verisimilitude by rigorously confining every detail of his picture to the range, and also to the capacity, of the eye fixed on it. 'In the Cage' is a curiously perfect example of the experiment on a small scale, only one very restricted field of vision being permitted. In his longer and more eventful novels, where the transition from one consciousness to another became necessary, he contrived it with such unfailing ingenuity that the reader's visual range was continuously enlarged by the substitution of a second consciousness whenever the boundaries of the first were exceeded. *The Wings of the Dove* gives an interesting example of these transitions. In *The Golden Bowl*, still unsatisfied, still in pursuit of an impossible perfection, he felt he must introduce a sort of *co-ordinating consciousness* detached from, but including, the characters principally concerned. The same attempt to wrest dramatic forms to the uses of the novel that caused *The Awkward Age* to be written in dialogue seems to have suggested the creation of Colonel and Mrs. Assingham as a sort of Greek chorus to the tragedy of *The Golden Bowl*. This insufferable and incredible couple spend their days in espionage and delation, and their evenings in exchanging the reports of their eaves'-dropping with a minuteness and precision worthy of Scotland Yard. The utter improbability of such conduct on the part of a dull-witted and frivolous couple in the rush of London society shows that the author created them for the sole purpose of revealing details which he could not otherwise communicate without lapsing into the character of the mid-Victorian novelist chatting with his readers of 'my heroine' in the manner of Thackeray and Dickens." [3]

By her own example, Edith Wharton was to encourage other American women to write truly out of their personal experience and observation. Willa Cather, Susan Glaspell, Ellen Glasgow, Ruth Suckow and many others in some degree owe to the pioneering of Mrs. Wharton their freedom to speak on subjects of which they had first-hand knowledge. Miss Cather, the most gifted of them all, and possessed of an even richer store of material than her master, avowedly followed in the steps of the older writer, and went on to create novels and stories of a profounder significance and a wider range of human relevance. But the distinction remains to Mrs. Wharton of being the pioneer and the exemplar of what might be accomplished by an American woman in a field where her English forerunners had long ago distinguished themselves.

The problem of the beginning writer was never more clearly exemplified than in the case of Willa Cather. Edith Wharton's attempt to find individual expression in the shadow of a great influence like that of Henry James was typical; but at least Mrs. Wharton knew early what she wanted to do, and the advances evident in her books are less a matter of progressively firmer grasp of materials than an increasing mastery of craftmanship. Miss Cather, on the other hand, not only had much to learn as a craftsman but also had to improve her knowledge of life, to acquire a subject matter of importance. She started, like Mrs. Wharton, by admiring James above all other writers; and in her first novel, *Alexander's Bridge* (1912), proved the truth of her own later observation, when she said,[4] "I think usually the young

---

[3] From *The Writing of Fiction* by Edith Wharton. © 1925 By Charles Scribner's Sons.
[4] From Preface to *Alexander's Bridge* by Willa Cather. © 1933 by Houghton Mifflin.

writer must have his affair with the external material he covets; must imitate and strive to follow the masters he most admires, until he finds he is starving for reality and cannot make this go any longer. Then he learns that it is not the adventure he sought, but the adventure that sought him, which has made the enduring mark upon him."

But Miss Cather also had the advantage of advice from another writer whom she greatly respected, which must have made a profound impression on her. "I had the good fortune," she says, "to meet Sarah Orne Jewett, who had read all of my early stories (and saw) where my work fell short. She said: 'Write it as it is, don't try to make it like this or that. . . . You'll have to make a way of your own. If the way happens to be new, don't let that frighten you. Don't try to write the kind of short story that this or that magazine wants; write the truth. . . .' I dedicated *O Pioneers* to her because I had talked over some of the characters with her, and I tried to tell the story of the people as truthfully and simply as if I were telling it to her by word of mouth." By the time she had written that novel, Miss Cather's knowledge and experience of the world were greatly improved, for she had waited, after the publication of some early stories, nearly ten years before presenting to Miss Jewett and the world her first important novel. That period of observation and incubation may have been the result of another piece of advice, for Miss Cather also says, "One of the few really helpful words I ever heard from an older writer I had from Sarah Orne Jewett when she said to me: 'Of course, one day you will write about your own country. In the meantime get all you can. One must know the world *so well* before one can know the parish.' "

Nevertheless, her first works were extremely derivative; and the earliest of them, a book of poems called *April Twilights* (1903) was in the very worst sentimental tradition. Her first novel, *Alexander's Bridge*, was Jamesian, and its locale was Boston and Europe, about which she knew little, and most of that little had come from books. Its theme, which might have come straight from Mrs. Wharton, concerned a moral choice forced upon a man whose marital relationships were unsatisfactory. But, in 1913, when *O Pioneers* appeared, she had indeed written about her own country, the flat Midwestern prairies where she had grown up; and here the fledgling writer had made a most auspicious beginning, in a novel that was immediately recognized as a minor sort of masterpiece, more than a work of "local color," more than another saga of the indomitable tamers of the wilderness, a work of mature imagination with universal overtones.

In the figures of Alexandra Bergson and Marie Shabata, Miss Cather created the two archetypal women whose existence, as much as any other factor, made possible the winning of the frontier. Alexandra, the strong, determined woman with a sense of property and business acumen resembling a man's, and Marie, the wild, passionate creature for whom men fight and foreswear reason—these are characters of elemental grandeur whose creation could only be possible in the hands of a mature artist. Alexandra's brother Emil, and their friend, Carl Lindstrum, are almost equally well realized; and it is the fortunes of these four which make the human drama of *O Pioneers*. We are given all the elements of a four-part tragi-comedy, in which one pair of lovers comes to a tragic end, and the other finds a temperate happiness through acceptance of life's limitations. The story of *O Pioneers* is altogether this concern with individual destinies, but as the protagonists play out their parts against a vast backdrop of hostile nature on the Nebraska tablelands, we gain a compelling insight into the pioneer life and what it means to carry on a perpetual struggle with land and sky in order to wrest a livelihood from acres that had never known the tenancy of man.

As one of the earliest of the "pioneer" novels, *O Pioneers* is certainly among the best, and it undoubtedly inspired many other writers of the Midwest to try their hands at similar stories. If anyone had thought that the dreary Western plateaus, with their scattered settlements peopled by ignorant, "uninteresting" men and women, were not material for fiction, Miss Cather had disabused them. The time was to come when others, who had perhaps even truer experiences of frontier hardships, would write better novels, and Ole Rölvaag's *Giants in the Earth* (1927) is a case in point; but at any rate Miss Cather was still one of the pioneers herself in finding for fiction a valid new realm of unexploited materials.

O Pioneers is a book full of faults, at least in comparison with other books by the same writer; yet it contains also some of the most restrained and sensitive prose Miss Cather ever wrote. Its male characters, especially Carl Lindstrum, are little more than puppets; it lacks the sense of progression that a chronicle novel vitally needs; it suffers from a disunity of theme (the epic of frontier-taming and the love story do not supplement each other); it sometimes wanders into bypaths. But it also has warmth, gusto, tenderness, and a largeness of humanity such as few books by women writers have ever shown.

In a sense even more ambitious was Miss Cather's next book, *The Song of the Lark* (1915), which followed the career of an untutored daughter of pioneer parents to the heights of achievement in the world of music. Thea Kronborg's journey from a childhood on the prairies to success as a Metropolitan Opera star is a case history in one of the arts, and it has many great passages; but as a whole the work contains little of the large, brooding humanity of the preceding book. However, in *My Antonia* (1918), the full tide of Miss Cather's genius was running again. The novel marked a return to the materials of *O Pioneers*, and a strengthening of grasp upon them, a refinement of the art that had nearly succeeded in making that book a masterpiece.

My Antonia was the second of a series of novels that Miss Cather was to write in which she traced the complete life story of a person, the fictional biography which was to be her most successful form. From Thea Kronborg in *The Song of the Lark* through Antonia Shimerda, and Professor St. Peter in *The Professor's House* (1925) to Father Joseph in *Death Comes for the Archbishop* (1927), these lengthy chronicles of a life are surely among the great achievements of Miss Cather's art. With *A Lost Lady*, they are the novels by which she will be remembered. They contain a full sense of felt life, they enclose areas of wide understanding, they call up to our recreated imagination visions of our own life, and they illumine our experience in flashes that are fine and true, as the great novels of all time alone can do.

When Professor St. Peter reaches that autumnal stage of life when he knows that he must henceforth be content to live without delight, we have a moment of recognition and belief, which opens up a new vista of truth. When the alarms and skirmishes of life are past, the professor begins, like all of us, to look back and relive his youth. He becomes a boy again.

It is this ability to capture essences of mood and a rare knowledge of the exact cast of thought and attitude in her characters' outlook at any given stage of their development which distinguishes Miss Cather's work at its best moments. Even in some of the least successful novels, these small miracles of observation and attitude appear with surprising frequency. In *One of Ours* (1922), *Shadows on the Rock* (1931) and *Sapphira and the Slave Girl* (1940), novels which represent a recession of Willa Cather's artistry, there are felicities enough to make a reputation for another writer.

But curiously enough, as in Edith Wharton's case also, the apex of her art is reached in a brief novel, hardly more than a novelette. *A Lost Lady* (1923) is an almost perfect story, showing all of Miss Cather's strengths, and succeeds greatly beyond its modest intentions. Unlike *Ethan Frome*, it is not a *tour de force* but a plain, straightforward story encompassing a woman's entire life, and devoid of the sentimentality or melodrama which vitiates the older novelist's story. In many respects it is one of the best-realized short novels in our literature, and is certainly more truly "American" than any of the equally fine novelettes by Henry James, with which it can often stand comparison.

A Lost Lady exists for its picture of a woman, one of the best-drawn portraits of a *femme fatale* we have. Oddly enough, this woman, Marian Forrester, is nothing more than the wife of a railroad contractor in a little town on the prairie. Yet with such an unprepossessing background, Miss Cather makes of her one of the recognizably great creations in the tradition of such women. It is also a study in disillusionment, the awakening of a youth to whom this woman had stood as one of the bright, fair visions of earth, and his discovery that she was largely compounded of dross.

We first meet Mrs. Forrester as Niel Herbert, a little boy, having suffered an injury, is taken into the Forrester home while the doctor is called. To Niel this house had represented something fine and great; standing on its little knoll, surrounded by trees and grassy meadowland, it had represented to him the far-off and fabulous luxury of great cities. The common people of Sweet Water had never entered it, and because they were excluded they had built up all kinds of false notions of its splendor. Marian Forrester, a good many years older than the boy, but much younger than her husband, seemed a wondrous creature to him. There was something fine, sweet, tempered and indefinable about her that set her apart. As Niel grew up he continued to worship the ideal of beautiful womanhood, embodied in Mrs. Forrester.

Captain Forrester himself was a man of incorruptible honor, and on the whole one of Miss Cather's best male creations. Her men, however, do not have the fiber and believability of her women. Her knowledge of men is restricted; she sees them through a woman's eyes. For example, when trouble breaks out in one of Forrester's railroad camps, he is made to solve it in the briefest manner in a scene which to Miss Cather seems to tell all, but which tells very little.

Niel's real awakening to the nature of his lovely lady comes when, one morning, he goes up to the Forrester house, knowing that the Captain is out of town, and discovers another man has spent the night there. Niel knows then that what he had supposed to be the tempered steel of Marian Forrester was indeed brass. That moment witnessed the extinction of his loyalty, his illusion.

At the very time that his wife is betraying him, Captain Forrester has gone on a journey to fulfill the obligations of his honor. In a run on a bank of which he is principal stockholder, he converts all his wealth so that his depositors will not be ruined. And it is the contrast between the nobility of her husband and the baseness of Mrs. Forrester that proves to Niel how wrong had been his estimation of her worth. However, Niel's real quarrel with her is not her immorality but rather that she did not live up to the high ideal he had of her as representative of a special time and place in American life. After the Captain's death she does rescue some of our admiration, keeping on at the old house, living within the straitened budget left after the bank's demands are met, trying to live up to the old conception the town had of the Forresters as people of "quality." But Niel sees Marian Forrester is not cut of the same cloth as the Captain and those of his generation.

The "lost lady's" career fades away into that limbo of all unhappy realizations, and Niel's final intelligence of her is that she has married again, and at last has died, probably in South America. She never had entirely forsaken the true and noble life that she had once been part of, for she had always sent money for flowers to be placed on the grave of her former husband; she always knew where greatness and integrity lay, even though she could not hold to them.

After *A Lost Lady*, such novels as *Death Comes for the Archbishop*, *Lucy Gayheart* and *Sapphira and the Slave Girl*, though more ambitious, were disappointing; but if Willa Cather had written only this one short novel, she would have richly earned a place among our important women novelists.

ERNEST HEMINGWAY
And the "Fifth Dimension"

THE GREATEST American literary reputation since Hawthorne's is undoubtedly Ernest Hemingway's. It is probably the greatest that any American ever enjoyed. It was achieved while Hemingway was still quite young, and continues almost without diminution. The publication of every Hemingway book since *The Sun Also Rises* has been an event of literary importance, and the rumor of a new one in prospect has always raised the liveliest expectations. Only two books of the nine he has published since then have been disappointing; and his earliest pamphlet, which appeared in 1924, contained one of his finest stories, "My Old Man." From the appearance of that thirty-page booklet at the

Three Mountains Press in Paris, until *For Whom the Bell Tolls* in 1940, the Hemingway career has been an impressive one of continuing triumph and an increasingly sharpened art.

No other American writer has inspired so much imitation as Hemingway. Not only have young writers of his own country copied every mannerism, but English and Continental imitators have appeared by the score. The bald statements, simple declarative sentences, sometimes linked together with successive "ands," the repetitive rhythms and judiciously repeated key words, are almost the trade mark of a generation of writers. "Hard-boiled realism," once thought to be the touchstone of Hemingway's appeal, was developed with a nearly ritualistic fervor. Careful understatement and violence reported casually were the *leitmotif* of scores of "Hemingway novels." The corruptions of a John O'Hara or a James M. Cain could not, however, be regarded seriously, and no imitator has yet produced a fiction that has the greatness of the originals. The copyists of Faulkner and Wolfe have sometimes succeeded in equaling their masters, but not so the imitators of Hemingway.

The reasons for this are perhaps discernible. Few people are endowed with a temperament as sharp, clear and true as Hemingway's. It is a gift, like a musical sense possessed by a Beethoven, or a facility with the brush given to an El Greco. As Ford Madox Ford says, "It arises from how you look at things." For his time, Hemingway has looked at things in the way that has interpreted the world most successfully for the most people. His technical adeptness, the tricks he has learned of his trade, have been quite adequately copied by others; but the Hemingway temperament is something that cannot be copied. His famous insistence on the attempt to write truly of things as one felt about them, not as one was supposed to feel, has been tried many times; but only he has written of them as Hemingway felt about them, which is the secret of his greatness—the secret locked away in the Hemingway temperament which cannot be imitated.

Another factor that accounts for Hemingway's unprecedented acceptance as the spokesman for at least two literary generations is his time sense. He possesses a sense of contemporaneity even more acute than that of F. Scott Fitzgerald, who had it in a high degree. *This Side of Paradise* and *The Great Gatsby* were, respectively, the accepted portraits of the flapper and the speakeasy eras. But Fitzgerald's bright genius burned out like a meteor; while Hemingway has continued with only minor lapses to catch the spirit of his times. *The Sun Also Rises* was undoubtedly calculated to be a picture of the generation dubbed lost (by Gertrude Stein); and as it happened, the novel did become the *vade mecum* of the postwar disillusioned young men and women, for it perfectly articulated the generation's bewilderment turned to a facile cynicism, the sentimentalized self-pity, the alcoholic and fornicating escapism. Above all, Hemingway's laconic presentation made everything seem the more world-weary and so to speak, off-hand. At the same time, his writing was so fresh as to seem new and even shocking. His prose was clean, simple, accomplished. The viewpoint was all new and different. And it appealed to a generation's estimate of the world and itself.

This supreme sense of timing has nothing journalistic about it. It goes deeper than a mere facility for sensing the proper moment for cashing in on an evanescent public interest. Hemingway seems to have in his bones a feeling for the decade's salient meanings. When *A Farewell to Arms* appeared, it was evident that he had absorbed not only the outward surfaces but the spirit of a maturing "lost generation" which tried to find underneath the shifting values of its disenchantment something to which to cling. In this case, of course, it was the idea of love, which had been flouted in the earlier novel. The action of *A Farewell to Arms* antedates that of *The Sun Also Rises* in point of chronology, but its spirit and viewpoint actually carry on into a later time the attitudes of Jake, hero of the earlier book; and Frederick Henry of the later novel is certainly only a somewhat older incarnation of Jake Barnes. All the principal Hemingway heroes, it has often been observed, are one and the same person, and they are largely modeled upon Hemingway himself. So that, as the novels successively appeared, we could watch the growth and maturing of their author, and we could see that the Hemingway time sense continued in its unabated acuity, catching the basic values of the decades as they wore on. *To Have and Have Not* was of the mid-'thirties, reflecting the nascent political awareness of a generation; and though it faltered, it was a good rehearsal for the magnificent success of *For Whom the Bell Tolls*, which did contain the best statement of a new appraisal of political values in our time. And meanwhile the short stories had offered a continuing corroboration of Hemingway's extraordinary awareness of the forces at work in people and the world about him.

The pamphlet of 1924 entitled *in our time* was expanded and published with capitalization the next year in New York. This collection of remarkable stories gave a more or less consecutive picture of the youth and young manhood of Nick Adams, a product of the Michigan north woods and the European war. The stories, complete in themselves, were tied together with brief vignettes of the war, and the net result was a wonderfully realized recreation of typical experience in that time. The stories range all the way from the little boy's observation of his father as he performs a rude Caesarean operation on an Indian woman, whose husband, unable to bear the spectacle, cuts his throat from ear to ear, to the somewhat psychoneurotic reactions of a returned veteran unable to adjust to any of the old values held by his family. His mother asks if he doesn't love her.

" 'No,' Krebs said.

"His mother looked at him across the table. Her eyes were shiny. She started crying.

" 'I don't love anybody,' Krebs said . . .

" 'I'm your mother,' she said. 'I held you next to my heart when you were a tiny baby.'

"Krebs felt sick and vaguely nauseated."[1]

The linking interludes nearly all are of the war or of bullfighting, and serve both to forecast experience of the boy Nick and to explain the attitudes of the grown men who figure in some of the stories. Stories and vignettes are saturated with the sense of death; it is the proximity of death that heightens the drama

---

[1] From "Soldier's Home" in *In Our Time* by Ernest Hemingway. © 1925 by Charles Scribner's Sons.

or makes more intense the meaning in all of them. The famous
"Chapter III" is an exquisite bit of writing and serves as an epitome of the death sense of the whole book:

"We were in a garden at Mons. Young Buckley came in with
his patrol from across the river. The first German I saw climbed
up over the garden wall. We waited till he got one leg over and
then potted him. He had so much equipment on and looked aw-
fully surprised and fell down into the garden. Then three more
came over further down the wall. We shot them. They all came
just like that."[2]

It is already clear in this first book that Hemingway's models
were mostly his own contemporaries, Gertrude Stein, Sherwood
Anderson, Ezra Pound and T. S. Eliot. But though the simple,
almost childlike rhythms of Miss Stein and the repetitions of Anderson are evident, there is an even more familiar ring to some
of the passages. For example, in "My Old Man" the narrator
says: "This Kzar is a great big yellow horse that looks like just
nothing but run. I never saw such a horse. He was being led
around the paddocks with his head down and when he went by
me I felt all hollow inside he was so beautiful. There never was
such a wonderful, lean, running built horse."[3] That is Huckleberry Finn talk and owes nothing to any American but Mark
Twain. Hemingway has said that *Huckleberry Finn* is the best
novel by an American; but one imagines it is the colloquial and
honest style that impressed him, for of Mark Twain's satiric and
other intentions, Hemingway's work shows not an iota. For
style, the pure art of narrative, Hemingway has always felt an
almost religious veneration; and he shows in his early work that,
although life itself is unsatisfactory and essentially meaningless,
the creation of art can perhaps provide a reason for existing. If he
could recapture experience in art he could cheat the deathward
drive of all existence. As he said, "But the real thing, the sequence
of motion and fact which made the emotion and which would

---

[2] From Preface to "The End of Something" in *In Our Time* by Ernest Hemingway. © 1925 by Charles Scribner's Sons.
[3] From "My Old Man" in *In Our Time* bv Ernest Hemingway. © 1925 by
Charles Scribner's Sons.

be as valid in a year or ten years or, with luck and if you stated it purely enough, always, was beyond me and I was working very hard to get it."[4] For him, Mark Twain had made experience valid for always, and when he worked "very hard to get it" himself, he could compose such a Clemensian passage as this:

"While I had him on, several trout had jumped at the falls. As soon as I baited up and dropped in again I hooked another and brought him in the same way. In a little while I had six. They were all about the same size. I laid them out, side by side, all their heads pointing the same way, and looked at them. They were beautifully colored and firm and hard from the cold water. It was a hot day, so I slit them all and shucked out the insides, gills and all, and tossed them over across the river. I took the trout ashore, washed them in the cold, smoothly heavy water above the dam, and then picked some ferns and packed them all in the bag, three trout on a layer of ferns, then another layer of ferns, then three more trout, and then covered them with ferns. They looked nice in the ferns, and now the bag was bulky, and I put it in the shade of the tree."[5]

In addition to his desire to report truthfully his feelings and those of his characters, Hemingway wanted always to project something deeper in his fiction. It was a variant of the desire of Hawthorne and James to inspire a deeper consciousness of reality through an appeal to the nonobjective factors of experience. In Hemingway's words, he wanted to know "how far prose can be carried if anyone is serious enough and has luck. There is a fourth and fifth dimension that can be gotten. . . . It is much more difficult than poetry. It is prose that has never been written. But it can be written without tricks and without cheating. With nothing that will go bad afterwards."[6] Of course it had been written, and James especially had gotten that "fourth and fifth dimension" better than anyone before; and Hemingway himself

---

[4] From *Death in the Afternoon* by Ernest Hemingway. © 1932 by Charles Scribner's Sons.

[5] From *The Sun Also Rises* by Ernest Hemingway. © 1926 by Charles Scribner's Sons.

[6] From *Green Hills of Africa* by Ernest Hemingway. © 1935 by Charles Scribner's Sons.

was to get it in some parts of *For Whom the Bell Tolls*—the fifth dimension of a new kind of consciousness that looks backward and forward at the same time, and which extends the range of our human awareness as even poetry has seldom done. For what else but poetry is the bulk of Hemingway's and James's work, taken in its essentials? Both writers care far more for the crucial abstractions than for the surface of life; any appellation of "realism" to their work is false, for it is the idealization of emotions, the dramatization of abstractions, which interests them. Both build character and describe outward action; but what really interests them is an intangible sense of what it all means . . . and they are not actually good at characterization in the sense that Fielding and Tolstoy are good. It is the evanescence of temperament which absorbs them and sets their work apart from that of all their contemporaries. The "fourth and fifth dimension" is just that marvelous ability to fathom temperament, and nothing else.

The Sun Also Rises, while it does skillfully create character, and reports brilliantly the surface of conversation and somewhat hectic action, is an interesting novel by reason of its investigation of submerged meanings, and for what is symbolic in the relationships of its strangely assorted personnel. Its factual background continues the postwar adventures of the generic Nick Adams of *In Our Time;* in this case he is compositely the narrator, Jake Barnes, who has been emasculated by a war wound; Philip Cohn, a writer with an inferiority complex; Bill (popularly supposed to be modeled on Hemingway's friend, Dos Passos); and a number of other hard-drinking, fornicating young men without illusions. They all go to Spain for the bullfights, and they take with them Lady Brett Ashley, a promiscuous female with whom Jake might be in love if he could have at all satisfied her sexually. She sleeps with many of the men, and gains a moment of virtue when she renounces the seduction of a young bullfighter. "You know," she says after making the sacrifice, "it makes one feel rather good deciding not to be a bitch."[7]

---

[7] From *The Sun Also Rises* by Ernest Hemingway. © 1926 by Charles Scribner's Sons.

All the hitherto displayed elements of Hemingway's temperament are continued in *The Sun Also Rises*, and there also emerges,
as Edmund Wilson has pointed out, what James Thurber called
the war between men and women. It is a conflict that continues
through all of Hemingway and finds the ultimate artistic expression in the wonderful story "The Short Happy Life of Francis Macomber." Love is only another manifestation of the death
principle; whenever love appears, it presages doom for one or
both of its professors. Lady Brett's favors bestow only misery
upon her lovers; she can give a reprieve to the young matador
which amounts to a last-minute pardon; but she is herself
thwarted by the accident of Jake's mutilation. Through story
after story it is love that defeats his heroes, and this is a paramount theme in the collections, *Men Without Women* (1927)
and *Winner Take Nothing* (1933); love is seen as a physical contest, one manifestation of the cruelty of the world which will
at last do a man in, and for which there is no remedy.[8] Those
heroes who do win victories, win them only in the moral sphere;
and Francis Macomber, Jake Barnes, Frederick Henry, Robert
Jordan, along with their many counterparts, succumb to the violence of love or "things as they are" despite their frequent
triumph as men of integrity in a moral universe.

Symbolically, Brett Ashley stands not only for the principle
of love but of total animal destruction; and the men who swarm
around her like gadflies meet destruction at her hands; Jake's victory over her is in a sense accidental, but it is conclusive. Even if
love had been possible, Hemingway indicates it would have
failed. " 'Oh, Jake,' Brett said, 'we could have had such a damned
good time together.' 'Yes,' I said. 'Isn't it pretty to think so?' "[9]

A Farewell to Arms (1929) might chronologically be taken
to precede *The Sun Also Rises*, for it is a history of Jake Barnes
in an earlier incarnation, a morally wounded young man in the

---

[8] The Old Lady in *Death in the Afternoon* asks Hemingway, "Have you no
remedy then?"—referring to the looseness of style in writing. "Madame," he
replies, "there is no remedy for anything in life." From *Death in the Afternoon* by Ernest Hemingway. © 1932 by Charles Scribner's Sons.

[9] From *The Sun Also Rises* by Ernest Hemingway. © 1926 by Charles Scribner's Sons.

midst of war, in love with a somewhat less bitchy Lady Brett, named Catherine. In this novel the central interest is the Romeo and Juliet theme with its tragic ending; but this is the least satisfactory aspect of the book, and the love story is not only trite but so sentimentalized as to be preposterous. Once again it is the aura of death pervading all the action and the magnificent writing that brings painfully alive the horror of war, its waste and destruction of moral values—that is the real fulcrum of the novel. Instead of bullfighting, we have skirmishes and retreats. Valor in the face of certain physical destruction, and moral victories over fear and senseless sacrifice of life, provide the usual Hemingway satisfactions. What remains clearest as a disclosure of attitudes is that the hero, Frederick Henry, became the nihilistic Jake Barnes as a consequence of his war experiences. They convinced him that society and its standards were worthless; that sensation was all that was valid; and that as far as any norm of conduct is concerned, "what is moral is what you feel good after." They inspired his flat rejection of accepted shibboleths, his notorious "nada hail nada full of nada," the ultimate refusal of all values. And yet there was an element of pose in all this; and the defiance of custom and moral law was only an inverted desire to accept a faith that had seemed less than the least it promised. Likewise, the "hard-boiled" attitude of all the writing was a cloak for a strong strain of sentimentality. The brave philosophy of understatement revealed a deeply wounded sensibility, and the invincible refusal to show any emotion was only the measure of an overdeveloped emotionalism. When Frederick said farewell to the dead Catherine he was acting out his part of Jack London's "blond beast"—the manly man overcome by powerful grief but resolute in his refusal to show it. "I went to the door of the room. 'You can't come in now,' one of the nurses said. 'Yes I can,' I said. 'You can't come in yet.' 'You can get out,' I said. 'The other one too.' But after I had got them out and shut the door and turned off the light it wasn't any good. It was like saying good-by to a statue. After a while I went out and left the hospital and walked back to the hotel in the rain."[10]

<hr>

[10] From *A Farewell to Arms* by Ernest Hemingway. © 1929 by Charles Scribner's Sons.

This strain of sentimentalism, coupled with a strong taste for sensationalism, for action regardless of relevance, has always been a great weakness in Hemingway, and in his next novel, *To Have and Have Not* (1937), these and other typical Hemingway frailties came into a most unfortunate conjunction. Without doubt it is the poorest novel he has written, and about on a par with the graceless dull boasting of his catch-all volume of big-game hunting, philosophy and writing manual, *Green Hills of Africa* (1935). Harry Morgan, the Key West rum runner, like his namesake, is a modern buccaneer who lives by his wits and physical endurance. Unlike the pirate, however, he is impecunious to a degree and must be classed among the "have-nots." In contrast to his exciting life are the idle rich, decadent Florida week-end visitors, who spend their time getting drunk, fornicating and following various perverted pleasures. They are incredibly despicable. But Harry Morgan is not by any means a sympathetic character either. Mrs. Morgan seems to appreciate him for the best thing he has: a great "talent for the bed." Harry Morgan fights his way through life, but is finally betrayed by those who should have stood by him, and exploited by those whose pleasures he assists. As he dies, he comes to realize that "No matter how a man alone ain't got no bloody f———— chance," and Hemingway observes, "It had taken him a long time to get it out, and it had taken him all his life to learn it."[11] This marks the conversion of an intransigeant individualist to another doctrine, and of course it signaled the same reorientation in Hemingway. For a long while, during the 'thirties, the social question must have been troubling Hemingway, who had long ago said: "Religion is the opium of the people. . . . Yes, and music is the opium of the people. . . . And now economics is the opium of the people; along with patriotism the opium of the people in Italy and Germany. What about sexual intercourse; was that an opium of the people? Of some of the people. Of some of the best people. But drink was a sovereign opium of the people, oh, an excellent opium. Although some prefer the radio, another opium of the people. . . . Along with these went gambling, an

---

[11] From *To Have and Have Not* by Ernest Hemingway. © 1937 by Charles Scribner's Sons.

opium of the people if there ever was one. . . . . Ambition was another, an opium of the people, along with a belief in any new form of government."[12] But now he had changed his mind, or rather, was beginning to find where he had really stood all the while, and *To Have and Have Not* was a clumsy attempt to make a statement of his position. He had never been won over by the Marxist proselytizing so universal in the 'thirties; but for a brief time *To Have and Have Not* had seemed to signalize his acceptance of Marxist gospel, which went even further in the inconsiderable play, *The Fifth Column*, written as a result of his activities as sympathizer and correspondent in the Spanish Civil War.

All of this writing, however, proved useful for what it provided as background for his next novel, *For Whom the Bell Tolls* (1940). On the whole, in spite of a generally lowered prose quality, it is the most satisfactory extended piece of writing he has done to date. This is the story of a group of Spanish Loyalists and their ostensible defeat by the forces of reaction and superior military equipment. It is the story of Robert Jordan, an American schoolteacher who enlists on the side of the Republicans and gives his life to the cause. It is the story of an idyllic love between Jordan and the mousy Maria (called most appropriately by him "little rabbit") which is the least successful thing about the novel. As a love story, *For Whom the Bell Tolls* falls far below *A Farewell to Arms*, but neither novel is strong for its tensions of love, which seem actually thrown in as a sop to public taste. Again, what makes this novel meaningful is the conflict between the life force and the much more powerful pull toward death. Robert Jordan reclines on pine needles as *For Whom the Bell Tolls* begins, and he is in a similar position as it ends; in between there has been for him only this long tendency toward death, as inevitable as the resolution of Greek drama.

The magnificent success of *For Whom the Bell Tolls* is due to the finally achieved characterization of wholly rounded people. A host of Spanish peasants come to life in a way that none of the earlier Hemingway people live. Pilar and Pablo, the leaders

---

[12] From "The Gambler, the Nun and the Radio", in *Fifth Column and the First Forty-nine* by Ernest Hemingway. © 1938 by Charles Scribner's Sons.

of a guerilla band, are masterly studies beside whom even Robert Jordan is but a phantom. El Sordo, Joaquin, Lieutenant Berrendo, and a dozen others have three solid dimensions and are more absolutely memorable than the characters of any contemporary American novel, with the possible exception of *The Grapes of Wrath*.

Hemingway's social conscience had been fully aroused by the time he got around to writing this book. He had gone through the phase of uncritical enthusiasm which marked *To Have and Have Not* and *The Fifth Column*. He had achieved the detachment and objectivity required to see the nature of social conflict in its real aspects. The result was a novel of clear and forceful meaning, that could be taken at its face value, a revolutionary document of persuasive eloquence, as well as a story of men in action, pitted against unfair odds, to be sure, but nevertheless in recognizably human situations. What defeats these earthy, ribald peasants, these thoroughly good if fallible men and women, is not so much their personal fallibility as the overall incompetence and inextricably tangled purposes of separately well-intentioned men aggregating a mass of ill-intentioned results.

The single most interesting feature of the book is its successful embodiment of the conflicts within Hemingway's own temperament. Robert Jordan is Jake Barnes and Frederick Henry ten years more mature, which is to say, he is Hemingway himself, with all his retinue of paradoxical tendencies. He is the man who would tear down all extant morality and deny the worth of any human endeavor. But he is simultaneously the yearner for a better existence for mankind. He is the big-game hunter who delights in killing for its own sake, and yet he is the tender lover of all that is soft and malleable in women. He is the hard-drinking sophisticate and also the clear-headed man of action. He is the melodramatist who plots scenes as operatic as El Sordo on a hilltop, or Maria and Robert in a sleeping bag, and concurrently he is the fierce opponent of all kinds of self-dramatization and rhetoric. Nevertheless, Robert Jordan, while possessing more than a little of all these mutually exclusive tendencies, is not an unsuccessful portrait. The psychology of a man who is willing to give his life in an impersonal cause, and who loves common men because they are human, is convincingly presented in this last incarnation of the Hemingway hero. If the brotherhood of man, as expressed in Donne's lines, is slightly to be taken as a super-imposition of Hemingway's convictions and not entirely supported by the action of the book, it is still well enough represented as to be acceptable. We believe with Pilar, the mannish female who rules the guerillas, that Robert Jordan is a good man and that, given his complex temperament, he would act as he did; that love of a woman, devotion to a cause and a belief in human decency are sufficient reasons for sacrificing the lives of others and of oneself. No amount of artful contrivance could carry these things into conviction; they must be the growth of an integrity that is inherent.

This is the path taken by Hemingway, then, since the early nihilism of *In Our Time*. He has come full circle from a renunciation of all human motive and a complete affirmation of death as good, though wearing a guise of ill. Death is still the reward of the good man, but death in itself is not good. The earlier characters pitted themselves against death as in a game that had to be played, and if you played it well you enjoyed the excitements attached to any game of chance, all the while knowing that the outcome would be failure. Now, you play the same game perhaps, but the reason you achieve any satisfaction from the play is altogether different. Now it is because you are playing to change the stakes, if not for yourself, then for others. Getting outside of your own miserable ego has become the goal. To shed the sickly soul of the sophisticate and be one with good, if fallible, humanity is the salvation of Robert Jordan. He tries to do it through Maria in the sleeping bag, and Hemingway tells us he succeeds; but we do not necessarily feel it to be true. He tries to do it through identifying himself with his simple, honest, if fallible, companions, and Hemingway shows us his success; we do not need to be told. To liberate the ego is to liberate the world.

It is unfortunate that, with this broadening of Hemingway's sympathies, and the enlarging of his humanity, he seemed to have lost some of his superlative skill as an artist. *For Whom the Bell Tolls* is less perfect from a technical standpoint than any of his novels except *To Have and Have Not*. It gives an impression of having been written hurriedly, of suffering from lack of planning. There is less genuine style in it than in any other long writing of Hemingway's. It is unsymmetrical, and expends itself at length upon episodes that merited little attention, and passes hurriedly over sections that should have been developed. The story of Maria in the hands of the Fascists, while excellent of itself, is disproportionately extended and retards the movement of the real concerns. The prose is looser than any Hemingway had written previously, and he hangs participial phrases upon participial phrases in an incredibly lax way, piling adverb on adverb and stringing adjectives in a line almost as inexorably as Faulkner has done. Describing El Sordo's painful mounting of the hill, he can write: "He climbed as hard as he could with the bullets spatting on the rocks, with the two sacks heavy on his shoulders, and then, holding the horse by the mane, had shot him quickly, expertly, and tenderly just where he had needed him, so that the horse pitched, head forward down to plug a gap between two rocks. He had gotten the gun to firing over the horse's back and he fired two pans, the gun clattering, the empty shells pitching into the snow, the smell of burnt hair from the burnt hide where the hot muzzle rested, him firing at what came up to the hill, forcing them to scatter for cover, while all the time there was a chill in his back from not knowing what was behind him."[18]

But carelessness is only part of the reason why the style is not up to Hemingway standard. As Ray B. West jr. has suggested, Hemingway, in attempting to affirm and accept in the novels *To Have and Have Not* and *For Whom the Bell Tolls* and the play *The Fifth Column*, rather than to deny and reject, as in the earlier short stories, *The Sun Also Rises* and *A Farewell to Arms*, was not able to develop adequate expression of his new attitudes. It was, Mr. West says, a "failure of sensibility," by which is

---

[18] From *For Whom the Bell Tolls* by Ernest Hemingway. © 1940 by Charles Scribner's Sons.

meant "that perceptivity or natural awareness of the artist for the variety and range of sense objects surrounding him in nature and which he consciously or unconsciously organizes or synthesizes into an artful pattern or form."[14] When he wrote as a conscious "lost generation" sophisticate he was able to enclose his awareness of the world in an imagery at once forceful and immediate. He shocked us, or set forth in startling new conjunctions the ideas latent in a world-attitude appropriate to the 'twenties, when he said: "I was always embarrassed by the words sacred, glorious, and sacrifice and the expression in vain. We had heard them . . . and had read them, on proclamations, now for a long time, and I had seen nothing sacred, and the things that were glorious had no glory and the sacrifices were like the stockyards at Chicago if nothing was done with the meat except to bury it."[15]

Set beside that powerful passage another statement of conviction—but how different—in *For Whom the Bells Tolls*, as Robert Jordan tells himself: "You believe in Liberty, Equality and Fraternity. You believe in Life, Liberty and the Pursuit of Happiness. . . . You have put many things in abeyance to win a war. If this war is lost all of those things are lost."[16] Here, in Mr. West's words, is an argument that "might have come from the platform of any patriotic orator, and it is a failure, not because it is an affirmative value, not because it is a patriotic sentiment, but because it is conventional and trite." Hemingway relies upon generalities which are not stated with originality or sharpness enough to carry the emotional potential with which he wanted them to be charged. When in his new vein he wishes to indicate that a materialistic explanation of phenomena leaves some factors of experience unaccounted for, he has Robert Jordan soliloquize: "Listen, one thing. Do you remember? Pilar and the hand? Do you believe that crap? No, he said. Not with every-

---

[14] From "Ernest Hemingway: the Failure of Sensibility," by Ray B. West, Jr., in *Sewanee Review*, Winter, 1945.

[15] From "A Natural History of the Dead" in *Fifth Column and the First Forty-nine* by Ernest Hemingway. © 1938 by Charles Scribner and Sons.

[16] From *For Whom The Bell Tolls* by Ernest Hemingway. © 1940 by Charles Scribner's Sons.

thing that's happened? No, I don't believe it. She was nice about it early this morning before the show started. She was afraid maybe I believed it. I don't though. But she does. They see something. Or they feel something. Like a bird dog. What about extra-sensory perception?"[17] And so, with the puerile statement that Pilar's supernatural powers may be equated to feeling or seeing something "like a bird dog," Hemingway has done his best to convey what amounts to a tremendous shift in his philosophy. How ineffectual it is beside the simple observation, in his earlier phase, that the death of a hero in war is like "the stockyards at Chicago if nothing was done with the meat except to bury it."

Whether this indicates a failure of sensibility, or simply a too hurried and slipshod embodiment of his new attitudes, *For Whom the Bell Tolls* succeeds least in its philosophical aspects. It is still a strong social document and its characterization is, for the most part, magnificent.

The "conversion" Hemingway seems to exhibit in the novel cannot be detected in his most recent stories, and two of them stand as the finest achievements in all the range of his art: "The Snows of Kilimanjaro" and "The Short Happy Life of Francis Macomber." In these, the overall point of view is similar to that of the earlier short masterpieces, "The Killers" or "The Undefeated," but there has been an increment in selectivity, in finding the best vehicle for embodying the exact fine shades of meaning. In "Francis Macomber" Hemingway found the perfect "objective correlative" for stating his theme: moral triumph achieved by man at the moment of death. Macomber and his wife are on a hunting expedition in Africa and as the story opens he has just shown himself to be a coward in the face of death: he runs from a lion he is supposed to shoot. His wife's contempt is made concrete by her sleeping that night with the professional hunter who accompanies them. But when, later on, Macomber redeems himself by standing up to a charging water buffalo, she shoots her husband in the back of the head.

---

[17] From *For Whom the Bell Tolls* by Ernest Hemingway. © 1940 by Charles Scribner's Sons.

More interesting technically is "The Snows of Kilimanjaro," where another big game hunter lies dying from a gangrenous infection of the leg, in the company of his wife, waiting for a plane to take him to the coast for treatment. The action takes place almost entirely within the man's conscious and subconscious mind as he goes back over his life, recounting the good things he has done and explaining the situation in which he now finds himself, married to a woman he does not love and the victim of a boredom that has reached the proportions of despair. He waits for death that goes "in pairs, on bicycles, and moved absolutely silently on the pavements." In his death trauma he believes the rescue plane has come and that he is taken aboard it and flying. "They were going to the East it seemed, and then it darkened and they were in a storm, the rain so thick it seemed like flying through a waterfall, and then they were out and Compie turned his head and grinned and pointed and there, ahead, all he could see, as wide as all the world, great, high, and unbelievably white in the sun, was the square top of Kilimanjaro. And then he knew that there was where he was going."[18]

In this story, more perhaps than in any other writing, Hemingway got the "fourth and fifth dimension" of prose, which speaks simultaneously on several levels and whose effect is to leave us aware of an experience at once more real than reality, and with overtones that can only be called extra-natural, of this world and beyond it. It is probably this infrequent quality in Hemingway which prompted Malcolm Cowley to call him a "haunted and nocturnal writer"—a characterization that at first glance seems absurd, but for which a case can be made.

What Hemingway's future will be remains one of today's most interesting critical questions; in the opinion of many he is perhaps the novelist most likely to continue to produce, not only because he has been the most disciplined artist in fiction since Henry James, but because he resolutely searches himself for attitudes of integrity. He possesses supremely the contemporaneous sense, and he continues to be active in a moving world.

---

[18] From "The Snows of Kilimanjaro" in *Fifth Column and the First Forty-nine* by Ernest Hemingway. © 1938 by Charles Scribner's Sons.

The Education of
THOMAS WOLFE

IN THE comparatively few years of his creative life, between
1929, the year of *Look Homeward, Angel* and his death in 1938,
Thomas Wolfe worked continuously on his one great theme:
the struggle of the romantic "I" against an alien society. In a
sense, Wolfe's whole pilgrimage was a Rousseauean justification
of the artist in a commercial civilization, an attempt to project
the concept of the individual as a sort of romantic superman
against the unfriendly environment of an acquisitive culture.

This typical nineteenth-century theme became meaningful for
the fourth decade of the twentieth century because, though it
had been a time-honored vehicle for countless other noncon-
formist egos, in Wolfe it found once again a temperament so
sensitive, so intense, so prodigal, that a new sense of relevance
emerged. Wolfe interpreted anew all the traditional drama and
significance of the individual's battle with society. His originality
consisted in the recreation of old attitudes amid new conditions.
Goethe's Werther had done the same for an earlier time, and
there will no doubt be other Eugene Gants to do it for times to
come.

Like Stephen Crane and Frank Norris, Wolfe remains one of
the American novelists whose achievement is incomplete, whose
performance promised more than it fulfilled. Less precocious
than either, he was not as disciplined as Crane or as doctrinaire
as Norris. The range of his sympathies and experience was probably on a par with theirs, and his only superiority lay in his having lived longer than either. As a creator, he was less inventive
(probably of the major figures in recent literary history Wolfe
was the least resourceful in pure invention) but he drew upon
his experience for a richer fabric of common meaning than did
Norris or Crane. And as a worker in prose, he curiously resembles
both; he has to some extent Crane's felicity with language, and
Norris' broad power to invoke material on the realistic level. His

173

books, however, are narrowly autobiographical, and he was seldom able to transcend the immediate significance of experience, for unless a thing had happened to him, he was unable to write convincingly of it. Even the lengthy portraits of his relatives are seen from without; and only Eugene's personal travail has the immediacy of interpretation that lifts the Wolfean chronicle to what might be regarded as universal applicability. Wolfe himself realized the limitations of his material and anticipated criticism. In a foreword to his first novel he wrote, "If any reader, therefore, should say that the book is 'autobiographical' the writer has no answer for him: it seems to him that all serious work in fiction is autobiographical—that, for instance, a more autobiographical work than 'Gulliver's Travels' cannot easily be imagined."[1] Of course he is right; but surely from *Look Homeward, Angel* to *You Can't Go Home Again* Wolfe hewed more closely to the pattern of his own life than any novelist has ever done in a manner so extensive, minute and painstaking. It is as if he were in his own mind justifying himself to the world, in a million words retelling everything that had happened to make him what he was—explaining the phenomenon of Thomas Wolfe in his time and place. Fortunately it matters to us what happened and why Wolfe was what he was; and this incredibly gifted and preternaturally a-typical artist, in his peregrinations through existence, may stand for the modern Romantic Young Man jousting with Fate, almost to the degree that he himself conceived that typification. Thus he was justified in his use of his own life and that of his friends and relatives as the materials for fiction, simply because he lifted it all into a realm of general applicability.

In every year a handful of young men appear with first novels written with painful accuracy upon their authors' youthful adjustment of life, and *Look Homeward, Angel* may be regarded as only another among the spate of such books. There was certainly little of the freshness and originality of such first books as *in our time*, *Dubliners* or *Swann's Way*. But if Hemingway,

---

[1] From Preface to *Look Homeward, Angel* by Thomas Wolfe. © 1929 by Charles Scribner's Sons.

Joyce and Proust had developed a new medium for expressing their view of existence, they too had only delved into the same storehouse of accumulated memory and experience. And none of them had been able more completely to recall and recreate the buried life. Wolfe's advantage was that he knew it all and wanted to tell it all; and without their discipline or selectivity managed to shovel it all into one immense volume that still was readable, and indeed in many ways remarkable. For what he lacked in the power of writing suggestibly, he made up for in the ability to remember to the last word and breath what had been done, said, and felt about everything that he had ever heard or seen or experienced. And so *Look Homeward, Angel* stood out above the ruck of autobiographical first novels, simply because Wolfe had a superaverage facility of recall and a roaring, headlong rhetoric in which to charge all of his material with more emotional and more strongly felt impact than any of his compeers displayed. It was fundamentally that he possessed a temperament of abnormal fecundity which reacted with painful sharpness to any experience, and thriftily treasured up both the circumstances of the experience and the reaction.

"A destiny that leads the English to the Dutch is strange enough," begins *Look Homeward, Angel*, sounding a diapason that Wolfe was able to sustain through the four panels of his sprawling history, "but one that leads from Epsom into Pennsylvania, and thence into the hills that shut in Altamont over the proud coral cry of the cock, and the soft stone smile of an angel, is touched by that dark miracle of chance which makes new magic in a dusty world."[2] This destiny of which Eugene Gant-Thomas Wolfe was a part includes the circumstances of the major conflict within the hero's divided ego: the coexisting urges inherited from his father's line and the legacy of his mother's hot Southern blood. Oliver Gant, the father, came from the North; and he had the Yankee spirit of enterprise, of flight, of a victory sighted on an ever-receding horizon. Without roots always searching for something he could never find, he was

---

[2] From *Look Homeward, Angel* by Thomas Wolfe. © 1929 by Charles Scribner's Sons.

homeless, a dreamer led on by the vision of the golden city. Eliza, the mother, was deeply Southern in her materialism, a fierce, unbounded determination to accumulate the solid things of this world, purblind in her earthiness, and yet wise with the wisdom of an old wife. Behind her in the Pentland line were ignorant, lusty men with the taint of insanity on them, hot, passionate Pentlands; and from them Eugene believed he had inherited a strain of unpredictable impulse and irrationality. With such a heritage the romantic "I" could be expected legitimately to suffer all the derangements of schizophrenia. In the blood of the children of this union warred the traditional elements of North and South, besides many other strange and unmalleable factors.

Old Gant's propensity to dream and evasion is objectified for us in his occupation as a stonecutter and maker of cemetery memorials; Eliza's materialism is apparent in her avid desire to build a fortune upon real-estate investment. Altamont (Asheville, North Carolina) is on the verge of a rapid growth, and opportunities for money-making in property are not lacking. Eliza makes the most of them, although she is greatly hampered by the dissolute ways of Oliver, who, thwarted now in his quest for the mythical golden city by an ever-increasing brood of children, spends much of his time in frequenting whorehouses and saloons. The result is that Eliza's somewhat temperate materialism becomes intensified, and she develops into miserliness, while Oliver sinks deeper into his dreams through drink and profligacy. The ill-assorted pair indulge in gargantuan battles, and the children grow up in this environment of bitter recrimination. Eugene, the youngest and most sensitive of them, becomes the Recording Angel of their tragedy; but he is by no means merely an observer; he is tempered and transformed in the crucible of the family inferno. And the Gant home is truly an inferno from which all the children seek to escape. There is no feeling of security or certainty in the family group; scenes are witnessed that brand and sear the minds of them all: Luke, the stuttering, good-natured son of Eliza who is marked to rise in a materialistic world; Helen, the daughter of Oliver, a gentle soul broken on the rack of her parents' disagreements; Ben, the youth too good for this world; Grover, meek and mild; and Eugene, wandering like a young wraith in this Bedlamite labyrinth.

But the only thing wraithlike about Eugene is his loneliness and incertitude. Physically he is huge, powerful, clumsy, and he seems to share many of his father's traits; he dreams of escaping, of finding the golden city, of cutting loose from the pettiness and horror of his life. He has ambition enough for twenty men, and appetites that can only be called Rabelaisian. He feels himself a Gulliver among Lilliputians; he is aware of greatness within him. To Eliza's credit it must be said that she senses this too, and Eugene is the only one of the children she sends through college. The fact that he is singled out makes Eugene an object of some resentment within the family; but this is the least of his concerns. He is such a finely attuned instrument that every experience of life becomes soul-shattering, the matter for a dozen pages of impassioned prose. His story from birth to early manhood is a record of tremendous reactions, of superhuman response to all stimuli; smells, sounds, sights are recorded with extraordinary intensity and richness; the everyday occurrences of family life are detailed in a rhapsodic prose that recalls Herman Melville, and the general texture of all the writing about Eugene is probably as lush, ornate and heavily burdened as any in our language. Unimportant incidents rebound upon Eugene's sensitive antennae with just about the same force as decisive ones; and this striving for overwhelming effect has a general tendency to vitiate all of his reported experience. The sight of the fields on a summer's afternoon or the smell of a flower in springtime has power to invoke in Eugene such response that he cannot react much more strongly to the betrayal of a youthful love; and this continual overwrought state of his awareness minimizes the drama that his chronicle should rightfully have. Nevertheless we believe in Eugene, and, especially, we accept the reality of his family and environment to a degree that offsets the flaw of exaggeration.

Oliver Gant's rant and rhetoric are among the most memorable things in *Look Homeward, Angel.* " 'Jesus God!' Gant yelled frantically, wetting his big thumb swiftly on his tongue, and glancing upward toward his Maker, with an attitude of exaggerated supplication in his small gray eyes and the thrust of his huge bladelike nose. Then, letting his arms slap heavily at his sides, in a gesture of defeat, he began to walk rapidly back and forth, clucking his deprecation loudly. Eliza stood solidly, looking from one to another, her lips working rapidly, her white face hurt and bitter."[3] This passage is an epitome of the recurring presentation of the father and mother and is repeated with slight variation a dozen times. The Dickensian trick of tagging characters is perhaps the chief fault in character presentation in the novel; when we meet any of the numerous personae, we are usually confronted with identical information as to their distinguishing habits. But in each case the tags are so apposite that we scarcely mind. Eugene has the characteristic of craning his neck at all affronts to his sensitivity, but it is so illuminating and believable that we accept the tag without resentment. Luke's stammer, Ben's casting up his eyes, Helen's "Mama, in heaven's name—", Eliza's "Why, pshaw!" and a dozen other inevitable labels become a part of the fabric of their owner's lives. Eliza's detailed colloquialisms as she ruminates upon past experience read like old wives' tales and superbly vivify the ancient heritage of family chronicles.

It is not alone the excellent character building that made the novel an immediately perceived minor masterpiece, but its romantic and even sentimental overtones. While Eugene is the typical sensitive spirit buffeted by a rude world, a consecrated vessel in the hands of barbarians, he is also the symbol of a philosophical attitude that has wide acceptance in our civilization. In little prose poems scattered throughout the book we are given the essence of this life-attitude, shared by so many in a society that has battened on materialism, grown so complex and become so misdirected as to mistake the importance of the "I" in a welter of extraneous pursuits. Wolfe sent a penetrating cry into this maze of crawling humanity, sounding the clarion for

---

[3] From *Look Homeward, Angel* by Thomas Wolfe. © 1929 by Charles Scribner's Sons.

a return to the inviolable ego. We are lost and alone though surrounded in our man swarm by millions of our kind, all of whom are at heart seeking identification with one another. We have lost our way in scrambling for the wealth and ease of a scientific age. The spirit has shrunk to impotence. Yet within each of us is the romantic need for assurance and certitude, that we are not lost or lonely, that there are others of our kind who can be found. We are searching for a father, a moral identity that will not change, and to which we can attach ourselves. We want authority upon which to lean. "... a stone, a leaf, an un-found door; of a stone, a leaf, a door. And of all the forgotten faces. Naked and alone we came into exile. In her dark womb we did not know our mother's face; from the prison of her flesh have we come into the unspeakable and incommunicable prison of this earth. Which of us knows his brother? Which of us has looked into his father's heart? Which of us has not remained forever prison-pent? Which of us is not forever a stranger and alone?"[4] This is the yearning of an ego for identification, for some received and acceptable authority, for a resolution of its frustrated gregariousness. And it was a yearning so universal that its sentimentality was disregarded in a cynical time. It became a viable *modus cogiti* and added poignancy to the romantic chron-icle of the Gants. Of course it is readily seen that for Wolfe the attitude arose from his own distressed experience as a child grow-ing up between the poles of disparate parental temperaments. But he projected it on a scale that altogether transcended its origins. The "search for a father" was, in his case, exactly the need for security which he never had in his youth. But the search for authority, certainty, a power outside ourselves, is an abiding urge of the human race, and since in our age the authority of religion had been removed, there was validity in this concept. However romantic or sentimental Wolfe's statement of it, the condition was acutely diagnosed, and the terms of its presenta-tion were acceptable.

In great contrast to the work of Hemingway, Faulkner, Dos

---

[4] From *Look Homeward, Angel* by Thomas Wolfe. © 1929 by Charles Scrib-ner's Sons.

Passos and other contemporaries, Wolfe's novels showed an almost absolute disregard of form. Shapeless and chaotic, *Look Homeward, Angel* resembles a block of life in which selectivity is wholly absent. This seeming shapelessness is even more accentuated by the high level of emotionalism that runs through the novel, by the undistinguishable powerful impact of all experience, as mentioned before. But in a larger sense Wolfe's novels have form of the kind associated with romantic music. There are recurrent themes, and long swells of counterpoint and development; and the four panels of this gigantic novel do have a beginning, middle and end. Not as ingeniously composed as Proust's similarly immense novel, Wolfe's work resembles *Remembrance of Things Past* not only in the symphonic method of its composition but in the overall rationale of its conception. Wolfe's books may be taken to represent their author's effort to recapture experience, to recreate the impressions and reactions of his life and thus make time stand still. It may be taken also as an "Education of Thomas Wolfe" in a more poetic and symbolic way than Henry Adams conceived his autobiography. For Wolfe was always trying to learn what his life meant, and to universalize its meaning. Until we had the last panel of the work before us, there was little indication that he would ever discover a meaning; but then it was clear that he had orientated himself in his world. And it is in this discovery of meanings, and the blocking out of patterns in his life, that we find a recognizable form in the novels of Wolfe. It is probably not the kind of form that Henry James or Ernest Hemingway would accept, but we might be justified in saying Joyce or Proust would have detected it.

The influence of Joyce upon Wolfe, as upon Dos Passos and Faulkner, is verifiable. Probably Stephen Dedalus' quest for his father, and his identifying Leopold Bloom as a compromise "spiritual" father, indicated to Wolfe a theme that he could develop in his own fashion. Certainly the Irishman's prodigal virtuosity must have prompted Wolfe to some of his own feats of word magic; and the chants and soliloquies in his novels sometimes have a Joycean flavor.

After *Look Homeward, Angel* had established him as one of

the potentially great novelists, Wolfe spent five years in dogged toil upon a successor which would clinch his claim to greatness. He wrote millions of words and suffered ten thousand agonies in an attempt to impose form upon his reminiscences. Of course without the aid of a perspicacious editor (Maxwell Perkins) he might never have gotten *Of Time and the River* into even its present shape of coherence. As the book now stands, it is still the least satisfactory section of this huge novel, for it alternately rambles, bogs down, soars, and progresses by zigzags toward the first of two goals Eugene Gant has set himself in life: the achievement of a great love. It is overwritten and undisciplined, ambitious and disappointing. The two-hundred-page prose poem devoted to a description of train travel is a case in point; ten or twenty pages would have been impressive, but there is no restraint in Wolfe, and we put the book aside in exhaustion. The Dickensian character-building has gotten out of hand, and Uncle Bascomb, Professor Hatcher and Francis Starwick jerk like puppets through interminable scenes. Everything is magnified and blown up. Eugene is a fabulous young Faustus devouring experience and laying siege to the domain of all knowledge like Gargantua. The gigantism already apparent in the first novel here gets entirely out of hand.

We follow Eugene as he attends Harvard; we are present at the death of old Gant—an excellent if slightly overwrought scene in which all the old man's enormous drive and misdirected energy are drained from him by the slow death of cancer, and there is a final reconciliation between him and Eliza—"No one can cook a chicken like your mother." We are present when Eugene is first attracted to Starwick, a Byronic youth whose artistic life appeals so greatly to the raw youth from North Carolina. Eugene eventually joins the faculty of New York University and continues his quest of learning. He and Starwick later travel together to Europe and fall in with a motley crew of characters, including two women from Boston. With one of them Eugene imagines himself in love; but he finds that it is Starwick and not he whom she favors. Starwick, however, shows himself to be incapable of loving a woman; and Eugene by this time has seen through the precious posing of the sterile artist type that Starwick represents; as the novel ends he returns to America determined to write a great novel.

In his mania for absorbing all experience, Eugene of course finds that love is of vast importance in man's life; so far, however, his attempts to form a grand passion have always met with failure. At the close of *Of Time and the River* (1935) he feels some intimations of his destiny as he catches sight of Esther Jack, who is, indeed, after the hero, the principal character in the next novel, *The Web and the Rock* (1939).

By the time *Of Time and the River* appeared, critics were saying that Wolfe could report only the things that had happened to him. Stung by this allegation, he announced that his next novel contained characters quite different from any he had previously created; they were objective delineations and would prove his versatility. *The Web and the Rock*, however, turned out to be a continuation of Eugene's pilgrimage and education, though now he was called George Webber and had altered in outward appearance. Esther Jack was still the name of the woman with whom George, formerly Eugene, fell in love, and indeed all the circumstances of the story remained identical. We were taken back again to George's boyhood and shown more members of the Pentland clan (now renamed Joyner), and in this book there were no further slips of the pen, as in *Of Time and the River* where occasionally the first person pronoun had crept in to replace the third. Meanwhile, in his thirty-eighth year, Wolfe had died, and the remaining section of his long novel was pieced together by other hands.

The Web and the Rock explores the second of Wolfe's two important symbols: time as a river, and the city as a rock. Both are actually aspects of the same thing: Wolfe's mania for multitudes, for number, for the flow and flux of things. He wanted to swallow external reality whole. He hoped to make himself the container of all that is. And part of his education was the discovery that this could not be done by any man. It was not until his final novel, though, that he explicitly admitted his discovery, and *The Web and the Rock* continues the Faustian pilgrimage.

This time the attainment of love and fame preoccupy him to the point of madness. His assault upon the "golden towers of the shining city" is but one expression of his mania for fame; it is also, as Maxwell Geismar has said, the mark of his fundamental provincialism, in its best sense—the wonder and awe of the country boy before all the enticements and marvels of a wider life. The suffering of Eugene-George and his sense of betrayal arise exactly from the disparity between the provincial's dreams and harsh reality.

Esther Jack at last becomes the typification of this betrayal, and in *You Can't Go Home Again* George's bitterness inundates her as the chief object of his betrayal, for by then he has found that neither love nor fame is enough, or are any anchorage at all to which man may secure his life. The love story of these two, as it unfolds in *The Web and the Rock*, is a moving one; and Esther is one of Wolfe's triumphs in character creation. She is George Webber's "jolly little Jew," talented, feminine, self-sacrificing, and withal worshiping and worshipful. Still she is a married woman, and he can never bring himself to respect her for allowing him to love her. He cannot respect the society of which she is an exponent and which condones adultery. In his mind Esther becomes the epitome of the decadent idle rich and the dilettante artists. He sees more and more clearly that this stratum of society battens upon the poor whom it exploits. When he sounds this note, we begin to have an intimation that Webber-Wolfe has found himself at last. The moment this note is heard, we catch a gleam of hope for this hitherto hopelessly self-centered ego. The toils of fate which have bound the romantic I are beginning to loosen, even by one cord, when George can look beyond his tortured self and see men as suffering individuals separate from himself. Heretofore he had been fanatical about Mankind; and Time and Number had been a mania; but always it was an abstract interest. Now the super-ego stirs sleepily within this mighty introverted I.

But it is a momentary stirring. George Webber must continue his odyssey and his quarrels with the world, his jousting with Fate and his agonized struggles with his mistress. It is not so easy to abandon a romantic love; Esther Jack is his Beatrice and his Heloise; he cannot disavow the tenets of his persuasion without a major dislocation of his life. But this does finally come, halfway through *You Can't Go Home Again* (1940), in what are undoubtedly Wolfe's greatest pages, the story of the party at the Jacks'. In them he breaks with Esther after clearly seeing the corruption, gaudy show and ultimate heartlessness of her world —a world that threatened to suck him down and destroy him as an artist and as a man. "For he had learned tonight that love was not enough. There had to be a higher devotion than all the devotions of this fond imprisonment. . . . He had sensed how the hollow pyramid of a false social structure had been erected and sustained upon a base of common mankind's blood and sweat and agony. . . . And that was where Esther and this world of hers came in. In America, of all places, there could be no honest compromise with special privilege. Privilege and truth could not lie down together.—He who lets himself be whored by fashion will be whored by time. (Esther) would never understand—never understand tomorrow—that a tide was running in the hearts of men—and he must go."[5]

So, he had found through bitter travail that love was not enough; and upon the heels of this realization came another equally difficult awakening. The avid quest of fame that had lashed Eugene Gant on through a thousand early pages met with success; when George Webber published his novel, *Home to Our Mountains*, he was famous overnight; and the greatest popular novelist of the time acclaimed him. This was Lloyd McHarg, "a great man, a man famous throughout the world, a man who had now attained the highest pinnacle of success to which a writer could aspire." And this McHarg had invited George to stay with him in London, during a triumphant visit in which he was to receive a coveted prize. At first hand George was able to witness the effects of fame and to assess its worth. His observation was that McHarg's fame had not brought him happiness, that even the greatest reputation did not insure a man against

[5] From *You Can't Go Home Again* by Thomas Wolfe. © 1940 by Harper and Brothers.

misery, that McHarg had taken Europe by storm and had worn himself out in the process, that what it all amounted to was a great emptiness when McHarg had had to go "to Baden-Baden for a 'cure'—cure, call it, if you will, for wine, women, and members of the press—cure, really, for life-hunger, for life-thirst, for life-triumph, for life-defeat, life-disillusionment, life-loneliness, and life-boredom—cure for devotion to men and for disgust of them, cure for love of life and for weariness of it—last of all, cure for the cureless, cure for the worm, for the flame, for the feeding mouth, for the thing that eats and rests not ever till we die. Is there not some medicine for the irremediable? Give us a cure, for God's sake, for what ails us! Take it! Keep it! Give it back again! Oh, let us have it! Take it from us, damn you, but for God's sake bring it back! And so good night."[6]

Esther Jack is the symbol of love's failure; McHarg of fame's insufficiency. And in the last section of *You Can't Go Home Again* we find a third symbol upon which Wolfe sounded his final affirmation. That is his editor, friend and critic, the man who stood in his mind as a second father, and whom he calls Foxhall Edwards. "Fox" is a man who has few illusions; he sees reality for what it is, but he would not change anything because any other order would be as bad; for him work is enough and let the status quo remain. Webber for a long while admired this stoicism and imitated it; but finally, after breaking the bonds of love and seeing through the chicane of fame, he renounces Edwards and all his philosophy. Let those who can stomach things-as-they-are, and continue to live with themselves; Webber, sloughing off the armor of the romantic I, turns his face toward a more heartening view of man's future. He identifies himself with his brothers, with America, with the promise of democracy. First, he must convince himself of man's claim to worthiness, and writes a magnificent chant that begins with a condemnation and ends on a paean. He offers a picture of the child, the youth, the man, each an Edwardsian characterization. As man, "he is busy, he is full of plans and reasons, he has work. He gets children, buys and sells small packets of everlasting earth, intrigues against his rivals, is exultant when he cheats them. He wastes his little three score years and ten in spendthrift and inglorious living. . . . At the end . . . his weary and lifeless eyes look out upon the scenery of strange lands for which in youth his heart was panting. Then the slow death, prolonged by costly doctors, and finally the graduate undertakers, the perfumed carrion, the suave ushers with palms outspread to leftwards, the fast motor hearses, and the earth again." [7] And yet, and yet, Webber-Wolfe retorts, man "needed speech to ask for bread—and he had Christ! He needed songs to sing in battle—and he had Homer! He needed words to curse his enemies—and he had Dante, he had Voltaire, he had Swift! . . . He needed a temple to propitiate his God—and he made Chartres and Fountains Abbey! He was born to creep upon the earth—and he made great wheels, he sent great engines thundering down the rails, he launched great wings into the air, he put great ships upon the angry sea! . . . so this is man—the worst and best of him—this frail and petty thing who lives his day and dies like all the other animals, and is forgotten. And yet, he is immortal, too, for both the good and evil that he does live after him. Why, then, should any living man ally himself with death, and, in his greed and blindness, batten on his brother's blood?" [8]

Once more Webber goes to Europe, and in Germany he senses the rise of a mortal sickness among men that could destroy them; in that country he concluded that America is the hope of the world, that "we are lost here in America," but that we shall be found. This is a somewhat mystical affirmation, but it cannot be doubted that Wolfe had come around to a concern in the destiny of others which transcended the concern for his own.

Diffuse and overwritten, at times sentimental and turgid, the novels in which Thomas Wolfe traced his education remain one of the impressive fictional achievements of the twentieth cen-

---

[7] From *You Can't Go Home Again* by Thomas Wolfe. © 1940 by Harper and Bros.

[8] From *You Can't Go Home Again* by Thomas Wolfe. © 1940 by Harper and Bros.

tury. The steady progress toward an externalization, an understanding of the forces outside Wolfe's torrential ego, are the most remarkable indications of a growth that was cut off just at the moment when it might have produced exceptional results. It is a far cry from the romantic realism of Washington Irving to that of Thomas Wolfe, yet the century that witnessed the metamorphosis saw other changes no less incredible. Whatever Wolfe may have inherited from his literary progenitors, he was seeking until the very last a reorientation that would be valid for his day. In his own work he seems to have subsumed the entire tradition, running the gamut of romanticism to a superior realism that acknowledged the presence of Whitmanesque ideals. His success was only partial, but as far as he went, he is still the best modern representative of the long line of writers who dedicated themselves to an interpretation of life on the levels of the real and the ideal.

JOHN STEINBECK
Realistic Whimsy

IF IT IS possible to believe that there are "born writers" one might be justified in saying that, of all the writers stemming from the Irving tradition, John Steinbeck seems the most naturally gifted, the best endowed with creative talent, and certainly the writer with the most evident love for his fellow humans. He is also one of the most versatile in the use of his medium, so much so that it took him nearly a decade to find himself, and to bring to artistic realization the forms in which he could work most successfully.

All these things might legitimately be said to Steinbeck's credit; on the other hand, criticism has often been uneasy before some aspects of his work. There has been something Dickensian about Steinbeck's writing, and the Dickens parallels are indeed so striking that one may almost predict Steinbeck's future by reexamining the great Victorian's career. Both have an enormous gift of story-telling. Both have a catholicity of sympathy and a "common touch" which embrace a large proportion of humanity. Both can create character with ease, although this creation often tends to lay emphasis upon certain characteristics or "humors", and sometimes seems to construct types rather than true individuals. Both love exaggeration and the sort of humor resulting from it. Both are at bottom sentimentalists, and the gravest weaknesses in their work derive from sentimentalism. Both insist upon well-wrought plotting; although in this respect Steinbeck has, of course, followed the modern tendency to dispense with the more mechanical operations of story complication. But they are story-tellers, and one has only to compare any Steinbeck novel with any of Wolfe's books to show what being a story-teller means. Finally, the Dickens parallels might be summed up in the fact that, of all our serious writers, Steinbeck has won the widest popular following, the forecastable result of all these factors.

Steinbeck's first novel, *Cup of Gold*, appeared in the same year (1929) with *Look Homeward, Angel*. It received little attention, and perhaps merited only as much as it got. By comparison with Wolfe's novel it was a minor performance; but perceptive critics saw that a new talent of potential stature had arrived. This early novel was a sort of journeyman effort, and in it one might have observed a writer trying to form his art, uncertain of his direction, and influenced by the successful novels of the immediately preceding era. There was more than a little of James Branch Cabell in *Cup of Gold*—the half-mystical, half-whimsical legerdemain of which Cabell was a supposed master, with its Merlin-the-magician, its predictions, the lightly satirical touch, and the occasional brittleness of style. It is subtitled "A Life of Sir Henry Morgan, Buccaneer, with Occasional References to History." The story is of the rise of the boy Henry from obscurity in the Scots Highlands, to the mastery of West Indian seas as a semi-legal pirate who attacks the ships of Spain. His eventual capture of Panama, the "cup of gold," and with it a woman who legend says is the vessel of all power in a materialistic world, coincides with his realization that the magician's prediction, years earlier on a mountain top, have come true. Merlin had said, "You are a little boy. You want the moon to drink from as a golden cup; and so it is very likely that you will become a great man—if only you remain a little child. . . . But if one grow to a man's mind, that mind must see that it cannot have the moon and would not want it if it could."[1]

The conception of the book was boyish (Steinbeck was twenty-seven when it was published) and the execution was not particularly original; but passages here and there, reread in the light of Steinbeck's subsequent development, show the fortes of which its author was in possession. The most interesting of these is what might be called the phantasmal or extrasensory. Like Hawthorne, Steinbeck was to keep his eye upon the physical manifestation always, yet there continued to lurk a sense of "otherness" beyond what could be seen and verified. If anything was clear at all, it was that Steinbeck would never be a literary naturalist, for all his eventual interest in biology.

In the next book, *The Pastures of Heaven* (1932), he explored new areas, using people and experiences he knew in his own world; but it is more illuminating to consider with *Cup of Gold* the third book, *To a God Unknown* (1933), since it seems to provide a developmental extension of the first novel. That is because *The Pastures of Heaven* is not a novel but a series of sketches, and was the first of the books in a sequence that has proved to be Steinbeck's real metier.

The central character in *To a God Unknown* is Joseph Wayne, a man of the soil, who has come west to settle in a fertile California valley called Nuestra Señora. Wayne is descended from a line of farmers, and he has a mystical feeling about the earth, and about his father, whose spirit he feels hovers about the California land. He goes so far even as to think that the paternal spirit finds shelter in a particular spot—an oak that stands in his yard. Wayne's brothers, one of them a Christian, the other a "sinner," regard him as a half-mad pagan influenced by the Indian myths and the surviving Aztec superstitions with regard to the fecundity of the soil. Wayne is a symbol of man's relation to the earth, and this mystical notion, extremely difficult to present

---

[1] From *Cup of Gold* by John Steinbeck. © 1929 by John Steinbeck.

with sympathy, is handled in a masterly way. There is none of the glossy satire, the uncertainty of attitude, of *Cup of Gold.* Whatever one may think of the validity of the concept, this earth-worship and its attendant aura of supernaturalism is presented with a sureness and apposite detail that is for the moment entirely convincing. The difficulty of treating this theme in such a way was enormous; only a master could have carried it through, and Steinbeck had proven his extraordinary virtuosity with these two novels. They had also given his readers causes for bewilderment, since he was already showing unmistakable signs of being a writer who would not be categorized. It was this versatility, though, which might have caused critics to recognize his potentialities for the development that came swiftly in the last half of the '30's.

And they might have seen, after *The Pastures of Heaven*[2] that Steinbeck's development would be one of the most heartening in recent fiction. For this book was to introduce something new in contemporary literature. It was to be the precursor of a succession of stories, whimsical and exaggerated in their human typifications, but recognizably indigenous to a region previously unexplored. While the sketches in *The Pastures of Heaven* were interrelated and had as background the Salinas valley country of California, they could each stand separately. Each was a small masterpiece, beautifully written, its material excellently controlled; but none of them transcended the intrinsic surfaces. There was, for example, the story of Molly Morgan, an orphan schoolteacher whose life revolved within the orbit of a beautiful memory. From childhood she had worshiped the ideal of a father whose bright presence, when he occasionally came home from wandering, let the sunshine into an otherwise drab world. When he and her mother both disappeared, she still continued to cherish the wonder of that father image. And then one day into her life came knowledge of a drunken bum bearing unmistakable evidence of being her father. She refused to corroborate the evidence. She ran away, taking the image with her.

---

[2] © 1932 by John Steinbeck.

The technique of this story is interesting; the method by which Molly's early life is shown through flashbacks placed for advantageous contrast against the progress of current action has similarities to Hemingway's "Snows of Kilimanjaro." But, to compare it only with that story, "Molly Morgan" is essentially journeyman work, and doesn't compare with many of Steinbeck's own later stories, such as "The Chrysanthemums" or "The Red Pony." The story of the idiot, Tularecito, is another harbinger of greater things; here Steinbeck gives us an early treatment of a subject that seems to fascinate him, that of the childlike individual, struggling against the complex world of normal persons. Tularecito, the "little Frog," is a subnormal creature found in the sagebrush one night; but he has a prodigious talent with the brush; and he is furthermore one of God's innocents who believes everything he is told. His innocence proves to be his undoing; he is told there are gnomes abroad, if he will only dig into the earth to find them. Thinking that he may have more natural affinities with gnomes than with men, he digs, and in a fight that arises over his persistent digging in other people's ground, half kills a man with a shovel. There is nothing for the people of Napa to do but commit him to an insane asylum.

It would be easy to say that Steinbeck is inordinately interested in the moron mentality, and that might be true, but it is only symptomatic of a wider interest. From this same sympathy derives his compassion for all humanity caught in its self-made toils of complexity and chicane. Tularecito, the simple paisanos, Lennie, and the Joads—they all are Steinbeck people and they bear close relationships to one another because Steinbeck is earnestly concerned with the problem of innocence enmeshed in an uncomprehending world. He is not necessarily a champion of the underdog *per se;* he is rather concerned with the question of how the pure in heart are to survive in a civilization that places a premium on sly multifariousness. He seems to say that salvation for the simple man lies in a complete repudiation of the standards of our living. Danny, Pilon, Pablo, the Pirate, and all the other personae of *Tortilla Flat* are inveterate nonconformists, and they are happy. They have their own standards, and whatever society may think of them, they achieve happiness by adhering to those standards. The tragedy that overtakes Lennie and George in *Of Mice and Men* eventuates because they cannot realize their dream of an independence from society; and the same is true of the whole Joad clan and all the Okies of *The Grapes of Wrath*. If the terms in which this idea is presented sometimes seem stagey, that is not the fault of the premise. For it is a premise upon which other writers have built great fiction; Dostoevsky and Stendhal especially come to mind.

The Pastures of Heaven seemed to have been a tentative study then for Steinbeck's first popular book, *Tortilla Flat* (1935). Basically it employed the same formula, with more success. The lovable and, by society's yardstick, dissolute paisanos living in carefree squalor on Tortilla Flat are funny only when their behavior is measured by civilized standards. However, the appeal of the novel lies not in its philosophy but in its sometimes tender, sometimes ribald humor. It is, above all, a superbly told story. Not only are its incidents amusing, its whole rationale and conception are highly original. Steinbeck adopts a mock heroic tone on occasion to give meanings not explicit in the story; and if we are seeking *Tortilla Flat's* "philosophy" it can be found at once in this light yet telling tone—as if, indeed, its author were attempting a modern Arthurian cycle in the humorous vein. Perhaps the rendering into English of the peculiarly ingratiating Spanish idiom had something to do with this effect, as it had also in the case of Hemingway's *For Whom the Bell Tolls*—an effect picturesque and appealing, and useful for what it did to help establish the individuality of the characters. Their language helps make memorable Pilon and Danny in even as short a passage as this: " 'When one is poor, one thinks, "If I had money I would share it with my good friends." But let that money come and charity flies away. So it is with thee, my once-friend. Thou art lifted above thy friends. Thou art a man of property. Thou wilt forget thy friends who shared everything with thee, even their brandy.'

"His words upset Danny. 'Not I,' he cried. 'I will never forget thee, Pilon.'

" 'So you think now,' said Pilon coldly. 'But when you have two houses to sleep in, then you will see. Pilon will be a poor paisano, while you eat with the mayor.'

"Danny arose unsteadily and held himself upright against a tree. 'Pilon, I swear, what I have is thine. While I have a house, thou hast a house. Give me a drink.'

" 'I must see this to believe it,' Pilon said in a discouraged voice. 'It would be a world wonder if it were so. Men would come a thousand miles to look upon it. And besides, the bottle is empty.' "[3]

The comic sense in *Tortilla Flat*, like that in some of Dickens' novels, gains complete mastery of the material, and verisimilitude suffers from it. We do not quarrel with this exaggeration, however, since we are being treated to what amounts essentially to a fable. And this fable is simply the superiority of true innocence to any manner of sophistication.

This same theme served to embody the real values of the more mechanical (and immensely more popular) novel that followed, *Of Mice and Men* (1937). Written in terms of theater, it is the most artifical of all Steinbeck's novels; and the central situation in which a harmless moron, Lennie, who worships his more socially adjusted friend, George, commits a crime—that of murder—through no intention of his, is entirely in the tradition of the melodrama. This is a negligible novel, seemingly written with a determined eye upon the cash register.

In the interim between *Tortilla Flat* and *Of Mice and Men*, Steinbeck published *In Dubious Battle* (1936), a novel anticipating *The Grapes of Wrath* in that it dealt realistically with social issues. The book was strong in an era when sociological novels were popular and weak, for it painted in no black and white contrasts the purity of those who wanted to change the world. The idea of revolution in the 'thirties, which was the subject of innumerable novels, and at last touched even such a hitherto thorough-going individualist as Hemingway, had not won Steinbeck over to its bright and false promise. He had op-

---

[3] From *Tortilla Flat* by John Steinbeck. © 1935 by John Steinbeck.

portunity to investigate a strike in the California fruit orchards, and in his novel temperately presented the case for and against the workers. It won him no plaudits from the extreme Left, aᵞd it probably lost him the endorsements of the Right. But it was an honest piece of work, and remains a perceptive study of strikes and strikers, but without the deep human significance and broad social overtones of the triumphant sociological novel of the decade, *The Grapes of Wrath* (1939).

This epic of migration, hardship and ultimate unresolved social contretemps, is about as formless as a novel could well be. It sprawls, recovers direction, and sprawls again. It preaches, adjures and thunders against injustice. It is primarily a picaresque tale, but Smollett or Le Sage would have been astounded at the type of adventures it chooses to tell. It is succinctly the story of a dust-bowl farming family from Oklahoma, the Joads. The land has become unproductive, and the owners have ousted these tenants. They are lured to California by handbills telling of high wages to be earned picking fruit. Their story is that of migration across country, and subsequent disappointment and betrayal when they arrive in an overcrowded, cheap labor market. The bare outline seems to offer little for a novelist of Steinbeck's talent to work upon. But that outline is as misleading as possible, for the story has unusual range and it is written with such force and conviction and furious anger that it ranks as one of the major fictional documents of an entire era.

There are literally dozens of characters in *The Grapes of Wrath*, and many of them are little more than two-dimensional. such people as the preacher, Grampa, the one-eyed man, and even Al and Rosasharn are Dickensian, for they appear always with their single refrains and impress their individuality upon us through a simple set of thought and action patterns. But some of them transcend these limitations: Ma Joad, principally, for she has the broad, earthy humanity of great fictional creations; and her sense of the family's unity is the fullest and most memorable single feature of the book. It is she who holds the clan together through its many tribulations, and in her mouth the philosophy of the Okie is articulated. Al and Tom and Pa Joad are as well realized as any strong male types in Hemingway, and they are considerably more identifiable as persons the normal reader may know. On the whole, Steinbeck has done his best work in character creation in this book. These people are less exaggerated, less picturésque, and the story itself less contrived than any other work of his.

In addition to telling the story of the Joads, Steinbeck chose to universalize their experience by the interesting method of periodically inserting short inter-chapters. They interrupt the flow of action, but they have use in that they offer a broader prospect of the time, and show what was happening all over America to cause the Joads and their kind to be in this predicament. As separate technical writing achievements, these inter-chapters are superb. The one called "The Turtle" with which the novel opens is a perfect example of tone-setting, and a sensitive, exact miniature that might stand as an epitome of Steinbeck's prose mastery. In describing minute biological action he is unsurpassed among our novelists. The vignette called "Two-a-Penny" is another wonderfully wrought picture, a short story as tender, warm, and at the same time charged with bitterness, as any story in our literature. Only a man of great heart and good will could have written such a restrained and beautiful fragment.

Anger at social injustice was the prime mover in this book; and for that reason its propagandistic aspect seems to have concerned some critics who felt that Steinbeck stacked the cards against his characters. They could not accept the explosive conclusion in which Rosasharn, her baby having died, gives her breast to a starving man. Admittedly the Steinbeck melodramatism weakened *The Grapes of Wrath*; but it was legitimately used because, from beginning to end, the novel was conceived as a tract for the times. In the hands of a less accomplished artist, it would have been merely another propaganda novel; in Steinbeck's hands the enormous sympathy, the philosophic overtones, the pervading spirit of humanity informed the melodramatic elements with something more important than their surfaces and very nearly excused them. Steinbeck's unparalleled interest in people was almost enough by itself to insure him against the first pitfall of the propagandist; it meant that his people would not be mere animated arguments or stiff exemplifications of "good" in conflict with equally simple examples of "evil."

This ability to see in the round worked to Steinbeck's disadvantage in his next novel, *The Moon Is Down* (1942), where he attempted to show the situation in a Norwegian village under Nazi rule. His Nazi officers are represented as men of two minds, yet his Norwegians are almost perfectly "good"; and the melodrama again obtrudes in the stagey formulation of plot pattern which was, as in *Of Mice and Men*, planned with an eye to the theater. Steinbeck has written motion-picture scenarios ("Lifeboat," "A Medal for Benny," etc.) which are no worse than this novel; and all the faults imputed to him—sentimentalism, exaggeration, too neat plotting, etc.—are observable in these manufactures that lie outside the realm of literature.

It was heartening then, in *Cannery Row* (1945), to find him returning to his most satisfactory manner. The famous versatility of this novelist had been well established; and it was with pleasure that we saw how easily he could continue in a vein once marked out. Like *Tortilla Flat*, this novel has a set of happy vagabonds for its personnel, workers at the fishing wharves and sardine canneries, as well as, more importantly, non-workers. Mack, Hughie, Hazel and Gay, a loose association of bums, live rent-free in a shack owned by Lee Chong, Chinese storekeeper of Cannery Row, and they have named their abode the Palace Flophouse and Grill. Mack and his friends are philosophers, eating when food is available, drinking a marvelous mixture of highball-dregs salvaged by one of their number who works occasionally at the La Ida bar; but when neither food nor drink are to be had, they sleep.

Central to their lives is Doc, who runs a marine laboratory, a man with face "half-Christ and half-satyr." More or less incidental to their existence is the Bear Flag Hotel where Dora presides over her "girls." The story is of an attempt by Mack and the boys to stage a party for Doc; they succeed only in wrecking his laboratory, but on a subsequent try they establish a legend in Cannery Row.

On the face of it, *Cannery Row* is a pointless and rambling tale; but its great distinction and real value lie in the warm humanity suffusing it, and the humor—Dickensian, but with twentieth-century franknesses that would have dumbfounded Dickens. The grim social commentator of *The Grapes of Wrath* again becomes the humorist of *Tortilla Flat* and writes one of the funniest stories since Mark Twain's "Celebrated Jumping Frog." The boys' frog hunt even rivals that classic of pawky American humor; but there are scores of similar, inimitable touches; the case of the Flag Pole Skater is in point, or the chapter on Dora's girls, or that on Doc's ride to La Jolla. The novel is, in fact, crammed with fantastic vignettes.

The characters and events in this and other Steinbeck novels are bizarre; but curiously enough, they are for the most part referable to reality, for Steinbeck has created them upon a basis of people and happenings in his native Salinas valley. The trouble is, perhaps, that this material has not been sufficiently refined in the crucible of the artist's temperament, has not been refracted with enough imaginative care; that Steinbeck has too literally reported the life he has seen. That is why he more than seldom skirts the limits of whimsy and falls into bathos, much as Dickens did; and that the humorous aspect of his work, like that of William Saroyan's, tends to sentimentality. This, I believe, is Steinbeck's continuing danger; if he pushes his *Cannery Row* technique too far, he can end by writing whimsy that will please neither the whimsical nor the tough-minded; and that will be unfortunate, for Steinbeck gives promise still of being our most gifted all-round novelist, with the greatest feeling for the basic human values, the surest sense of the novelist's obligations to drama, and the most lavish story-telling ability since Mark Twain's.

REALISTS

HOWELLS' GRASSHOPPER

THE DOMINANT LINE taken by American fiction in the twentieth century has certainly been that of realism. Romanticism, that hardy perennial, has of course flourished side by side with the more rigorous growth; but it has seldom risen to artistic eminence. Even the novels of Cooper, in which it found most respectable representation, spawned a method that degenerated in the hands of imitators. The side currents of mysticism as shadowed forth in Hawthorne and James, or of the apocalyptic as represented in Poe and Melville, also tended in some sense toward a realistic exposition of at least the surface of their content. In the years between 1798, when Brockden Brown published *Wieland,* and 1881, when Howells' *A Modern Instance* appeared, American fiction had made striking advances and had produced two long masterpieces. *The Scarlet Letter* and *Moby-Dick,* to say nothing of the short stories of Poe. By 1881, however, the mines opened up by the "schools" of romantic realists and the apocalyptics seemed to have been exhausted. A new vein was required, and once more by the example of what was being done on the Continent our fiction took the cue. Howells promulgated his creed of realism and set about by his own novels to exemplify his meaning and fulfill his demands.

It is difficult to determine by what avenue Howells arrived at his intensive realistic dogma. His reading in European literature doubtless was the most important factor; but temperamentally he was always impatient with fanciful, heroic and glaring deeds, written or actual. The "insipid face" of reality held more charm for him than any amount of romantic bravura. Among his most impassioned literary emotions was an abhorrence of Scott; his earliest enthusiasms were for Pope, Shakespeare, Chaucer, Dickens and Heine. He championed the Russian novelists, and Tolstoy became his literary god. We see how natural it was that Howells early and flatly broke with the schools of romanticism, "local color," mysticism, apocalypticism, and every other current that flowed through American literature, and established himself as the anchor of dogged realism. If his own novels had not been first in the field (Edward Eggleston's *Hoosier Schoolmaster* and John De Forest's *Miss Ravenal's Conversion* had preceded him), they were the first to make great pretension to "literature", and most of all were reinforced by an unwavering literary philosophy. Late and soon Howells insisted on the values of a "truthful" representation of life; during his more than sixty years of active literary endeavor he never wearied of dinning into his readers' consciousness the transcendant desirability of the Howellsian realism. He spoke so engagingly of it that those whom he could not win by example were not lost to him from an inordinate zeal. And, in fact, the timid realism he preached could hardly have been unacceptable to even the genteel morality of the post-bellum nineteenth century. Howells richly merits the well-known reproach of having drawn up a program only to erase half of it in the process. To him a realistic representation of life meant, on the whole, only its "smiling aspects." He was willfully blind to the evil there is, which a mordant realism would in later years possibly overemphasize. He shied away from the French Naturalists, whose "realism" was certainly uncompromising, because they dwelt too much on the sordid aspects of life. But he was able to find some sophistical consistency in his philosophy, contending that the moods in which men perpetrate crimes, fall victim to vices, exhibit their sensual or passional natures, lie within the province of romance. In other words, when he called for "truth" in the depiction of life, he did not admit that what was immoral was true: it belonged with the categories of fancy. Crippled thus essentially, Howells' moral nature showed itself allied to that of the New England transcendentalists whose optimism overlooked what it did not desire to recognize. A good man, Howells was a bad theorist. If he had been as thorough-going as his program demanded, he would have been the America Zola; he became instead our masculine Jane Austen.

Nevertheless, Howells was the fountainhead of realism in American fiction, as he was its prophet, salesman and exemplar. The writers who followed him largely turned away from his cautionary advices: they would not be circumscribed; they sought to apply his critical dicta not only to the smiling aspects but to all of life. Hamlin Garland, Brand Whitlock, David Graham Phillips, Frank Norris, Stephen Crane, Dreiser—all owed their freedom to speak frankly of life to the efforts of the older man who, though he wrote hardly more decisive work than closet romances, spoke of what really happened in them, while being careful to stay within a small circumference of decorum.

If we agree that realism had triumphed by 1900, what were the causes of this shift from what must be characterized as idealism in the work of Emerson, Melville and Hawthorne? Realism, with its insistence on material values, grew rapidly after the triumph of industrialism following the Civil War. But in Europe also there was a concurrent development of realism in fiction. What were the basic factors that could raise a Howells to the status of prophet and made the celebration of the present with its burden of ordinary experience the triumphant philosophy of late nineteenth-century literature?

Undoubtedly the preoccupation with moral problems that was a characteristic of the Puritan heritage gave the New England writers of the classic period their best subject matter. A system of rigid deism did not, of course, obtain; but every writer felt the obligations of his uneasy Puritan conscience, and often made strange shifts to placate it. Puritanism and a firm belief in God certainly motivated most of them. Through Emerson, Thoreau, Hawthorne, Lowell, and lingering on in Melville and Whitman, these spiritual reliances were important manifestations basic to their philosophies. But the pushing west of the frontier brought about changes, and the emergent realists, Eggleston, De Forest, Mark Twain—and Howells (born and reared in

Ohio), relied more upon a pragmatic view of reality, though God was by no means absent from their interpretation of it. With the advent of Norris and Dreiser, the influence of Zola and Naturalism overwhelmed the paler program of Howells, and the "ideal" vanished, or very nearly. Still later, the disillusion following the first World War strengthened the materialist bias of such writers as Dos Passos, Hemingway and Faulkner.

Howells himself might have been scandalized by Norris and Dreiser, but he would have been chagrined if he had been able to foresee what became of their immediate successors. Hemingway and Dos Passos, tremendously influential though they have been, did not have the last word. Wolfe and Steinbeck, through very different approaches, turned their backs squarely on realism's ultimate philosophy. They both reaffirmed a faith that was not materialist in nature. Though far from voicing the Emersonian belief in the "oversoul" or the mystical hope of Whitman, they imply acceptance of a value system transcending "mere biology." This is even more evident in some modern poets, MacLeish, Ransom and Tate, for example. Some of them (and, for that matter, Hemingway and Dos Passos) went through a period of adherence to naturalism as a philosophy, yet seemed in their later works to have repudiated it and formed new concepts in which some form of the ideal is not absent. This will be more clearly seen in subsequent chapters.

Actually the two major causes of the triumph of Howellsian realism, and its apotheosis, naturalism, were the intensification of nineteenth-century industrialization and the widespread acceptance of the theories of Darwin. Science, confident of its ultimate mastery of society's material conditions, assumed the successful management of all departments of human welfare. It was believed that the machine would deliver civilization from its drudgery, while in fact it reduced the greater proportion of mankind to slavery. Enthusiasm for science, and a rational explanation of human behavior indicated that literature could also become "scientific." American writers of the middle period, believing in Natural Selection, had no use for Emersonianism. Idealism declined, materialism advanced. But it was Howe l's himself, uneasy at the results of laboratory practice applied to art, who put his finger upon the weakness of realism and its progeny in the realm of philosophy, writing in 1891, "When realism becomes false to itself, when it heaps up facts merely and maps life instead of picturing it, realism will perish, too."

From the appearance of his earliest novel, *Their Wedding Journey* (1871), Howells' predilection for the homely truths of existence was apparent, but in no novel during the next ten years did he achieve utterance sufficiently memorable to have impressed his "truth-telling" doctrine upon the novel-reading public. And it was not until twenty years after his first novel that he published his considered program in *Criticism and Fiction;* but during those years he made steady advances in not only the elucidation of a critical theory but the exemplification of it in his own work. The fact that he was incredibly prolific, a "one-man literary movement," apparently militated against the artistic perfection of any single work. He published more than one hundred books, of which thirty-eight were novels. He wrote rapidly and easily, and many of his novels were extremely popular. Today, however, realism being no longer a rallying cry, the novels seem less extraordinary than they once did; of the thirty-eight, there are possibly but five that can be read with any degree of pleasure today; and among his books of criticism and reminiscence only two or three. In fact, Howells appears to be more important as a historic figure in our literature than as a creator. He certainly, to a greater degree than any other "shaper" we have discussed, molded the course of a great tradition in our literature.

While his early novels reported with fidelity on a very limited segment of experience (mainly boy-meets-girl and do-they-marry situation) they were pale Victorian idyls. But in *A Modern Instance* Howells grappled with a knottier problem and broke the ground for his realistic pronunciamentoes. This novel represents, in many respects, his furthest advance into a timid naturalism, for it deals with definitely unsavory, unhappy events in the dissolution of a marriage. He never again treated of illicit love or divorce, holding that it was immoral in a novelist to do so. Such is the measure of his "realism", which, as we shall see, stopped somewhat short of its logical development.

A Modern Instance pictures the ill-starred marriage of Marcia and Bartley Hubbard, the misery of a divorce in the courts, and the destruction of Bartley, whose many small vices added up to a great and fatal one. Bartley Hubbard is a scoundrel, but Howells treats him sympathetically for the most part, indulgent of his crooked business practice but unforgiving before his moral lapses in the marital relationship. It is, of course, the questionable economic manipulations this side of the law that open the breach between Marcia and her husband, but it is Bartley's own egoistic drive which causes him to withdraw from Marcia, whose love and self-immolation ought to have been rewarded by something better than the ineffectual adoration of Ben Halleck. Halleck long and anonymously worships Marcia; and after the divorce is obtained, we expect him, an honorable, thoroughly deserving man, to marry her. But Howells will not have it. He condemns Halleck even for privately coveting Marcia; his passion is defined as guilty—a rare resurgence of the Puritan conscience cropping out in a "realist." Howells' comment, however, appears to be not altogether Puritan but Tolstoyan: he wishes to prove the point by this questionable means that any marriage, even a loveless one, is sacrosanct.

Technically the novel is not well constructed, and while it certainly has greater drive and more incident than any of the preceding novels, there is a tendency to the monotonous, as there is, curiously, in all the Howells novels. The dead level of statement, the eschewing of explosive or bizarre or highly dramatic events (all ruled out by definition), are not conducive to liveliness. But the great structural flaw in *A Modern Instance*, as in most of the novels, is a dichotomy of plot somewhere past the middle. We are treated to an exigent dramatization of the divorce court, then suddenly involved in the machinations of shady business men. What interest had been secured is diverted and discouraged; the final impression is blurred.

A Modern Instance appeared originally in *Century Magazine*, and it marked a phase of transition in both Howells' life and work. He had just resigned editorship of the *Atlantic Monthly* and moved to New York; a new era of cosmopolitanism was about to open for him. Accordingly, in his next important novel, *The Rise of Silas Lapham*, he came out from the pleasant backwater of Boston into the glare and welter of the modern commercial world. Though its setting is Boston, this novel holds up to gentle ridicule both the empty culture of the Back Bay Brahmin and the loud vulgarity of the parvenu class, represented by Silas himself. It must be admitted that Howells' sympathies are divided; Silas is treated the less mercifully to start with; but toward the end, when he has suffered for his ignorance and aggressiveness, his is the more admirable character. The other pole of society is represented by the Coreys, who on the whole are more gently handled; but Bromfield Corey, the fine flower of Brahminism, is censured for his disdain of the common man; the caste system (which fascinated while it irked Howells) comes in for some pointed criticism. Actually, however, *Silas Lapham* is not the novel its purported theme might have made it. There are indications that Howells intended it to be a decisive story of conflict between the old and the new in the Boston of the 'seventies, a clash between the rising commercial class and the old families; but what it finally resolves itself into is simply another typical Howells love story. Young Tom Corey falls in love with Silas' elder daughter, Penelope, but declares his passion so unobtrusively that the Laphams think he is wooing the younger, Irene—who thinks so too. After some slight attempt at raising a moral issue in this misunderstanding, Howells resolves the contretemps by sending Tom and Penelope off to Mexico, where they are married—happily, we conjecture; but it is a complete evasion of the issues, for the real conflict might easily be assumed to have begun when the daughter of *nouveau riche* Lapham and the son of Brahmin Corey must settle down to life together.

Lapham is a well-wrought character, probably Howells' best. In the era of his "rising" he is least convincing, his rise too rapid and his knowledge of the paint business meager and gingerly. When he falls on hard days he begins to develop; a new earnestness, soundness and genuineness enter. By the time he has been brought low, we feel of him—as we do of Hardy's Henchard or, even, if we make proper adjustments in the level of our criteria, of the heroes in Greek tragedy—that he is overwhelmed by the fate that is character.

Howells' admiration for Mark Twain was at its height when he was writing this novel; and it is not difficult to see evidences of this admiration in *Silas Lapham*. Principally it is to be observed in the dialogue which, whenever vulgarity is to come from the mouths of the Laphams, or Bartley Hubbard (he enters briefly, like the many other Howells characters who have a habit of reappearing throughout all the novels), relies more than a little on the "warn't's" and "got to go and get's," and other peculiarly Clemensian bits of idom. Actually, however, Howells is not at home with such Americanisms, and they have a curiously stilted look, surrounded by irreproachable English. Howells' ear for common speech was remarkably inaccurate; it is as if he had relied on his readings in the work of men who had an ear for it, failing in the end to fuse slang with everyday speech. The influence of James can also be traced; but here, of course, Howells fell so far below his younger rival that comparison is very nearly invidious. Stylistically, Howells is not greatly inferior to the James of the early and middle periods, but if we set side by side such creations as Lydia Blood of *The Lady of the Aroostook* and Isabel Archer, both women of considerable force, Howells' somewhat similar method and incomparably feebler performance are equally indubitable.

Tepid as they may seem to us now, *A Modern Instance* and *Silas Lapham* represent Howells' most vigorous attempts to come to grips with the problems of life. Had he wished or been able to continue in that vein, no doubt his work would have greater interest for us today; instead, he chose to treat of the more temperate moods and politer mores of his time. *A Hazard of New Fortunes*, *The Quality of Mercy* and *A Traveler from Altruria* are the only subsequent novels sufficiently charged with vitality to warrant our acquaintance. And even these rise so little above the level of a score of others, *The Kentons*, *A Chance Acquaintance*, *The Son of Royal Langbrith*, etc., etc., that it is difficult to assign reasons for their superiority. Perhaps *A Hazard of New*

Fortunes is chiefly memorable for its characterization of Fulk-
erson, the genial humbug and original amoral man in American
fiction; Micawber-like yet without exaggeration, he typifies a
kind of ubiquitous businessman we have come to know better in
the guise of "Get-Rich-Quick Wallingford" and other scamps
of popular fiction. Also this novel's intimate picture of the journalistic world of the 'eighties is as revealing as any we have; and
finally, its concern with socialism and the workingman foreshadows the last phase of Howells' realistic philosophy, which
brought forth the Utopianism of *Altruria* and a continuing interest in ameliorating the miseries attendant upon a nascent capitalism. Its weaknesses are diffusion, lack of integration, unresolved threads of narrative, and in exacerbated degree the structural faults common to almost all the novels.

More interesting for the possibilities it held is *The Quality of
Mercy*, the only extended crime story Howells wrote. Starting
well, it pursues the defaulter Northwick, who has stolen money
from his partners and flees to Canada. Northwick's daughters and
his younger sister, Suzette, thinking he has been killed in a train
accident, attempt to rehabilitate his memory by clearing his
name in the courts. Suzette falls in love with the son of Northwick's defrauded partner and marries him. The greater part of
the novel is devoted to this love story, with, incidentally, a secondary one as well; while the really interesting issues are held
in abeyance and rather summarily dismissed when Northwick is
discovered to have taken a different train, his conscience burdened by his crime, and he acknowledges his guilt. On his way
home to accept punishment, he dies. If we had been permitted
to follow Northwick more consistently, and if the moral choices
devolving upon his sister and daughters had been more logically
consequent upon his crime, *The Quality of Mercy* would have
attained to real importance. The "truth" for Howells, however,
could not have been that uncompromising, and the novel fails, a
victim to his moderation.

One aspect of the "crime" ought not to be overlooked. In ac-
counting for Northwick's defalcation, Howells is careful to note
that it is the economic order which is to blame for tempting and

destroying the man whom circumstances render incapable of withstanding the promise of easy riches. Northwick is essentially a passive character, acted on by the social organism. This conception of criminal responsibility was somewhat in advance of the time and altogether a piece of insight, though it is possible Howells was only first to introduce in America a theory of which Tolstoy was the great champion.

A Traveler from Altruria (1894) goes even further into social and political nostrums and is the fullest exposition of Howells' opinions on these matters. Long preoccupied with the problems of unemployment and sympathetic to the claims of the worker, Howells' leftward thinking was reinforced by the philosophy of his idol, Tolstoy. *A Traveler from Altruria* is a more literate *Looking Backward*. As a novel, it leaves much to be desired, being for the most part mere transcripts of conversations between Mr. Homos, Howells' "lovably childlike" visitor from the Utopian commonwealth of Altruria, and various American colloquists: writers, business executives, lawyers, doctors, ministers and scholars. This device enables Howells to put into his hero's mouth the various socialist programs for the liquidation of capitalism's iniquities, but it does not make a dramatic novel. Still, the book is interesting as an exposition of the humanitarian, egalitarian principles of the American 'nineties. Its sequel, *Through the Eye of the Needle* (1907), attempts to show what life is like in Altruria; but monopoly and sameness prevail, for all the conflicts of the world as we know it have been resolved. On the basis of this performance, we are forced to assume that, if socialism should produce the perfect society, novelists, along with the exploiters of humanity, would become extinct.

The springboard of the Howellsian platform is *Criticism and Fiction* (1892), a little collection of Easy Chair essays originally published in *Harper's Magazine*. Its essential doctrine is that ". . . in proportion as we gain a firmer hold upon our own place in the world, we shall come to comprehend with more instinctive certitude what is simple, natural, and honest, welcoming with gladness all artistic products that exhibit these qualities."[1] Wordsworth asked for similar criteria in poetry nearly a hundred years earlier. The "simple, natural and honest" in art have been called for recurrently, and always the discovery that they are desirable creates a new flurry. But Howells was thoroughly anti-romantic, anti-classic, and anti-idealistic. Though the wire-and-cardboard grasshopper, prettily painted and perfectly indestructible, was ideal or heroic, impassioned or romantic, and had served to represent the notion of a grasshopper ever since man emerged from barbarism, it seemed to him a poor substitute for the simple, natural, real-life grasshopper. Every true realist "in life finds nothing insignificant. . . . He cannot look upon human life and declare this thing or that thing unworthy of notice, any more than the scientist can declare a fact of the material world beneath the dignity of his inquiry."[1] That is Howells' program, yet it was too inclusive for his own practice; and he often concurred in the condemnation of "objectionable French novels" (those of the naturalists); still, so fervid was his rejection of romanticism that he could find it in his heart to say that "French naturalism is better at its worst than French unnaturalism at its best."[1] For the realistic novelist's "soul is exalted, not by vain shows and shadows and ideals, but by realities, *in which alone the truth lives.*"[1] (My italics.) Uneasy as he may be in the company of Zola, he quotes with approval the Spanish critic, Valdes: "No one can rise from the perusal of a naturalistic book with a vivid desire to escape from the wretched world depicted in it, and a purpose, more or less vague, of helping to better the lot and morally elevate the abject beings who figure in it. Naturalistic art, then, is not immoral in itself, for then it would not merit the name of art; for though it is not the business of art to preach morality, still I think that, resting on a divine and spiritual principle, like the idea of the beautiful, it is perforce moral."[1]

Howells has nothing good to say about even the best of the romantic novelists; he can barely abide Balzac; he abominates Scott; and his contemporary "purveyors of slush" and the "sensation mongers" are scathingly treated. "Let fiction cease to lie about life," he says; "let it portray men and women as they are, actuated by the motives and the passions in the measure we all know; let it leave off painting dolls and working them by springs and wires; let it show the different interests in their true proportions; let it forbear to preach pride and revenge, folly and insanity, egotism and prejudice, but frankly own these for what they are, in whatever figures and occasions they appear; let it not put on fine literary airs; let it speak the dialect, the language, that most Americans know."[1] Emerson trumpeted forth a similar call; and Carlyle before him; but Howells, speaking for the novel, incessantly rang the changes. His principle, "truth," was simplicity itself, a creed that needed no great intellectual profundity to grasp; and it was not original with him. He freely gives credit to Emerson, John Addington Symonds, Valdes, Canon Farrar and Carlyle for their prior and, in most cases, profounder citations of the need for realism. But he was the great prophet of it in the novel; and *Criticism and Fiction* is his statement of policy.

Howells' limitations were many, and in some respects he was peculiarly unfitted for the role in which he cast himself. We have seen that he was squeamish, that his taste shunned what was unpleasant, though his intelligence told him that he ought to recognize it. He did not conceal his penchant for the "more smiling aspects of life" which he believed "are the more American." Our novelists, he said, "seek the universal in the individual rather than social interests. It is worth while, even at the risk of being called commonplace, to be true to our well-to-do actualities; the very passions themselves seem to be softened and modified by conditions which formerly at least could not be said to wrong any one, to cramp endeavor, or to cross lawful desire."[1] He acknowledged that there must always be sin and suffering in the world, but he insisted that "in this new world of ours it is still mainly from one to another one, and oftener still from one to one's self."[1] We must admit that the general position seems more tenable today than it did in the depression years. One reason why it seemed wrong to him that the artist should picture reality in its less "smiling aspects" may be the result of his tender-minded concern for the young woman who reads novels. "If the novel were written for men and for married women alone, as in continental Europe, it might be altogether different. But the simple fact is that it is not written for them alone among us, and it is a question of writing, under cover of our universal acceptance, things for young girls to read which you would be put out-of-doors for saying to them."[1]

Howells' meager acquaintance with classic literature is notorious, and by it we may account for his under-estimation of classicism in art. He could make a sweeping indictment of classical literature like the following and stand pat on it. "At least three-fifths of the literature called classic, in all languages, no more lives than the poems and stories that perish monthly in our magazines. It is all printed and reprinted, generation after generation, century after century; but it is not alive; it is as dead as the people who wrote it and read it, and to whom it meant something perhaps; with whom it was a fashion, a caprice, a passing taste. A superstitious piety preserves it, and pretends that it has aesthetic qualities which can delight or edify; but nobody really enjoys it; . . . it is trash, and often very filthy trash, which the present trash generally is not."[1]

Anyone who believed in realism as firmly as Howells would have had to admit that, when the art had become sufficiently perfected, it would approximate a record of life itself. But what else does good biography attempt to do? And so we are not surprised to find him conceding that "when the great mass of readers, now sunk in the foolish joys of mere fable, shall be lifted to an interest in the meaning of things through the faithful portrayal of life in fiction, then fiction the most faithful may be superseded by a still more faithful form of contemporaneous history." A gloomy outlook for fiction, representing an inconsistency in Howells, because, as we have noted, he contended that realism would be untrue to itself *only* when it heaped up facts, which are the most faithful, though ultimately false, record of human events.

Defining the critic's function, Howells took the position of the usual nineteenth-century naturalists, echoing Sainte-Beuve and Saintsbury. "It is really (the critic's) business to classify and analyze the fruits of the human mind very much as the naturalist classifies the objects of his study, rather than to praise or blame them . . . it is his business . . . to identify the species and then explain how and where the specimen is imperfect and irregular."[1] He would endorse the laboratory method altogether; and such notions as "creative criticism," advocated by Lowell and Stedman or any of the essayists who chose a book as vehicle for a rambling excursion of their own, were offensive to him. "The critic . . . must perceive, if he will question himself more carefully, that his office is mainly to ascertain facts and traits of literature, not to invent or denounce them; to discover principles, not to establish them; to report, not create."[1] It is to be doubted whether, in his own practice, he adhered to these rules. *Criticism and Fiction* contains little direct criticism of individual works, while *My Literary Passions* and *Literary Friends and Acquaintance* are oftener the record of personal reactions than of scientific investigation.

American fiction since 1880, in its broadest stream, has shown an overwhelming preference for the live Nightingale of Andersen's fable and the real grasshopper of Howells'. Realism went on to a new forthrightness in examining not only the grasshopper's "simple, natural and honest" exterior but its viscera. It left Howells far behind, and in so doing showed that while his grasshopper had the outward appearance of the real thing, it was only a stuffed specimen, without insides.

MARK TWAIN
Realism and the Frontier

WHILE HOWELLS was calling for the emergence of a true American realism and sometimes lamenting the slavish attitude of American writers toward the British novelists, at least one native story-teller was working importantly with materials that were unmistakably American. Mark Twain had begun by joining that large class of humorists which included Petroleum V. Nasby,

---

[1] From *Criticism and Fiction* by William Dean Howells. © 1891 by Harper and Brothers. © 1919 by Mildred Howells and John Mead Howells.

Josh Billings and Artemus Ward—a well-established group of public entertainers who reflected in their writings the ebullient spirit of the '70's and '80's. They wrote drolly of many subjects, were keenly analytical on topics of the day, and yet were careful to reflect only the majority opinions. Optimistic, complacent, and far from profound, this journalistic humor of the era was a typical manifestation of an expanding, self-confident society. It poked fun at anything that betokened a divergence from the norm of ordinary middle-class American life. At the beginning of his career Mark Twain's special qualities were admirably suited to participation in this breezy journalism.

After a boyhood in Hannibal, Missouri, that was perhaps typical of the period, Samuel Clemens was apprenticed out to a local printer at twelve years of age. In the country newspaper office he learned to turn out whimsical jokes and sketches that showed he could do equally as well as his masters. But the small town offered no room for his expanding ambitions; he wanted to see the world and to make money. He went to New York, Philadelphia and other big cities, earning his living as a printer; but eventually he came back to the river that had appealed so to his romantic imagination as a boy. He learned the profession of pilot, and in the years during which he navigated the river boats up and down a twelve-hundred-mile stretch of the Mississippi, stored up experiences that were fruitful for his future career.

This stage in the evolution of the first "American" story-teller was ended with the coming of the Civil War. Clemens served for a time in the Confederate army, and at the war's end went west, joining the thousands of his countrymen who sought adventure and gold in the new Eldorado. And here again he was fortunate in gaining a typical experience of the time. After trying his hand at mining, he began to write for the Virginia City, Nevada, *Enterprise*. He wandered to San Francisco, met and worked with Bret Harte, and while in California heard the tale which he fashioned into an early masterpiece of humor, *The Celebrated Jumping Frog of Calaveras County*. From the moment that this engaging sketch was printed, and reprinted throughout the country, Sam Clemens became Mark Twain, the "Wild Humorist of

the Pacific Slope," whose writings began to attract national attention. He launched upon the series of humorous lectures that continued throughout most of his life and gained him almost as much
fame as his writings.

In 1869 Mark Twain emerged with *Innocents Abroad* as the
American frontiersman capable of expressing the outlook which
gave America its brash, swaggering self-confidence, showing not
only the effete East but Europe as well how little it thought of
the conventions of older cultures. *Innocents Abroad* was an in-
stantaneous success; the American public was delighted to see
fun made of the many landmarks and customs of antiquity, was
transported by its rough contrasts, and found uproarious the
brawling, headlong humor implicit in them.

Roughing It (1872) continued this irreverent pilgrim's travels,
but with a difference. Here Mark Twain returned to his own
frontier, and the experiences shared by many of his fellows. He
had had time to evaluate the meaning of much that he had seen
and done; and in this book he took liberties with fact, shaping
his memories into a more artistic pattern than he had been able
to do in the preceding book. Filled with extravagant speech and
blustering burlesque, *Roughing It* continued to resemble the
rowdy journalism of the American West; but it was all set down
in a spirit of tolerance, and though it showed crudities, they
were of a different kind than had been explicit in the story of
Mark Twain's European travels. The picture of life on the still
expanding frontier, its on-the-spot reporting of Mormonism, the
stories of life in Virginia City, the gold camps and early San Francisco—all are fresh and vibrant with life. In this book Mark
Twain was beginning to get the feel of fiction and to utilize
imaginative reconstruction in pointing up incidents and creating
character. There were passages reminiscent of Artemus Ward,
perhaps, but the old-time funnymen of the American newspaper
could never have conceived, much less created, the sense of
bustling excitement and vivid life, or the feel of spacious, unten-
anted earth and sky that Mark Twain evoked in *Roughing It*.

By the time Clemens had convinced the East that he was not
a literary buffoon, that East had already fastened upon him and

attempted in its way to "civilize" him further and bend his genius to its own standards of taste. He fell under Howells' notice, and there followed a lifelong association between the two very dissimilar writers, with Howells always taking the part of mentor. Mark Twain deferred to him as the literary pundit of the age, and there is no way of determining to what extent Howells' influence shaped this boisterous genius away from its natural bent. Clemens married in 1870 a woman who acted in the capacity of censor, further abetting Howells and the Boston culture. Between Olivia Langdon and W. D. Howells, the "Wild Humorist of the Pacific Slope" was trimmed and tamed. Undoubtedly this repressive influence had a great deal to do with the truncation of the career that began with such fireworks and spluttered out so dismally toward its end.

In 1873 the result of the first of these new influences might have been seen in *The Gilded Age*, a novel with a curiously Victorian air, that was meant to be a social satire. A collaboration, it had neither the advantage of Mark Twain's best qualities, nor those of Charles Dudley Warner, who was a competent but hardly inspired artist. Still there was enough anger and idealism in Mark Twain that his satirical picture of such scoundrels as Senator Dillworthy was a scathing indictment of the corruption in high government circles. And in the creation of its chief character, Colonel Beriah Sellers, the novel succeeded in epitomizing a type of lovable post-bellum American. The sections that show Mark Twain's hand are, of course, the best; but the novel itself failed for obvious reasons.

Three years later Clemens published *Tom Sawyer*, and went back to his Hannibal origins for the best boys' book any American had written. Apparently he wrote it partly as a corrective to the Sunday School type of story, and because he sensed in his boyhood a mine of humor through which to tell truthfully how a small boy thinks, feels and acts. *Tom Sawyer* is not an even work; it falls off at the end into a typical blood-and-thunder tale; but many of its events are in the finest realistic tradition and the book itself has entered into our consciousness as a classic of the literature of boyhood.

During his forties, when he was at the height of his powers,

Mark Twain wrote the two books upon which his serious reputation will rest; one of them a work of casual reminiscence,
Life on the Mississippi (1883), the other a novel considered by
many the best American novel of the century, *Huckleberry Finn*
(1885). There is no denying that the prose style of these works
has influenced modern writers (especially Hemingway, and
through him the most influential novelists of this century). It
is colloquial, natural, in harmony with its content, and by long
odds the clearest, easiest prose to come from any native writer.
Its even rhythms and lack of pretention are as far as possible
from the "literary" language of such people as Henry James or
even Howells. One feels that Clemens wrote as he must have
talked, and that his talk was indeed as good as it has been reported. Honesty and the plain realism of every-day life are
the keynotes of this style; and the only advance that any writer
has made upon it in the decades since has been a willingness to
speak of some phases of human experience that Samuel Clemens
could not discuss. Even he, however, showed his impatience with
convention in the famous privately circulated *1601*, written
overtly as a joke but probably the result of a chafing at the proscriptions imposed by the polite tastes of his day, and the censor-
ship of his wife.

Life on the Mississippi grew out of his experiences as a pilot,
and is written with warmth and love. An unsentimental nostalgia
for past time, the sensuous evocation of the river, the land and
the people produced a document of negotiable value; and when
one compares this book with *Roughing It*, that other evocation
of past experience, one sees what a different Mark Twain was
writing, now that he had discarded the swaggering bravado of
his Western newspaper ways.

It would be hard to find a more perfect example of indigenous
American writing, or a more honest account of a typical remembered incident than this, from *Life on the Mississippi*:

"It was always the custom for the boats to leave New Orleans
between four and five o'clock in the afternoon. From three
o'clock onward they would be burning rosin and pitchpine
(the sign of preparation), and so one had the picturesque spectacle of a rank, some two or three miles long, of tall, ascending

columns of coal-black smoke; a colonnade which supported a sable roof of the same smoke blended together and spreading abroad over the city. Every outward-bound boat had its flag flying at the jack-staff, and sometimes a duplicate on the verge-staff astern. Two or three miles of mates were commanding and swearing with more than usual emphasis: countless processions of freight barrels and boxes were spinning athwart the levee and flying aboard the stage-planks; belated passengers were dodging and skipping among these frantic things, hoping to reach the forecastle companionway alive, but having their doubts about it; women with reticules and bandboxes were trying to keep up with husbands freighted with carpet sacks and crying babies, and making a failure of it by losing their heads in the whirl and roar and general distraction; drays and baggage-vans were clattering hither and thither in a wild hurry, every now and then getting blocked and jammed together, and then during ten seconds one could not see them for the profanity, except vaguely and dimly; every windlass connected with every fore-hatch, from one end of that long array of steamboats to the other, was keeping up a deafening whizz and whir, lowering freight into the hold, and the half-naked crews of perspiring negroes that worked them were roaring such songs as 'De Las' Sack! De Las' Sack!'—inspired to unimaginable exaltation by the chaos of turmoil and racket that was driving everybody else mad. By this time the hurricane and boiler decks of the steamers would be packed black with passengers. The 'last bells' would begin to clang, all down the line, and then the powwow seemed to double; in a moment or two the final warning came—a simultaneous din of Chinese gongs, with the cry, 'All dat ain't goin', please to git asho'!'—and behold the powwow quadrupled! People came swarming ashore, overturning excited stragglers that were trying to swarm aboard. One more moment later a long array of stage-planks was being hauled in, each with its customary latest passenger clinging to the end of it with teeth, nails, and everything else, and the customary latest procrastinator making a wild spring shoreward over his head." [1]

---

[1] From *Life on the Mississippi* by Mark Twain (S. L. Clemens). © 1917 by Harper and Brothers.

Without wholly premeditating the effectiveness of his device, Clemens used the first-person narrative method in *Huckleberry Finn*, and created a character to stand beside Melville's Captain Ahab, Dreiser's Hurstwood, or James's Isabel Archer, as one of the great fictional creations in our literature. Huck Finn has the additional advantage of being more easily identifiable as a human being than any of these; and in the whole range of our fiction it is to be doubted if one character exceeds in all-round fullness and life the urchin Huckleberry Finn.

How did Mark Twain succeed so well in breathing life into this backwoods boy? Largely through the narrative device of having Huck tell his own story. It was possible to characterize him in every word of the novel, for every word came from Huck's mouth. James knew the artistic advantage of this method; he exploited it to the full, and it has been used by nearly all our best writers; but Clemens undoubtedly felt instinctively the usefulness of the method. [1] It fitted both his subject and his own excellences perfectly. Strongest when writing colloquially (perhaps this was his real affiliation with the Petroleum V. Nasby school of humorists), Mark Twain utilized every strength by making his narrative ability fit the story he wanted to tell. And *Huckleberry Finn* plainly proved the worth of his insistence on purely American speech, wholly American backgrounds, and altogether American materials for his fiction. Had he been a more self-conscious artist, he would undoubtedly have continued in this remarkable vein; that is to say, he would have seen the value of his materials, and insisted on using them; he would have avoided his subsequent retinue of historical novels and travelogues with trumped up plots; but Mark Twain was not a self-conscious artist.

Huckleberry Finn, on its literal level, is simply a rattling good yarn about a village ne'er-do-well's son who runs away from his foster home at the Widow Douglas', and in company

---

[1] In 1875 Mark Twain wrote Howells, saying that he thought he might have been mistaken in not writing *Tom Sawyer* in the first person. "By and by I shall take a boy of twelve and run him on through life (in the first person) but not Tom Sawyer—he would not be a good character for it."

with a runaway slave, drifts down the Mississippi aboard a raft. His adventures provide American fiction with its one truly great picaresque novel. But it is, of course, much more than an adventure story for boys, since Huck's experiences in most cases have a double significance; sometimes satiric, as in the incidents of the Grangerford-Shepherdson feud sequence, and again symbolic, as in the story of the Duke and the Dauphin. Huck is the mouthpiece for a great deal of unconscious social commentary, and his code is at variance with the accepted morality of the typical small town of the Gilded Age. There is limitless humanity in the book, and the ethics of the unschooled urchin are invariably shown as superior to those of his betters. The exposition of this superiority is entirely artistic, for the author never steps in to point out his moral; and Huck Finn's own words carry their weight of double meaning with immense effectiveness. For example, he realizes that he has helped a slave to run away, and at one moment his sense of the moral proprieties prompts him to let Jim's owner know; and at the next he has listened to his own conscience in the matter. In the end he tears up the letter he planned to send to Miss Watson. "I was a-trembling, because I'd got to decide, forever, betwixt two things, and I knowed it. I studied for a minute, sort of holding my breath, and then says to myself:

" 'All right, then, I'll *go* to hell,'—and tore it up.

"It was awful thoughts and awful words, but they was said. And I let them stay said; and 'never thought no more about reforming." [2]

The mature reader never has any difficulty determining that Huck's moral decisions are the right ones, and they show how wrong are the laws and taboos of the genteel among whom he is a pariah.

But the true beauty of the novel is its wonderful evocation of the river, and night, and the sounds and smells of the earth in boyhood. The freshness and wonder of all these things as known in our youth are recaptured more poignantly in *Huckleberry*

---

[2] From *Huckleberry Finn* by Mark Twain (S. L. Clemens). By permission of Harper and Brothers.

Finn than in any other novel, with the possible exception of Thomas Wolfe's best works. In a paragraph Mark Twain can resurrect that wonder and immediacy of sense impressions, smells, sounds, the texture of wind and sun and rain, as no other American has been able to do. And the writing is wonderfully fine, too, as it would have to be to make its effect with such economy. When Huck is on the river at night, for example, his words are almost magical, yet they are simple and in character:

"The next minute I was a-spinning down-stream soft, but quick, in the shade of the bank. I made two mile and a half, and then struck out a quarter of a mile or more toward the middle of the river, because pretty soon I would be passing the ferry-landing, and people might see me and hail me. I got out amongst the driftwood, and then laid down in the bottom of the canoe and let her float. I laid there, and had a good rest and a smoke out of my pipe, looking away into the sky; not a cloud in it. The sky looks ever so deep when you lay down on your back in the moonshine; I never knowed it before. And how far a body can hear on the water such nights! I heard people talking at the ferry-landing. I heard what they said, too—every word of it. One man said it was getting toward the long days and the short nights now. T'other one said *this* warn't one of the short ones, he reckoned—and then they laughed, and he said it over again, and they laughed again; then they waked up another fellow and told him, and laughed, but he didn't laugh; he ripped out something brisk, and said let him alone. The first fellow said he 'lowed to tell it to his old woman—she would think it was pretty good; but he said that warn't nothing to some things he had said in his time. I heard one man say it was nearly three o'clock, and he hoped daylight wouldn't wait more than about a week longer. After that the talk got further and further away, and I couldn't make out the words any more; but I could hear the mumble, and now and then a laugh, too, but it seemed a long ways off." [3]

The "realism" of *Huckleberry Finn* is by no means absolute, and the reappearance of Tom Sawyer in the concluding chap-

---

[3] From *Huckleberry Finn* by Mark Twain (S. L. Clemens). By permission of Harper and Brothers.

ters, the eventual resorting to plot complication, mar what otherwise is a fine novel. It remains, in spite of this, one of the great
American novels, and its realistic elements proved fruitful for all
the following generations of writers in that vein.

Mark Twain's writing career after 1885 is disappointing,
not because what he wrote was not good, but because it was not
great. Here was probably, with Melville and Whitman, the
most gifted and powerful creative genius America ever produced, and yet after *Huckleberry Finn* it gave the world nothing
of absolutely first-rate quality. Why? Was it again the dichotomy between the free, untrammeled impulse toward creation,
manifested in his earlier books, and the repressions of a culture
he could not assimilate? It is certain that Sam Clemens was a
product of the frontier; he was self-educated, learned his craft
through frontier journalism, and in his days of growth regarded
himself as simply an entertainer. But in his middle life, with
the incidence of Howells and eastern recognition, he was made
to understand that he was a literary man. He went on to make as
much money as possible, and he continued to write entertain-
ingly—but he was under the shadow of a cultural pattern alien
to him. He knew that there was little of the "artist" in his make-
up; his vivid imagination, his boisterous spirits, his hatred of
shams and affectation, and his misunderstanding of the things
that mattered to others who had attained a more formal state
of culture—these were all products of his essential frontiersman's spirit. Even his empirical philosophy, uttered in the bitter
posthumous books, seemed original to him, and this philosophy
was remarkable, in that it had been spun out of his own brain
with little aid from books.

The problem of Mark Twain is a knotty one, and it has not
yet been unraveled. Given the limiting factors of his environment in the mature years, he achieved much; and if none of his
books is entirely satisfactory, any one of them contains more life
and earnest native American stuff than a dozen of the better-
made novels of his time. He achieved the distinction of being
recognized, not only at home but in England and on the Continent, as the greatest American humorist, and his shorter fiction

abounded with such humor as is a joy forever. Both as a writer and as a personality of unusual distinction, he became a symbol of the cruder kind of American writing that was, in the popular mind, art. It is not too much to say that he is still the great folk hero of American literature. But with all his force and genius, it is strange that he never quite overcame the limitations imposed on him. There is somehow an indication of magnificent failure about Mark Twain. And its cause seems to rest in a division within his own consciousness. He seemed never at home, either in the world of catholic thought, or in the cruder and more primitive climate of the frontier. He stepped outside the boundaries of his early culture, but he never entered within the charmed circle of his aspirations. There was no middle ground for him to stand on between the brash optimism of his early works and the bleak pessimism of his last.

We can trace this development from the enthusiastic promise of his frontier days, through the successes of his middle period, to the dark resignation and determinism at the end of his life. After *Life on the Mississippi* and *Huckleberry Finn*, we had the largely diffuse, if occasionally brilliant, novels like *A Connecticut Yankee* (1889) and *Joan of Arc* (1895). In these he defended the ideals of American democracy; in the former satirizing the ancient aristocracy, with its notions of *noblesse oblige*, and in the latter apostrophizing The Maid for her devotion to truth in an age that worshiped property and practiced deceit.

Like all realists, Mark Twain's humanitarianism led him to take his stand with the workers and the dispossessed of the earth. Howells' eventual turning to socialism was the apparently necessary result of his insistence on truth; Mark Twain's honesty likewise eventuated in his taking up the cause of the underdog. *A Connecticut Yankee* and *Joan of Arc* showed that, though he had moved away from explicit realism in his fiction, his interest in people forced him to recognize the plight of the common man in the age of emerging industrialism. As Howells said, "He never went so far in socialism as I have gone, . . . but from the first he had a luminous vision of organized labor as the only present help for workingmen." The more we examine the work of the realists, the better we see that they are alike in their leanings toward the political left.

Another evidence of Mark Twain's central position in the stream of American realism is his final attitude toward life. He felt that the bright optimism of his frontier days had been a mirage, and that he had been betrayed. It was the cry of an outraged idealist who declared, "I have been reading the morning paper. I do it every morning—well knowing that I shall find in it the usual depravities and basenesses and hypocrisies and cruelties that make up civilization, and cause me to put in the rest of the day pleading for the damnation of the human race." [2] His fatalism, and the philosophy which he built up to support it, best seen in *The Mysterious Stranger* and *What Is Man?*, show him to have suffered a complete reversal of attitude from the brave days of his robust youth. As Van Wyck Brooks sums it up, this sort of despair "springs from a kind of disappointment, and this is the characteristic American mood from Mark Twain and Henry Adams to John Dos Passos and William Faulkner. Our world has not lived up to its assumptions, and the single man feels helpless before the mass. . . . Fatalism presupposes hope, and any child can be a fatalist. Take away his kite or his train of cars, or lock him up in a closet, and he sees life stretching before him as an endless desert or prison." [3]

The black closing years of Mark Twain's creative and real life are a lesson in this sort of disappointment. The dream of a free America as it seemed in the '60's had dissolved; American life was set in the rigid mold of the industrial age; and in Mark Twain we have a man who had witnessed this metamorphosis. His is a relevant case history of a genius whose adjustment to reality was not adequate to correct his sense of outraged idealism.

---

[2] Letter to W. D. Howells in 1899.
[3] *The Opinions of Oliver Allston* by Van Wyck Brooks. © 1941 by E. P. Dutton & Co., Inc.

Naturalism Nascent
CRANE AND NORRIS

TOWARD the close of the nineteenth century a handful of American novelists, with the examples of Howells and Mark Twain before them, had begun to see that there was drama not only in romantic chronicles of events "far away and long ago" but in the everyday lives of the men and women around them. Howells had beat the drum for Tolstoy and the Russians, and a group of younger critics began to praise the French naturalists with greater enthusiasm than had Howells. James Huneker, Percival Pollard and Harry Thurston Peck discovered the "advanced" writers of the continent: Flaubert, Zola, Strindberg, Ibsen, Shaw and Hardy; and they were much less temperate than Howells in advocating a simulation of these realists by American writers. Mark Twain's success in writing of his own experiences of boyhood and life on the frontier had helped foster a school of local colorists: Bret Harte, G. W. Cable, Mary Wilkins Freeman and Sarah Orne Jewett. The local colorists were in some sense realists, but their tendency was to make quaint the background and milieu of their characters and to divorce their stories from the mainstream of American life by making it seem special and even esoteric. Most of them pointed up their dramas with romantic devices learned from Cooper and Scott, and almost caricatured their personae in the interests of a special regionalism. They exaggerated what seemed picturesque in the locale and in the types found there. The result was a kind of romantic realism that helped pave the way for the American naturalism that was the predominant note in American fiction of the first decades in the new century.

Conterminous with the emerging realism, of course, was the continuing romanticism of the widely popular fiction of the *fin de siècle* era. Winston Churchill, Owen Wister, Lew Wallace were the writers of best-sellers; and their influence was great in spite of Howells' preeminence and his championship of the new realism. And the apocalyptic writers like Bierce and Hearn continued their delving into realms of the psyche, oblivious to the literary currents flowing around them.

Breaking ground for the two most important realists after Howells was a small group of talented writers headed perhaps by Hamlin Garland. In 1891 he published *Main-Travelled Roads* and in 1895 *Rose of Dutcher's Coolly*, books which owed something to the pioneering of Mark Twain as well as that of E. E. Howe, whose black and bitter *Story of a Country Town* was far in advance of its day, and seemed to derive from the earliest of the realistic novels, De Forest's *Miss Ravenal's Conversion* (1867). Garland's work was an extension of the local colorists' methods, in that it showed signs of the French naturalists' influence and spoke forthrightly of many things Howells would have excluded from his own novels. Before Garland, Harold Frederick had published *Seth's Brother's Wife* (1887), and ten years later *The Damnation of Theron Ware*, strong studies of rural life and the falsity in a type of organized religion. H. H. Boyeson's *The Mammon of Unrighteousness* (1891) and H. B. Fuller's *The Cliff Dwellers* (1893) again proved that the ground for realism was fallow and awaited only the tilling of truly expert hands.

A young man, son of a Newark Methodist minister, proved to have the hand that could till this soil. Stephen Crane at twenty years of age had written a short novel that remains today the epitome of early American naturalism with its oblique debt to Flaubert and Zola and its sound characterization of completely indigenous types. *Maggie: A Girl of the Streets* was completed in 1892, published at Crane's own expense in the next year, and finally brought out in 1896 by Appleton's after *The Red Badge of Courage* had made him internationally famous.

The distinction of *Maggie* as a pioneering effort, and the reason why it met with scant appreciation in its time, lay in its amorality of viewpoint. Crane wrote with an objectivity that would have won approval from Flaubert; detached and amoral, Crane's attitude confounded his readers, who might have forgiven a treatment of sordid themes if enough emphasis had been laid upon moralizing. But Crane contented himself with an austere reportage of what he had observed in the Bowery, and the world of *Maggie* is sinful without realizing its sin, ignorant without the possibility of knowledge, devoid of hope without dreaming there can be a salvation. Mag herself is a good woman, but she is destroyed by the ugly superstitions and social taboos of an evil society. There are no gleams of light in her story, which begins casually and ends without one climacteric moment. It is a stringent tragedy, and it made capital of all the elements left out of respectable novels of the day. Maggie's brother, Jimmie, "menaced mankind at the intersection of streets . . . dreaming blood-red dreams at the passing of pretty women." His career is one of seduction and betrayal. Two of his victims "caused him considerable annoyance by breaking forth simultaneously, at fateful intervals, into wailings about support, marriage and infants." Yet he has stirrings of a rudimentary aesthetic sense, for one evening he said feelingly, "Deh moon looks like hell, don't it?"

Maggie works as a wage slave at five dollars a week, and in time is seduced by a bartender; and when her mother turns her out into the streets even Jimmie, who might be expected to remonstrate, does nothing to stop her. Maggie tries to entice men into her room, but feeble and ill-favored, she cannot even succeed as a prostitute, and she ends her misery in the dark waters of the river. Crane concludes this inexorable drama: "In a room a woman sat at a table, eating like a fat monk in a picture. A soiled, unshaven man pushed open the door and entered. 'Well,' he said, 'Mag's dead.' "

In 1895 Crane published *The Red Badge of Courage,* a monumental treatment of war, and in the opinion of most critics, the first great American war story. It was written by a twenty-two-year-old who had never been in battle and whose interpretation of the reactions of a man under fire were wholly intuitional; yet participants in the Civil War admitted that its picture was entirely accurate. Crane had read and admired *War and Peace* and Zola's *The Downfall,* and it cannot be doubted that these were his guides. Fear, unashamed desire for self-preservation, and a complete lack of appetite for glory are the motivating factors in its protagonist's experience. He runs from war; there is absolutely nothing heroic in his make-up. He is a molecule caught up in a vast explosion, and his chief thought is how to save himself. This conception of war was so totally fresh to American fiction that *The Red Badge* caught on with the public and sold phenomenally.

With the creation of these two novels Stephen Crane's bright genius seemed to have expended itself. They were the products of a precocious youth who was led by his success to England and a divorcement from his roots; like Bret Harte, Joaquin Miller, Harold Frederick and other Americans, he scattered his powers and wrote little once he had broken ties with his origins. The short stories and poems remain as fragmentary evidence of a continuing creative function, but Crane died young without fulfilling his wonderful promise—a rebel to the end; as an artist, instinctive, often irrational, more highly gifted than any in his generation, and cut off by death long before he had arrived at artistic maturity.

A more dogged champion of the new realism was Frank Norris, another youth whose energies and life lasted a brief term (his published work covered only six years). Norris grew up in San Francisco, spent a year or more in Paris, and for one year matriculated at Harvard. While still an undergraduate at the University of California he began his best-constructed novel, though it remained unfinished until 1899. Starting as an admirer of the medieval romance, in a few years he was the chief disciple of Zola, and his fiction bore witness to the duality of his enthusiasms. For Norris, naturalism consisted not only in delineating the everyday occurrences of life but in accentuating the terrible or tragic. As he said, "The naturalist takes no note of common people, common in so far as their interests, their lives, and the things that occur in them are common, are ordinary. Terrible things must happen to the characters of the naturalistic tale. They must be twisted from the ordinary, wrenched from the quiet, uneventful round of everyday life and flung into the throes of a vast and terrible drama that works itself out in unleashed passions, in blood, and in sudden death."[1] This sounds far more like a defini-

---

[1] The San Francisco *Wave*.

tion of romance; and in Norris' practice, naturalism inhered only in the fact that he used common people for his characters. What happened to them was wildly "unnatural" or at any rate beyond the norm. He wrote truthfully, however, of their milieu and tried his best to include in his report of them the things that were taboo in the polite fiction of the time.

Zola was certainly the important influence in the writing of Norris' first novels, *McTeague*, published seven years after it was begun, and *Vandover and the Brute*, published after his death. Kipling, Richard Harding Davis and Stevenson charmed him simultaneously; and his first published novel bears evidence of his thralldom. *Moran of the Lady Letty* (1898) is Stevensonian in its concept and execution, the tale of a modern Brunnhilde subdued by a society youth against a background of sea adventure. For this novel Norris "worked up" his material through his acquaintance with an old sea dog, Captain Joseph Hodgson, and to this extent he was imitating the methods of Zola. The story has a Kiplingesque pace and movement, but it hardly foreshadows the strengths of the writer who was to crown his career with such a novel as *The Octopus*.

But in 1899 Norris had completed *McTeague*, begun in his college days, and American naturalism came suddenly of age. *McTeague* owed much to the Continental influence, but it was specifically American in the unembarrassed melodrama with which it was imbued. It was the kind of novel for which Howells had been asking, and which he himself could never write, for it had the viscera and sinews he did not wish to recognize. It spoke brutally of brutality; it investigated the noisome corners of existence and dwelt at length upon unsavory events and unadmirable people. The story of a conscienceless dentist, on San Francisco's Polk Street, *McTeague* deals with murder and bestiality in a way that seemed intolerable to the readers of that day. A reviewer in the San Francisco *Argonaut* said: "Seven tenths of the story the normal reader will peruse with a mixture of depression and disgust. We have heard Zola called 'Apôtre de ce qui pue.' Similarly, Mr. Norris riots in odors and stenches. He might have changed his sub-title and called his book 'McTeague: A Study in Stinks.' " Of course the hue and cry was of no moment; and the figure of the gigantic dentist has a living quality found in few other novels of the period. In character creation the book excelled all of the author's other novels, and as Howells wrote in a lengthy review: "It abounds in touches of character at once fine and free, in little miracles of observation, in vivid insight, in simple and subtile expression. Its strong movement carries with it a multiplicity of detail which never clogs it; the subordinate persons are never shammed or faked; in the equality of their treatment their dramatic inferiority is lost; their number is great enough to give the feeling of a world revolving around the central figures. . . ."[2]

Although *McTeague* is essentially a realistic novel, it also exhibits to a marked degree the romantic leanings of Norris. Its painstaking portraits of the lower middle class and workers, shopgirls, stew bums, merchants and loafers are in the realistic tradition; but the big moments of the book derive rather from Balzac than Zola. McTeague's friendship for Marcus Schouler that turns to hatred, and the developing avarice of McTeague's wife, Trina, recall Eugénie Grandet and Rastignac. And, of course, the stark melodrama of McTeague's end in the desert of Death Valley, handcuffed to the body of the man he has killed, has little to do with any conception Howells had of the purposes of realism. Norris contended that a novel must move slowly, carefully, toward its climax, but that it must increase with great acceleration toward the "big" scenes and end in a blaze of shocking power. *McTeague* did just that. Strong and sensational, it certainly marked a development away from the tepid realism of Howells; but it owed much to his methods, which had made the path for what public acceptance there was for *McTeague*.

The interim novels, *A Man's Woman* (1899) and *Blix* (1899), between *McTeague* and *The Octopus* are a reversion once more to romanticism. The former stemmed from Kipling and Norris' own *Moran*, while the latter was a more or less idyllic resume of its author's love affair with his future wife. Neither is of particular importance, although *Blix* is interesting for its evidence of

---

[2] *Literature*, March 24, 1899, quoted by Franklin Walker in *Frank Norris: A Biography* (1932).

a lyrical strain in Norris, later to be explicit in the story of Van-amee and the two Angéles in *The Octopus.*

By the time *McTeague* had stirred the American public to a recognition of the possibilities of naturalism, Norris had already made plans for a series of three "big novels" to be called "A Trilogy of Wheat." In two years he had finished the first of them, *The Octopus* (1901), and drawn heavily upon all his re-sources in an attempt to create an American novel that would stand for a thousand years. Like Howells and Zola, Norris be-lieved that a novel should have a "purpose," that its excuse for being, in addition to its entertainment value, lay in its influence upon the thought and action of its readers. But his background as a moneyed young man gave him no particular sympathy with the working class, and he never had Howells' or Zola's interest in socialism. Still, by the time he had hit upon his "idea as big as all outdoors," i. e., his "Trilogy of Wheat," certain personal adjustments had caused his eyes to be opened to the problems of the moneyless and expropriated. His parents were divorced, he lost the prospect of inheriting a fortune and was forced to earn his own living. This personal experience, combined with a nat-ural sympathy for the sufferings of humanity, and a contagion of ideas gotten from his reading, may have been the reason why Norris chose the role of reformer in *The Octopus.* The story of the struggle between California ranchers and the Southern Pa-cific Railroad for control of the rich San Joaquin valley wheat-land had all the elements of a social war, and therefore a titanic melodrama seemingly tailor-made for his talent and interests. Once he had completed this panel of his trilogy, there remained for volume two the drama of trading in wheat on the Chicago exchange. Finally, there would be the story of wheat's consump-tion—and he planned to show how the California harvest should save from famine the hungry hordes of Europe.

This was certainly a series of novels with a "purpose." And yet, in Norris' lexicon, the propaganda novel was a failure if it did no more than present a wooden argument. First of all, the novelist must tell a story. He must tell the truth. And that truth, if properly told, would constitute the purpose. His growing in-terest in the economic struggle was intensified through his association with such people as Lincoln Steffens, Ida Tarbell and Ray Stannard Baker, whose "muckraking" books were soon to set a new standard in journalism. But Norris chose to remain firm upon an aesthetic ground, and he wrote: "The moment . . . that the writer becomes really and vitally interested in his purpose his novel fails. Here is a strange anomaly. Let us suppose that Hardy, say, should be engaged upon a story which had for its purpose to show the injustices under which the miners of Wales are suffering. It is conceivable that he could write a story that would make the blood boil with indignation. But he himself, if he is to remain an artist, if he is to write his novel successfully, will, as a novelist, care very little about the iniquitous labor system of the Welsh coal mines. It will be to him as impersonal a thing as the key is to the composer of a sonata. As a man Hardy may or may not be vitally concerned in the Welsh coal miner. That is quite unessential. But as a novelist, as an artist, his sufferings must be for him a matter of the mildest interest. They are important, for they constitute his keynote. They are *not* interesting for the reason that the working out of his *story,* its people, episodes, scenes and pictures, is for the moment the most interesting thing in all the world to him, exclusive of everything else."[3] There was little danger that Norris would turn tractarian; he was too much the story-teller, too inveterately fascinated by the dramatic. And his sympathies were not likely to be touched to a degree that his eye for melodrama would be dimmed.

At any rate, *The Octopus* is both dramatic and heavy with its message. Magnus Derrick, the wealthy rancher, is a character built upon large design, and his story is the familiar one of a great man undermined and vanquished by small and evil men. He fights valiantly to save the valley and its farmers from the tentacles of the railroad, but he is predestined to failure. This important thread in the novel is reinforced by several equally interesting strands—the story of Dyke, the engineer, fired from his job; and there are the love stories of the rancher Annixter and Hilma Tree, and Vanamee and the Angéles. There are even proletarians in the book—the pitiful Hooven family, and in con-

---

[3] *The Responsibilities of the Novelist* (1903).

trast to them the autocratic Cedarquists, nabobs of San Francisco. Finally, there are the rich and powerful railroad magnates, Shelgrim and S. Behrman. With this array of contending personalities, and the enormous struggle of property which they must personify, *The Octopus* had innumerable opportunities for drama, and Norris missed none of them. Because of the size of his canvas, he managed to get an epic sweep in this story; the importance of his theme took hold of his sympathies, and enabled him to impart a human warmth in his characterizations that was not apparent in *McTeague*.

But the faults of the novel are great. Its structure comes near to splitting upon the rock of his dual intentions: the naturalism of the "canvas (swarming) with actualities—plowing, planting, harvesting, sheep-herding, merry-making, rabbit-killing, love, labor, birth, death," side by side with the mystical unreality of Vanamee's communication with his Angéle. And the determinism of the events—in which the railroad is alternately shown to be an inevitable development, its evil effects not to be ameliorated, and simultaneously as having been the result of machinations by immoral men—vitiates the philosophy which ought to have been consistent. The railroad, he tells us, is something greater than the men who operate it and are its slaves; yet he pronounces a moral judgment on those men. And at the end, when we have been shown an inexorable functioning of the deterministic principle, with the triumph of the railroad over the ranchers, and the golden deluge of wheat as also a force greater than the men who produce it or those who distribute it, and mankind a puppet in the hands of a soulless force—then we are told what we are absolutely unprepared to expect from the premises or to subscribe to: "The larger view always and through all shams, all wickednesses, discovers the Truth that will, in the end, prevail, and all things, surely, inevitably, resistlessly, work together for good."

Flamboyant, enthusiastic, Norris was inconsistent and boyish.[4]

---

[4] Franklin Walker relates that Norris once wrote an editorial beginning with one point of view and ending with another. "He started it with enthusiasm, was interrupted, and returned to finish it with a fresh burst of energy, only to find on re-reading that he had completely reversed his opinion during the intermission."

His was not an orderly mind. When we inspect his literary style we find the natural consequence of this lack of discipline. Norris' style, like that of many naturalists, is slovenly, loose, turgid. He cares little for the *mot juste*, and he is far more interested in telling too much than too little. We have a deluge of adjectives, phrases, descriptive passages, like a barrage of heavy artillery—aimed more or less in the direction of interest, and through sheer weight of numbers covering their target. Those who are sensitive to fine prose find it difficult to read Zola, Norris, Dreiser, Farrell and their like. And Norris, like his compeers in naturalism, was the victim of still another weakness inherent in his literary philosophy. His novels were "thought up," prepared in advance with maps, character sketches and a program. The fusing quality of a supreme imagination seems lacking. We feel that the story is after all "made up," and this failure of imagination sets Norris on a lower level than the truly great novelists.

This failure is pointed up very clearly in *The Pit* (1903). Here Norris was hampered by the requirements of his preconceived theme, and the operations of the Chicago wheat market, the chicane of business, the confining elements of a different society and activity served him poorly. The wonder is that he made so much of a theme which was certainly uncongenial either to his interest or his talent. Curtis Jadwin, the market operator, is not the typical tycoon of the age, and he is no ruthless Cowperwood, but an amoral, blundering plaything in the hands of a force he cannot even comprehend. The corner in wheat that he is instrumental in engineering becomes a juggernaut for his destruction. Norris flounders in the narrow quarters of this novel, and we see that, to work successfully, he needed a broad canvas and the stuff of humanity with which to deal.

The contribution of Frank Norris to the naturalistic strain of our fiction is extremely significant. As a pioneer, he forced the acceptance of a more robust conception of realism than Howells could have endorsed. His treatment in *McTeague* of unsavory elements in our collective life, and his sprawling power in *The Octopus* to evoke the whole life and habits and backgrounds and even folk customs of a region, cleared the way for those who would work in the dominant mode for the next forty years. If he had lived he might have fused the diverse elements of his philosophy and his art, and created an enduring monument of American realism. Nevertheless, his service to American fiction was of the greatest importance; he stood by his guns in an unfriendly era, and as he himself put it, "I never truckled; I never took off the hat to Fashion and held it out for pennies. By God, I told them the truth!"

THEODORE DREISER
Philosopher

WHEN Theodore Dreiser died in 1946 his enormous reputation had already suffered considerable diminution from what it had been in the 1920's. In the literary weeklies and reviews dutiful appreciations appeared, but they were on the whole temperate; and Dreiser had evidently outlived the heyday of his fame. The frame of America's postwar literary mind was alienated from the heavy naturalism which had been Dreiser's forte, and while due acknowledgment was made to his pioneering of forbidden trails in the novel, the assessment of his art was severe. It repeated the hoary strictures on his stumbling prose, reiterated the old diatribes against his groping philosophy, and held up to ridicule the mechanistic concept of the universe which Dreiser had from his youthful reading of Huxley and Darwin.

And yet it was impossible for the honest critic to deny that Dreiser, more than any other twentieth-century American novelist, had worked greatly in the tradition of novelists of other times and lands. Perhaps we have never had a novelist who came nearer to Tolstoy, Fielding and Balzac as the chronicler of Life. For him the novel was a vast crucible into which could be poured everything—his observation of manners, characterization of men and women, thoughts on issues of the day, his entire reading of the meaning of existence. The novel, in Dreiserian terms, was a carryall, vast, sprawling, all-inclusive, to be written with sincerity, eschewing all tricks and contrivance. It was to enclose all the truths that its writer knew, and nothing could be alien to it. Its very artlessness was to be its strength; the only thing to be avoided was artificiality or deception. And, in the year 1900, when *Sister Carrie* made its inauspicious debut, this was something quite new to our fiction.

McTeague had appeared in the preceding year, but Dreiser had not read it. It is doubtful that, if he had known Norris' work then, it would have made much difference in Dreiser's development as an American literary naturalist. There probably has never been a writer as oblivious to currents of abuse or praise as Dreiser, and hence few writers as unlikely to be influenced by the work of others. His development must be accounted for in other ways. Norris acknowledged his debt to Zola; but Dreiser apparently owed no direct debt to anyone.

Because Norris, as reader for Doubleday, Page & Co., was first to perceive the merits of *Sister Carrie*, and urged its publication, there have been those who have argued a continuity, in Dreiser, of the Norris naturalistic tradition. But Dreiser had never met Norris and was unfamiliar with his work.[1] He was grateful for the recognition, and later he saw that they had indeed held similar views as to the philosophy of the novel. Nor was Dreiser acquainted with Zola, though he had read Flaubert. Perhaps the chief influence was Hardy, whom he read for the first time in 1896; and there are certainly points of likeness in *Tess of the D'Urbervilles* and *Sister Carrie*. If so, Dreiser's introduction to naturalism came in a roundabout way, from France, via England, without benefit of any American influences at all.

The really significant thing about Dreiser's literary origins lies in his personal background. The son of lower middle-class Teutonic immigrants, he grew up on the wrong side of the tracks in Warsaw, Indiana. Life as he saw it in his formative years was a drab battle with unfriendly elements, and took on principally the form of a perpetual warfare at the lowest economic levels. To eat was the primary struggle; and the aspiration of those in his circle was always to get money in order to rise above the animal

---

[1] Reported by Dreiser in a conversation I had with him in 1937.

existence. Growing up in a total isolation from the artistic, Dreiser's perception of beauty was a slow growth; it was unnurtured and formless; like his education, it was empirical in every detail. When finally he was able to get hold of books, he devoured everything in sight. He has recorded his delight in the discovery of E. P. Roe, Lew Wallace, Stevenson, Dumas, Tolstoy, Balzac, Poe, Hardy, Sienkiewicz, Scott, Kingsley, Dickens, Thackeray, Hawthorne, Irving, Bret Harte, Howells, Holmes and George Ebers. He says, "I used to lie under a tree and read *Twice Told Tales* by the hour. I thought *The Alhambra* was a perfect creation, and I still have a lingering affection for it."[2] His omnivorousness was not confined to belles lettres. He began to read philosophy, and at twenty-three discovered Spencer and Huxley, whereupon any piety he may have had was gravely undermined. Born to question the shibboleths of ethic and morality, sensitive to the divergence between what was reported to be true of society and that which he had endured in his own youth, he quickly turned his back on the platitudes of religion, and swallowed whole the determinism of the nineteenth-century scientists. He was swept clean, as he said, of the faith of his boyhood, medieval Rhenish Catholicism, and from then on dedicated himself to searching out the underlying causes for all human behavior.

The search was never rewarded. Dreiser was the eternal agnostic, the incessant questioner, fumbling for truth and finding it forever beyond his reach. About the nearest he came to conclusions was to say that we are like floss, adrift and at the mercy of currents we cannot understand. In his middle life, at the height of his intellectual powers, he could come no nearer to making a positive statement than this:

"I have lived now to my fortieth year and have seen a good deal of life. . . . But I am one of those curious persons who cannot make up their minds about anything. I read and read. . . . But I find that one history contradicts another, one philosopher drives out another. Essayists, in the main, point out flaws and paradoxes

---

[2] From *A Book of Prefaces* by H. L. Mencken. © 1922 by A. Knopf.

in the current conception of things, novelists, dramatists and biographers spread tales of endless disasters, or silly illusions concerning life, duty, opportunity and the like. And I sit here and read and read, when I have time, wondering."[3]

But it would be impossible for a novelist to write without having some basic beliefs, and Dreiser of course had them. While the world might have no meaning, or none that was intelligible to humanity, the actions of men had their causes, though they might be in the main ignoble ones. Within the bounds of social convention and moral taboo, men do whatever they can. They desire power and pleasure, and these drives are at bottom of all their actions. The strong man dominates the weak; it is not a question of goodness or badness. Since we are at best but marvelously complex chemical compounds, the successful among us are those who triumph over the failures. There is no understandable meaning in the universe; its vast uncomprehendable force grants us an allotted span of activity unless by the accidental operation of its forces we collide with its intentions, which we cannot know—in which event we are wiped out in the batting of an eye. This is determinism, of course, and it was a philosophy that Mark Twain, Crane and Norris all subscribed to in greater or lesser degree, and was the prevailing philosophy of the time.

Nevertheless, Dreiser is deeply concerned with the plight of man in this cheerless universe. He is suffused by a vast pity for man caught in the toils of circumstance. There is little that we can do about it, but pity tends to soften the harshness of our lot. As a novelist, it is pity alone that brings Dreiser's view of life within the bounds of human endurance. "Let no one underestimate the need, of pity. We live in a stony universe whose hard, brilliant forces rage fiercely. From the prowling hunger of the Hyrcan tiger to the concentric grip of Arcturus and Canopus there is the same ruthless, sightless disregard of the individual and the minor thing. Life moves in an ordered hierarchy of forces of which the lesser is as nothing to the greater. . . . And in the midst of the rip of desperate things—in odd crannies and chance flaws

---

[3] From *Hey, Rub-a-Dub-Dub* by Theodore Dreiser. © 1920 by the author.

between forces—there spring and blossom these small flowers of sentiment. Tenderness! Mercy! Affection! Sorrow! The Hindus worship an image of pain. And well they may. It is a classic amid the painless, the indifferent—Nirvana. Blessed are the merciful, for they shall receive mercy! No, no. Blessed are the merciful, for they create mercy. Of such is the kingdom of the ideal."[4]

Yet all of Dreiser's work is a direct refutation of this somewhat adolescent doctrine. The boundless energy that went into the creation of the seven monumental novels could hardly have been exerted if Dreiser had taken his own counsel. And the pity of which he is the champion, and for which he is justly admired, is the key to the resolution of his paradoxes. It proves that the tiger in man is by no means supreme, that it is just by the degree to which he is aware of his fellowship in pain that he shows his manhood, and places himself in a different category from the chemical reaction which Dreiser claims all life to be. The fact that his novels champion man against the forces that prey upon him is conclusive evidence that there rests in men a power resistant to the blind forces of the universe, that man does possess a will in defiance of natural law, and that there must be a potency within him not measurable in the scientist's laboratory. At the end of his life Dreiser recognized and, in *The Bulwark*, acknowledged these truths.

The great service of a concept of life such as Dreiser entertained was that it helped him to strip away without ceremony the false ideals and petty bourgeois morality that was stifling American fiction at the time he began to write. With an overall view so austere, he could never be concerned with the minor proscriptions of Puritan morality that hamstrung such writers as Mark Twain and W. D. Howells. His whole intention would be to reveal the true motives of men and spike the illusions men entertain. The "animal called man" would work out his destiny on the basis of his animalism: his twin urges for power and for pleasure. Being largely unaware of the taboos that a politer culture might have fastened upon him, Dreiser, the tireless, self-taught

---

[4] From *The Financier* by Theodore Dreiser. © 1912 by the author.

prober, would write of life as it seemed to him. A provincial, he would not be worried about breaking rules or wounding sensitive social tissues. He could be ashamed of nothing, for man is too puny a creature for shame. If the truth seemed brutal, that was no fault of his. He had not made the universe, and he could not be responsible for the wretchedness of the creatures inhabiting it. Neither could he blame men for being wretched; the "scheme of things" was responsible. In this detachment lay Dreiser's great strength. It made possible a literary naturalism of the first order, without benefit of strategy or a formal concept of the novelist's art.

In his twenties Dreiser worked on several newspapers in Chicago, Toledo, Cleveland and New York. He had aspirations to write for the stage, but fiction had never interested him. By chance he was encouraged to try his hand at short stories and sold the first four he wrote. Then in 1899 he sat down to write *Sister Carrie,* and completed about half of the novel in two months. He had little faith in it, and put it aside for a time. Six months later it was finished and on the press. Its publication difficulties are well known; after coming from the printer it was withheld at the request of offended members of the Doubleday family. A few copies were sent to reviewers who treated it respectfully, and it was published in England. Seven years later it appeared again in America, and won a good public. In the intervening years, however, Dreiser had been discouraged and published nothing. Such was the condition of American taste in those years. A story in which a bad woman went unpunished had little chance of being read. But such a novel could not be ignored, particularly when England gave it sanction. Still, it made its way so slowly that Dreiser realized little from it and resorted to hack writing for the next ten years.

As a first book, *Sister Carrie* is surely one of the most remarkable novels ever written by an American. In many respects it is the best novel Dreiser wrote, for it not only contains his most lucid prose, but a minimum of the philosophizing with which he has a tendency to burden his stories. It has a certain charm which none of the other Dreiser novels possess, and its insights are always true. Carrie as a woman is revealed whole, and she is marvelously alive. Almost overshadowing the story of Carrie herself is the wonderful narrative of Hurstwood—one of the most moving treatments of the theme of a man's fall since it was introduced by the Greek dramatists.

For all its length and seeming complexity, *Sister Carrie* is a simple story involving four major characters: Carrie, the waif from the hinterland who comes to Chicago seeking wider horizons; Drouet, the "drummer" who befriends her and makes her his mistress; Hurstwood, whose pursuit of Carrie is the initial link in the chain of his disasters; and Mrs. Hurstwood, an archetypal figure of the injured wife. The fulcrum of their relationship is the fatal attraction of Carrie; and the principal difference between Dreiser's treatment and that of a hundred other novelists who have dealt with a similar theme was that Carrie, the reagent for so much tragedy, herself went scot free. To be sure, Dreiser tells us at the end that she will never know either surfeit or content. "In your rocking-chair, by your window dreaming, shall you long, alone. In your rocking-chair, by your window, shall you dream such happiness as you may never feel." But at any rate, in the course of her story she is not made to suffer as the moralists of the day would have desired. She was, on the whole, successful and at no time particularly conscious of having sinned. Nor did the author make apparent his disapproval of her actions; in fact, he neither approved nor disapproved. This was the way things were. By withholding censure, many readers felt that he in effect condoned Carrie's conduct. This same objectivity in the other Dreiser novels led to much condemnation by self-appointed defenders of the public morals. It made Dreiser the object of vilification, and very nearly turned him from fiction altogether.

Yet *Sister Carrie* is a moral book. There have been many studies of broken marriages since the picture of Hurstwood's defection and headlong pursuit of an amoral woman—studies that make this one seem very tame indeed. There is not a line in this early "outspoken" novel that could be described as inciting to immorality; certainly nothing in the solemn account of Hurstwood's infatuation with Carrie, in his willingness to throw up all that had given his life meaning: social position, the esteem of friends, and personal honor. And of course his eventual defalcation with his firm's money points the moral of human frailty and the error of men making profit and pleasure their goals. Far from censuring these misguided creatures, Dreiser offers them his pity, and he broods upon their shortcomings, as if he were saying, "Here is life as I see it, but I cannot explain why it is thus and not otherwise; and why should we blame these unhappy beings? —they act as they do because life is this way."

It is difficult to see why the Mrs. Doubledays of that time could have found anything reprehensible in *Sister Carrie;* but one reason for our emancipation from that type of blindness is precisely because Dreiser and his followers continued to write truthfully of the life they had known and observed, and foreswore the cheap romanticizing of the popular novelists or the timid objectivity of Howells.

In a sense *Jennie Gerhardt* (1911) is the artistic fruition of the story for which *Sister Carrie* was a rough draft. In the eleven years that elapsed between the two novels Dreiser had increased his perception of life and in retelling substantially the same story, had managed to find new terms for it. Once again he presents an untutored country girl overwhelmed by the life of a great city, taken in by its false splendors, and brought to bed by men who have little understanding of her true quality. Jennie is perhaps more sentient than Carrie, and she has the finer nature. She finds wealth, and in wealth had hoped to find also a larger life; but although her experiences awaken her to a dim sense of possible beauty, she can never attain to such a state of grace. In the end she is left to rue the follies of her early action, and to realize that they precluded future happiness. Senator Brander and Lester Kane, the men through whom her life was both unfolded and soiled, are agents like Drouet and Hurstwood; and we are made to feel Jennie's tragedy as acutely as we do Carrie's. Jennie has been the center of our interest throughout the novel; and there has been no powerful interlude, like the story of Hurstwood, to distract our attention from her. Technically, then, *Jennie Ger-*

hardt is the better constructed, but it still does not have the warmth and gusto of the first book.

In *The Financier* (1912) Dreiser attacked one of the naturally big themes of his time. His selection of it, as much as his achievement, proves the unerring sense of contemporaneity that the great novelists possess. With all the shortcomings of *The Financier* and its continuation, *The Titan*, these novels still represent the most considerable treatment of the type of robber baron which America produced in the closing decades of the last century. Here Dreiser based his story on the facts in the career of Charles T. Yerkes (as he was later to base *An American Tragedy* on an actual criminal case) but he raised the story completely beyond the realm of prosaic biography and made of Frank Cowperwood a human being great in his weaknesses and strengths and, above all, recognizable as a man. The coexistent urges which, Dreiser says, impel all men to action, are of about equal intensity in Cowperwood. His will to power and his love of pleasure are the prime movers for all his deeds; anything that stands in the way is brushed aside, including honor and duty. There is nothing hypocritical about him. He acts according to his nature. "He saw no morals anywhere—nothing but moods, emotions, needs, greeds. People talked and talked, but they acted according to their necessities and desires."[5]

Cowperwood climbs slowly and steadily to positions of eminence and wealth by taking advantage of the weakness and ignorance of others. He is shrewd, affable, strong; and it causes him little discomfort to realize that his own success must always come at the expense of others' failure. This is as true of his activity in the realm of love as in business. When his wife no longer has power to move him sexually, he has no hesitation in casting her aside. He is completely consistent in his philosophy. Although he suffers reverses and goes to prison for a time, he never loses faith in his abilities or in the ultimate vindication of his philosophy. From one fall he goes on to new triumphs so that, at the close of the first volume, he sees himself on the threshold of

[5] From *The Financier* by Theodore Dreiser. © 1912 by the author.

even greater success, both as a tycoon and as a lover. All this, however, by no means represents Dreiser's views; and his contemporary critics went far astray in ascribing to him a philosophy paralleling his hero's. The future for Cowperwood might seem to include bright vistas: ". . . a world of mansions, carriages, jewels, beauty; a vast metropolis outraged by the power of one man; a great State seething with indignation over a force it could not control; vast halls of priceless pictures; a palace unrivalled for its magnificence; a whole world reading with wonder, at times, of a given name . . ." But, as the author's prescience told, there was also to be ". . . sorrow, sorrow, sorrow."

The Titan (1914) brings Cowperwood to the height of his vaulting career as master of a railroad empire; but it brings him low at last—the superman whose ambition could never be realized, since the mass of mankind is always greater than any individual. The forces of life and society are shifting and undependable, and the strong man cannot always remain strong. As age and the flux of social forces impinge upon Cowperwood, he finds himself unequal to the battle; at last his stockholders have their day in court. The mighty empire he has built crumbles about him.

The Financier and *The Titan* were to have been followed by a third volume, carrying Cowperwood's operations abroad, and showing him monarch of an international cartel. But for whatever reason, Dreiser postponed and finally abandoned this "Trilogy of Desire." Perhaps he knew that he had already said all that mattered about the archetypal buccaneer of finance. At any rate, he turned next to another type of American, the predatory artist whose primal urge was beauty and through beauty, pleasure. Eugene Witla of *The "Genius"* (1915) epitomizes again a kind of man whose meanings are found in the exploitation of his sensual nature. Witla is in effect an embodied five senses, dependent wholly upon sensuous stimulation for his ego-drive. *The "Genius"* is a long, muddy narrative that traces the child into man, and the man into his ripe maturity. In the course of this long chronicle Eugene has many affairs, paints many pictures, and emerges, like Cowperwood, a plaything in the "trap of circumstance." He tries through pleasure to alleviate the sufferings of his lot on earth, and in striving for beauty misses happiness; seeking an illusion, grasping at chance opportunities for gratification of his senses, he ends tragically, as all men must do who strive for unattainable ends.

The "Genius" is perhaps the least impressive of the novels for the reason that its chief character contains in himself little of the stuff that makes for drama. Witla is weak, and his vacillations are less exhilarating than depressing. Cowperwood is strong, and his conflict with the world makes for absorbing contests. Witla's weakness, his surrender to fleshly ease, and his recurrent attempts to impose himself upon the artistic world are finally monotonous. Dreiser takes occasion to interject a good deal of moralizing on platitudinous levels, slowing up an already interminable and lethargic story.

Nearly ten years passed before Dreiser published another novel. In the meanwhile he wrote books of travel, short stories, plays and autobiography. His fame was great, if disputed, and he was accepted as the leading naturalistic writer in America. The school of Midwestern writers, in revolt from the small town and from the increasing mechanization of American life, began its triumphant career under the banner of realism. Sherwood Anderson wrote his halting, tentative stories of escape; Sinclair Lewis satirized the more obvious shallows of American civilization in flippant novels; James Branch Cabell wove his delicate, preposterous web of historical satire; Edith Wharton, Joseph Hergesheimer, Willa Cather, Zona Gale and Floyd Dell wrote with varying degrees of success in realistic terms about the life they knew. Truly Howells' feeble grasshopper had now been dissected and classified with a thoroughness he would have found amazing.

With the coming of the first World War, a new generation of writers was to emerge, and their reading of life was to enhance Dreiser's reputation, for their findings were natural extensions of his. And during all this time Dreiser continued to probe gently, wonderingly, through the maze of his own mind—to look introspectively at his experience and set down in book after book what he knew and remembered. Few of these are of much interest now; the saving grace of his great compassionateness and his deep imaginative sympathy are largely absent from them; and they cannot be read for their style, which is indeed the deplorable and most serious weakness of Dreiser. In *A Traveler at Forty* (1913), *A Hoosier Holiday* (1916), *A Book About Myself* (1922) and *Hey, Rub-a-Dub-Dub* (1920) he explained his background and convictions, and revealed to the discerning mind how he had come to be what he was—an unsophisticated observer of a world about which he could draw few conclusions. But he also wrote, in *Twelve Men* (1919) and *A Gallery of Women* (1929), some individual studies of actual persons which, for their honest, painstaking care, are on a par with his novels. Their relative unimportance is due to their brevity; for Dreiser, like all naturalists, had to have a great canvas to work upon; his effects are cumulative. For this reason he was never at home in the short story. As with Farrell and Dos Passos, it is the weight of all the evidence that brings home to us Dreiser's meanings. In the shorter forms we are too conscious of the lack of grace, the uninspired stylistic medium, the episodic character of the writing.

During this hiatus in novel production, Dreiser must have been storing up energy to produce his *magnum opus*, with which he might hope to rest his claims to greatness: *An American Tragedy* (1925). There is evidence that he planned this novel carefully, gave it steady consideration and, when he came to work on it, wrote confidently in a way he had not done, probably, since the days of *Sister Carrie*. His imagination stimulated by a famous crime of several years before, he took the plain incidents and lifted them into a realm of universality, and yet he leaned heavily for a good proportion of the story upon printed records of the court trial. This was certainly evidence of the naturalist's interest in the brute fact, that what happened in life could be a transcript for fiction. In its essentials, the tragic story of Clyde Griffiths and Roberta Alden had been enacted in real life; now the artist had only to imagine the antecedents of Clyde's crime to make of the story a representative document for all time.

The great advantage of *An American Tragedy* over its predecessors was that it dramatized rather than reported its events. For the first time and the only time in Dreiser's career as a novelist he had a subject that could be presented dramatically for at least three-fourths of its length. As a result this novel, despite its tremendous size (840 closely printed pages), has much the best integrated dramatic structure of any Dreiser novel. The others are chronicles—espisodic, with long narrative passages in which events are told as being of the past, rather than immediately presented. But the romance of Clyde and Roberta, the error of Clyde's infatuation with Sondra, his decision to drown Roberta, who is with child by him, so that he may be free to marry Sondra, and the inexorable justice that descends upon him for his error —this is dramatic situation, and it demanded to be written with an eye always upon the moment. Basically the story is without novelty; in fact, at first glance it even appears unpromising. But in the hands of a writer of Dreiser's sympathies and tragic sense, it became a great one. He explored every possible mutation of his theme; he probed more deeply and developed greater significance from the simple human story than had been done by any American who handled a similar theme before him.

It has been said that Dreiser posited, in the environmental conditions for which he blames Clyde's crime, an explanation contrary to the evidence submitted by his story. If the boy had been reared in any other environment, these critics say, he would still have committed his crime. It is not the fault of the false American dream of higher social position, the lure of wealth and pleasure, that caused Clyde's downfall, but a weakness inherent in the boy. But the truth is, Dreiser never made such a claim. He shows us Clyde Griffiths a poor youth among boys of higher social rank, with money to spend, and Clyde's whole fault is his endeavor to enter the closed circle of wealth, represented by expensive motor cars, summer homes, lawn parties—and of course the lovely daughters of the rich. Clyde was weak from the beginning; like Eugene Witla, he gravitated to pleasure as a bee is attracted to a flower; and the pleasure he once received in the arms of Roberta seems a poor thing as compared to the more glittering allure of Sondra, whose beauty is reinforced by the accoutrements of wealth. The moment of moral decision for Clyde comes when, rowing on the lake with Roberta, he accidentally strikes her and upsets the boat. He can save her, but he allows her to drown. Nearly all of the latter half of the novel is devoted to a minute description of how Clyde was apprehended, and of his trial and conviction. He moves toward contrition and almost to a faith in God. Just before he goes to the electric chair he manages to say: " 'Mama, you must believe that I die resigned and content. It won't be hard. God has heard my prayers. He has given me strength and peace.' But to himself adding: 'Had he?' "

An American Tragedy contains the poetry of a great man's heart; in many of Dreiser's pages there is this beauty of feeling that, unfortunately, is seldom combined with felicity of phrase. Despite the awkward expression, this poetry of spirit makes itself felt; it is intangible and difficult to cite; but it is there. And the Dreiser who tells this story is the same questioning, doubting Dreiser of the early novels, unwilling or unable to offer a shred of comfort. He reports what to him are the facts of existence, and hard though they may be, we must confront them. Our pity and understanding will help blunt the sharpest edges of disaster; but disaster we must expect.

After the publication of this major work, nothing more of importance came from his pen until after his death. As America moved into the years of depression, Dreiser, whose interest in the working class had always been great and his sympathies greater, embraced the Communist Party. He made lecture tours and harangued the uplift societies on the inequities of capitalism. His attitude toward his own art was refreshingly offhand; and among our novelists his disregard for fame was so unusual as to be considered eccentric. He lived on into an era when the novel had become the vehicle of experiment, when younger men had preempted the scene and, acknowledging him their master, had done things in the field that were undreamed of in his time. Caldwell, Dos Passos, Fisher, Farrell and many others working in the naturalistic vein had made advances far beyond the frontiers established by *Sister Carrie* and *The Financier*.

When, in 1946, *The Bulwark* was published a few months after

Dreiser's death, it came like an anachronism out of the early years of the century. Here was a novel that spoke in the tones of the late Victorians, and seemed heavy-handed and old-fashioned; yet it was filled again with many of the strengths that had made Dreiser a towering figure in the novel, and indeed in one respect presented a significant alteration in his philosophy. Had it appeared between *The "Genius"* and *An American Tragedy*, when from internal evidence the greater part of it was almost certainly written, it would have created a profound impression. Coming from the presses in an era that was worlds away in temper and taste, it created hardly a ripple.

The Bulwark tells the story of Solon Barnes of Philadelphia, a Quaker, who, like Frank Cowperwood, became a financial power before the first World War. Unlike Cowperwood, Barnes is a man of integrity and ideals. The first part of his life is an idyl. Everything he cherishes as being worth while comes to him. He marries his childhood sweetheart, Benecia Wallin. He goes to work in Wallin's bank and ultimately is made a director. To him and Benecia are born five children, Isobel, Orville, Dorothea, Stewart and Etta, in whom he takes great pride. But—and this is the source of his tragedy—his children grow up in a different world from that he knew, and none of them accepts the moral order he stands for. Etta runs away from home and enters the artistic world of Greenwich village. Stewart, pleasure mad, is instrumental in the death of a virtueless young woman, and kills himself. Solon Barnes is bewildered by the inescapable realization that all his good intentions are mocked, that there is no way of securing good merely from good will. But, bludgeoned though he is by circumstance, he does not swerve from a belief in the ultimate certainty of divine truth—the "Inner Light." He remains a bulwark of faith in a world tottering to ruin.

The key to Dreiser's philosophy in all his earlier work is found in the brief afterword of *The Financier*, where we are given a sketch of the life and habits of a sea creature called the Black Grouper, whose peculiar mode of protecting itself is an ability to assume the color of its surroundings.[6] "Lying at the bottom of

[6] From *The Financier* by Theodore Dreiser. © 1912 by the author.

a bay, it can simulate the mud by which it is surrounded. Hidden in the folds of glorious leaves, it is of the same markings. . . . Its power to elude or strike unseen is of the greatest." Arraigning the concept of divine purpose informing the universe, Dreiser goes on: "What would you say was the intention . . . which gives . . . this ability? To fit it to be truthful? . . . Or would you say that subtlety, chicanery, trickery, were here at work? . . . Would you say, in the face of this, that a beatific, beneficent creative, overruling power never wills that which is either tricky or decepitve?"

As this is the paramount symbol of the earlier Dreiser, one can judge the extent of conversion undergone in the twenty-year silence between *An American Tragedy* and *The Bulwark*, by examining the explicit symbol of his later attitude. Solon Barnes, near the end of his trials, walks in his garden one day, observing the [7]"various vegetative and insect forms obviously devised and energized by the Creative Force that created all things in apparently endless variety of designs and colors." His attention is drawn to a "small twig that bore a small bud" upon which "was perched, and eating the bud, an exquisitely colored and designed green fly. . . . Why was this beautiful creature, whose design so delighted him, compelled to feed upon another living creature, a beautiful flower?" His conclusion, so vastly different from Dreiser's own brooding upon the subject of the Black Grouper: [7]"Surely there must be a Creative Divinity, and so a purpose, behind all of this variety and beauty and tragedy of life."

In his wondering, his awe, his final humility before the greatest questions that man can ask, Theodore Dreiser showed himself to be of the company of the great tragic writers. Like Etta, in the wonderful words with which *The Bulwark* ends, Dreiser seems to say,[7] "Oh, I am not crying for myself, or for Father—I am crying for *life*."

---

[7] From *The Bulwark* by Theodore Dreiser. © 1946 by Doubleday & Co., Inc.

JOHN DOS PASSOS
Literary Collectivist

THE NOTE of social protest that sounds with increasing portentousness through the works of all American literary naturalists became, in the work of John Dos Passos, strong and clear, and was the most noteworthy feature of his novels. Howells' socialism was a lazy intellectual conviction arrived at late in life. Mark Twain was sympathetic, but believed that society and its components were ultimately damned. Crane's interest in the poor was largely clinical. Norris never realized his burgeoning socialism and was too dazzled by the spectacle of power and drama in American life to probe very deeply. Dreiser gave his personal support to the Left, but in his work was content to depict the miseries of the disinherited. But Dos Passos made the battleground of class conflict his particular province and produced the first, and still the most artistic, long fiction based on broad social issues.

It would have been difficult to predict, from the early manifestations of Dos Passos' interests, that he would one day be considered a foremost champion of the underprivileged. He attended Choate and Harvard, and was one of the youthful aesthetes who joined an ambulance unit early in World War I. His first novel, *One Man's Initiation* (1919), expressed the typical sensitive young artist's reaction to the brutality and horror of war. Its hero, Martin Howe, hates everything about the war, principally because it interferes with his aesthetic appreciation of Europe. There is little evidence that the conflict meant anything more to Dos Passos than a nightmare hindrance to his absorption of beauty. He had grown up in the rarefied atmosphere of academicism ("four years under the ether cone", as he later said) and had been out of touch with rude life. It took a little time for the purple veils of aestheticism to be stripped from his eyes. And yet they were removed, and with finality, once he orientated himself.

249

This came about sometime before the publication of *Three Soldiers* (1921). It would be interesting to know exactly what precipitated the extraordinary change from the vague preciosity of *One Man's Initiation* to the hard-boiled realism of *Three Soldiers*. Partly, of course, it was a more mature estimation of the war experience itself, and perhaps it was also the example of such disillusioned fiction as was produced during the war in France and England. There was, probably, a warring dichotomy within Dos Passos' own personality all the while; even as a Harvard youth he must have been uneasy in the knowledge that he was, to some degree, set apart—the son of a Portuguese father, with ties of blood to the great immigrant hordes that made up America's polyglot people. He was an outsider, in a way, and he could look at the sons of the rich with an objective eye, in the times when he did not imagine himself to be one with them. He was different from them; and those differences came to the top when he finally broke with tradition and wrote the first tough, realistic, bitter World War I book, *Three Soldiers*.

It is difficult to estimate at this distance of time, with a greater war intervening, the unusual effect *Three Soldiers* had on the reading public of 1921. After a spate of romantically presented war stories celebrating war's opportunity for private heroism and its sacred nature, this novel burst like a bombshell into the post-war mood of disillusion, and probably helped increase it. Crane's *Red Badge of Courage* had similar repercussions, but this time the results were even more overpowering. No American had written so devastating a criticism of war's effects upon the individual, no American had dared to write so candidly about the individual's real attitude toward the army machine that destroyed his manhood as surely as its guns could destroy his body. The novel's three soldiers—Fuselli, the young San Franciscan of Italian parentage; Chrisfield, the Indiana-born farm boy; and Andrews, the New Yorker with a college education—all are ground under the wheels of the monstrous machine. Fuselli is the deluded neophyte; he wants to abide by the rules and win glory, as he has been told he may by the jingoes back home. To become a corporal is his driving ambition, but he goes through the same rigid processes of training and the mass molding which turns him into a hard-bitten cynic with an additional handicap of venereal disease contracted from a French woman. Chrisfield, the individualist, develops a burning hatred for a superior officer who has subjected him to various humiliations. His experience is to kill his officer in one of the most bitter episodes of war fiction. But Andrews is the fulcrum of the novel, for he is the man who is most worth saving, and for whom salvation is least possible. Sensitive and aesthetically aware, Andrews can find no one to talk with, no moment of inner peace; the grinding of the machine wears upon him with inexorable force. The mud, stench, blood and death are a continuing inferno for him, and only when he goes AWOL does he momentarily reach stature as a man. A musician, he has only the unquenchable desire to go on with his composition, a work to be known as "The Queen of Sheba." When the Armistice is signed, and he finds that he cannot obtain a discharge, he deserts. He seems to know that his desertion is only an interlude and that he has been on the treadmill too long ever to escape it. The old song, "John Brown's Body," choruses in his mind as the time of his recapture comes . . . and he is given into custody of the military police by his concierge. As he is marched away, his music on which he had been working dissolves into the limbo of forever unattainable ambition. "On John Andrews's writing table the brisk wind rustled among the broad sheets of paper. First one sheet, then another, blew off the table, until the floor was littered with them."

As for technique, which has always been of primary importance to Dos Passos, *Three Soldiers* foreshadows much of the fictional method employed through all the novels up to and including *The Big Money*. In every sense a child of his century, Dos Passos has been as greatly influenced by the technical innovations of his contemporaries as he has been interested in the immediate historical scene. In France, at the close of the First World War, a literary movement was on foot called Unamism, of which Jules Romains was probably the chief proponent. Dos Passos' interest in Unamism, whether he knew it by that name, was extreme, for it seemed to offer an ideal method of translating into fiction his broadening social interests. Unamism, as Romains had pointed out, was a literary philosophy which embraced social masses and performed a panoramic function in contradistinction to the traditional method of presenting the story of one character or group of characters in chronological sequence. *Three Soldiers* attempts, in a limited way, to fuse the experiences of three young men, and its sequences move intermittently from one to another, sometimes bringing them together, although essentially their stories are separate. The net effect is to create an impression of varied yet typical experience, to move on a number of levels simultaneously, and to receive as the most lasting sense a general understanding of what it all portends. If the method was dubbed Unamism in France, it became known later in the century as "collectivism" in America, where Dos Passos became its chief practitioner.

Manhattan Transfer (1925) was the novel in which the collectivist technique was employed to create an impression, not through the lives of three individuals, but a score and more, and through them the life of a great city. Again Dos Passos skyrocketed the literary world—this time with technical fireworks. *Manhattan Transfer* not only went through many printings but, what was more important, established its author as unquestionably the leading young novelist of the 'twenties. Its new approach to the materials of the novel lent a freshness which few American novels before had offered; there was no yardstick by which to measure the difference. The "collective novel" had arrived with a fanfare, and it was a success, though it puzzled many, and put off others who looked for the old continuity, the recognizable story-line, the plot with its climax and denouement.

Like *Three Soldiers*, this novel was objective, but much more rigidly so. Flaubert in his most expansive moods could hardly have imagined a work in which the author more rigorously excluded himself. Not only does Dos Passos keep himself out of it, he even eschews many of the ordinary explanations. For example, there is never an explicit statement of the time of the story; one must gather that from the nature of its events or from references to historic occasions often obscure, such as a brief mention of the Greater New York bill. As the time sequence develops, eras are telescoped, and the little girl who is born to Ed Thatcher is glimpsed in her mother's arms, later as a frightened child cowering under bedclothes when the light is turned off at night, and pages further as a rather dissolute young actress. Ellen Thatcher's biography is full enough, but it is given less in fullness than in climacteric scenes. And the same is true in the case of many other prominent characters: Bud Korpenning, the upstate boy who has murdered his father and is hiding in the man swarm of New York City, always trying to get "nearer the center of things"; Jimmy Herf, the young boy carried about by his mother, later going to college, taking a job on a newspaper, disillusioned through successive experiences; Congo Jake, the poor immigrant turned successful bootlegger; Blackhead and Densch, the entrepreneurs; and a dozen other characters from all levels of the city's life. They move quickly into view, without a preliminary unfolding of antecedents, caught in the glare of Dos Passos' spotlight, observed for a while, and then dropped, while his camera moves on to another contemporaneous group. The method at first seems confusing, the characters hard to remember; but as the book progresses, Ellen Thatcher and Jimmy Herf become the most important foci, and we do not lose this sense of their centrality. What it all means in the end is simply that here are people—here is a society hardly worth saving. We have been offered an exigent picture of metropolitan life in the early years of the twentieth century; and there is no denying that we feel the immediacy and the authenticity of it. But it is a depressing spectacle. That may not be Dos Passos' fault; and his book, far from being what Paul Elmer More called it, "an explosion in a cesspool," is a kaleidoscopic evocation of life in a city that includes despair, gaiety, aspiration, squalor, greed, cruelty—the gutter and the stars. Withal, it is a civilization set in a mold as rigid as the militarism that confined Fuselli, Chrisfield and Andrews, and that mold is the mechanicism of modern life which makes city-dwellers hardly more than robots, going through automatic motions, men and women riding an endless escalator or forever whirling around revolving doors.

The legitimate criticism of *Manhattan Transfer* has nothing to do with its moral validity, which is unassailable, but rather with a certain extreme philosophic determinism which makes all of its characters seem like biological specimens, moving as their environment dictates, without the rudiments of a shaping will, and without purpose except as directed by what might be called response to sensory stimuli. This is a recurrent weakness of all naturalistic writing, and is just as apparent in James T. Farrell as it was in Emile Zola. However, because Dos Passos, in the days when he was writing *Manhattan Transfer*, had a more or less well-defined social philosophy—a socialistic anarchism—he never entirely allows his despair to overcome him, or to sink his novel beneath a load of behavioristic pessimism. Jimmy Herf, who roughly corresponds to the traditional autobiographical "I", makes an affirmative effort at the close of the novel. He does at least turn his back on this welter of purposeless activity, he does repudiate the terrible waste of city civilization, by walking out of it. Ellen Thatcher thinks of doing the same thing; she knows there are [1] "lives to be lived if only you didn't care. Care for what, for what; the opinion of mankind, money, success, hotel lobbies, health, umbrellas, Uneeda biscuits . . .?" But she never escapes. Jimmy walks out into the dawn and, with three cents in his pocket, encounters a furniture van. " 'Say, will you give me a lift?' he asks the redhaired man at the wheel. 'How fur ye goin?' 'I dunno. . . . Pretty far.' "

Prefacing each chapter of *Manhattan Transfer* is a short prose poem, in which Dos Passos, the fine writer, the Harvard aesthete, still has his say. These poems are often very successful, and of all the naturalists, Dos Passos has been by far the best stylist, perhaps because he has not always been happiest in his role of realistic photographer. They often set the mood for the reportage that is to follow; some of them seem to announce the whole book's intention, as the one marked "Metropolis": [1] "There were Babylon and Nineveh; they were built of brick. Athens was gold marble columns. Rome was held up on broad arches of rubble.

---

[1] From *Manhattan Transfer* by John Dos Passos. © 1925 by the author.

In Constantinople the minarets flame like great candles round the Golden Horn. . . . Steel, glass, tile, concrete will be the materials of the skyscrapers. Crammed on the narrow island the millionwindowed buildings will jut glittering, pyramid on pyramid like the white cloudhead above a thunderstorm."

Here, in these vignettes, Dos Passos was developing one of the devices to be expanded later in his great trilogy; and in other sections of *Manhattan Transfer* may be found early, tentative trials of new materials for the greater work to come. The example of Joyce probably was not lost upon him, and the "Camera Eye" sections of *U. S. A.* are strictly Joycean stream-of-consciousness writing; but then, so are feebler efforts in *Manhattan Transfer*, where Dos Passos was still unable to fuse the imaginative recreation of thought processes into an artistic rendition of movement and thinking. As Ellen Thatcher thinks of her blighted life in the mold of the machine, she "sits back in the corner of the taxi with her eyes closed. Relax, she must let herself relax more. Ridiculous to go round always keyed up so that everything is like chalk shrieking on a blackboard. Suppose I'd been horribly burned, like that girl, disfigured for life. Probably she can get a lot of money out of old Soubrine, the beginning of a career. Suppose I'd gone with that young man with the ugly necktie who tried to pick me up. . . . Kidding over a banana split in a soda fountain, riding uptown and then down again on the bus, with his knee pressing my knee and his arm round my waist, a little heavy petting in a doorway. . . . I hope they haven't ordered dinner. I'll make them go somewhere else if they haven't. She opens her vanity case and begins to powder her nose." This is not successful "interior monologue" and is a far cry from the magnificent writing in the "Camera Eye," but it is an indication of a way of handling this fictional device.

All of these exploring attempts in *Manhattan Transfer* were suddenly tempered in the fire of genius to true steel in *The 42nd Parallel* (1930), the first volume of the *U. S. A.* trilogy that remains Dos Passos' masterpiece. It might be said that with *The 42nd Parallel* he founded a new school in the American novel. Its highly original technique influenced a score of younger men in the 'thirties—that decade so largely given over to an enthusiasm for the proletariat and the bright hopes of a revolution that would bring justice among men; and it announced the beginning of an attempt to formulate the successful "collective novel." Actually it was the first panel of the only collective novel that still seems first-rate.

Again we might consider what this "collective novel" is. It is collective in the sense that its groups of characters move in separate orbits and yet are dealt with consecutively within the confines of a single novel. The resultant effect is a very engrossing and convincing picture of all strata of American society, ranging in Dos Passos' case from unemployed proletarians to Park Avenue socialites, from movie actresses to publicity agents and the moguls of monopoly capitalism.

The enormous scale upon which Dos Passos decided to work, in *The 42nd Parallel* and its sequels, *1919* (1932) and *The Big Money* (1936), has no even remote counterpart among the work of other American novelists, and only Dreiser had ever tried to carve such a breadthwise slice of American life. But Dos Passos was incomparably more successful in getting the broad sweep of life into his pages, albeit the older novelist was better at indicating the subtle nuances of feeling and in developing a sense of the strivings and hopes of his people. In fact, among American novelists, Dos Passos alone worked in a vast and various field— picturing a society in the whole, much as Balzac had done. Dos Passos seems to have been on intimate terms not only with the paltry lives of the very poor, but with the broader horizons open to the rich. All his characters are acceptably real as they move in their circles. Dreiser, on the other hand, never seemed wholly sure of himself when dealing with the very rich, always showed himself to be an outsider, often awed and a little envious of his people of culture and wealth.

Dos Passos, in *U. S. A.*, is attempting to recreate his time, not in the circumscribed pilgrimage of a single individual (as, for example, Frank Cowperwood), not among individuals of a certain station in life or a single section of the land, or even of one level of society, not among people of one class, but among the people inhabiting the whole spatial breadth of the United States, the multitudes of its conglomerate citizenry from every rank and class, during decades of time, and including periods of industrial growth and dissension, war, recovery and boom, depression and rehabilitation. This is ambition on a magnificent scale.

But at the same time Dos Passos was striving for something more. He wanted to recapture the spirit and flavor of the times, and how better than through artistic use of news headlines, snatches of popular songs and catchwords in the parlance of the street? These sections of *U. S. A.* are the "Newsreels." They point up the action carried in the intervening chapters of narrative, each chapter being devoted to one of his many chief characters: "Mac" McCreary, Janey Williams, Eleanor Stoddard, J. Ward Moorehouse, Charley Anderson, Dick Savage, Joe Williams, Eveline Hutchins, Ben Compton, and a dozen more. The "Newsreels" are not always entirely satisfactory, for they do have the effect of scattering the attention and in some instances seem overlong; but at their best they provide an ironic commentary on American civilization, their choice being usually to bring out not only what is characteristic of the era but what is discreditable to it.

The innovations do not stop with the time-fixing stratagem of the "Newsreels." Periodically we are given sections involving actual representative Americans . . . Big Bill Haywood, Randolph Bourne, Henry Ford, Luther Burbank, Woodrow Wilson and others—industrial magnates, inventors, scientists, social theorists, presidents, artists—historical figures whose lives in some way reflect the aspirations and ideals of wide segments of the American public. These are frequently superbly written and are unquestionably the finest work, from a technical standpoint, that Dos Passos has done.

And even more than this, *U. S. A.* includes the highly personal and inward record of Dos Passos' own life. These sections are called "The Camera Eye." Here the Joycean stream-of-consciousness method has become completely assimilated, and there is no fumbling for the dreamlike compressions and abridgements, the sometimes fantastic telescoping of memory and experience. Almost always these vignettes have some connection with the narrative that surrounds them, and provide a different kind of commentary from that in the "Newsreels," for they are the sane, sympathetic reactions of a sensitive intelligence to the frenetic, illogical record of American life.

And so this is the amalgam which goes to make up the great collective trilogy, whose chronology is roughly 1900 to the brink of the 1929 economic collapse. *The 42nd Parallel* covers the American scene in the decade and a half preceding the first World War; the war itself is dealt with in the earlier works, *One Man's Initiation* and *Three Soldiers; 1919* deals with the repatriation of the army and the aftermath of the Armistice in this country; *The Big Money* encompasses the 'twenties, the postwar era of accelerating prosperity, decadence, and impending doom—represented by the hungry 'thirties and the second World War.

To follow all the separate lives that make up this vast chronicle is an experience corroborating one's personal observation. We take no exception to these chronicles, for they involve persons recognizably existent. Charley Anderson's is a case in point: he is the not uncommon farm boy with a knack for tinkering with machinery. Returning from France, he lands a job with an aviation firm, perfects an airplane motor of his design, rides high on the wings of financial expansion and success. There is nothing, however, to give him inner stability; money emphatically is not enough. He is out to get all he can from a world that has destroyed his equilibrium by thrusting him into the insane barbarism of war. And drink and profligacy destroy him.

Margo Dowling is another who moves steadily toward the same uncomprehended end, a girl seduced by her foster father, married to an extraordinarily charming and worthless Cuban musician, abandoned by him, living alternately the life of easy money and hard luck, supported by her physical beauty and quick wit, finally landing in Hollywood to become a popular movie idol.

Dick Savage is the Harvard undergraduate turned cynic, working for the great public relations executive, J. Ward Moorehouse, falling heir to his boss's job and squalid precepts. All of these characters turn to sensual pleasure and to liquor for amelioration of their unbearably specious living. All of them are hurtling down an incline of decadence and death. There are indeed few among all this company of American types who seem to realize any part of their potentialities, or who have any faith in anything. Those who do believe are quickly ground under the wheels of this iron civilization. Ben Compton, the radical, is one; Mary French, another. They are orientated to achieve some integration in their world, but they are from a stratum of society which makes it impossible for them really to join hands with the only class that has integrity, the workers. Mary French, the girl whose father and mother early separated, grows up in boarding school, and settlement house; her eyes turn from Jane Addams to Communism in her search for a life with meaning; but doubt, frustration and despair are ultimately her lot. There is one person in the trilogy, a minor character, who appears to have realized himself: Bill Cermak, Charley Anderson's mechanic. Cermak is a man of the working class, with a job to do and a serenity of mind no other character achieves. Dos Passos clearly intends to say that there is no health in our middle class, that the upper reaches of society are already rotten with decay, and that only the workers have life and sanity. They, however, are also victims of a sort of moral paralysis, and must move with the machine.

On the whole, *U. S. A.* presents a terrible spectacle of life being lived at breakneck pace, without aim, without much hope, with no inherent values—a frenzied existence on a dungheap of counterfeit, lies and deceit—the era of expanding capitalism, frozen into the mold of monopoly, ending in the decade of Coolidge prosperity, of gaudy parties, of the big money for those willing to meet the corrupt and corrupting terms of big business. In its way the spectacle is magnificent, as must have been the sight of Rome under Nero's torch—a world rushing headlong toward its doom—the doom that came all too swiftly in the 'thirties and 'forties.

One of the reasons for the great immediacy and continual motivation in Dos Passos' writing is that his narrative is always written in the dramatic present. Something is constantly going on. Like a conveyor belt, the movement is always onward, and Dos Passos has developed a prose instrument of almost miraculous mechanical efficiency—ideal for telling the story he has in mind. The older method of interspersing dramatic "scenes" with descriptive narration is abandoned. His story proceeds like the motion picture—always in the present, always with an eye upon the actors, always immediate. And yet there is a coldness about this delineation too, as if Dos Passos had no real liking for his people, as if his hatred of the society they lived in was also compounded of a distaste for those who comprise it. There is little warmth in *U. S. A.*, and its behavioristic pattern has led some critics to condemn it as embodying an externally applied theory, not borne out by the real facts of American life. In so roundly condemning our society, they say, Dos Passos has overstated his case. He has left no room for the unexplained outcropping of idealism, the occasional mutation, the miracle of his own admired Randolph Bourne, for example, who existed in this society and yet was a beacon light in its dark night because he held to an ideal. Dreiser's groping Jennie Gerhardts and Joseph Barneses, while stuck in the morass of our society, could still dream of the stars, and the determinism of their universe was not so complete as to deny them some aspirations to another set of values. It is this imposition of a preconceived design that weakens *U. S. A.* We believe in Dos Passos' people, but we feel that he has left out of his picture some authentic ameliorating aspects.

Of course, the hatred Dos Passos cherished for American life was itself a reverse idealism, and this was clearly shown in his next novel, *Adventures of a Young Man* (1939). It was a departure from the sort of writing he had been doing, a return to the traditional form in that it followed the career of a single "hero." On the whole, it was a far less impressive piece of work than *U. S. A.* And if Dos Passos had seemed to believe that the salvation of the American people lay in a turn to the Left, in some organized political action, this novel indicated he had lost that faith. Glenn Spotswood, son of a Columbia professor, early becomes interested in the Marxist class struggle. His interest is not confined to theory; he lives for a time as a working man in the Northwest, but eventually returns to school. After taking his degree, he is unwilling to enter a profession. Deeply concerned to change the structure of society, he joins the Communist Party and becomes an organizer in the coalfields. But being something of a humanist, Glenn dissents from the Communist proposition that "the end justifies the means." Nevertheless, when the Spanish Civil War begins, he joins the Republicans and fights with the International Brigade. He is arrested by the Marxists, apparently only because he is known to be out of sympathy with the Party. One of the soldiers of the so-called United Front tells him: "Here we fight several different kinds of war. We fight Franco, but we also fight Moscow. . . . They want to destroy our collectives. They want to institute dictatorship of secret police just like Franco. We have to fight both sides to protect our revolution." In the end, Glenn is shot in what amounts to an execution by the very side he was supposed to be fighting for. The implications are plain that Dos Passos, long interested in the Left, was bitterly disappointed in its operations as reflected in the abortive Spanish revolution.

And so, in *U. S. A.*, we had seen displayed one of the most mordant critical intelligences of our time. A modern Jeremiah had assessed American civilization, and without exception, his report was negative, his cumulative evidence seemed nearly irrefutable. In *Adventures of a Young Man* the only glimmer of affirmation, the dream of a perfect anarchism, was extinguished.

There was an impending crisis for John Dos Passos, to be reached between the publication of this novel and his next. It was the same crisis that confronted Hemingway, and it was met in a similar manner. Dos Passos, of course, had always been vitally interested in politics and the international situation, and for years he had been interspersing fiction with travel books and observations on men and affairs. As early as 1932 he had written *Orient Express*, in which he presented a kaleidoscopic view of Europe in the war's aftermath. Then, in 1934 came *In All Countries*, another excursion into the minds of plain men in many lands. *Journeys Between Wars* (1938) showed him still convinced that the essential hope for survival lay in collective action of some kind. But after the disillusion and disappointment reflected by *Adventures of a Young Man*, in 1939, there came a notable change. In what amounted to a repudiation of his former beliefs, Dos Passos viewed the rise of the totalitarian state and the menace of fascism, which he equated with the state socialism of Soviet Russia, and turned back to the "storybook democracy" of our own past. First, he wrote a brief biography, *Thomas Paine* (1940), and then in *The Ground We Stand On* (1941) affirmed nearly everything that he had denied in his great trilogy. So when his next novel appeared, we were prepared to find a new Dos Passos, a reorientated man, looking back to the American Dream as a thing that once had existed, or showed possibilities of having existed, and espousing a foundational philosophy which he had spent most of his life demonstrating had failed to materialize. And this new sense of values might have been a good thing for his art. He believed now, where he had formerly denied —but the affirmation did not create good fiction. That it may in some future time is possible; but on the basis of *Number One* (1943) we have little hope that it will.

It is true that the despair and denunciation of *Three Soldiers* and *U. S. A.* were the expressions of an outraged idealism. Dos Passos' moral yearning, which emerged as indignation, had certainly been the determinate in all his social criticism. And it became evident that he had never lost that yearning, but now the indignation was waning, and the yea-saying urge was strongly resurgent. It imposed upon *Number One* a resolution that was not deducible from the internal evidence.

In this story of a gangster politician's rise, Dos Passos wrote of another segment of our civilization as corrupt and detestable as any in *U. S. A.* Yet he posits as the outcome an aroused sense of personal responsibility and a recognition of the individual's sanctity in the mass. His politician, Homer T. Crawford (a character based on Huey Long and "Pappy" O'Daniel) rises to eminence and power through the aid of a paid underling, a cynical "idea man." The idea man has no illusions about his role, and when Crawford doublecrosses him, he might have accepted that with the same cynical satisfaction that previously motivated him; but instead he is awakened to his responsibility; he sees what he has done in aiding this mountebank to achieve power which is used to the detriment of the people. He awakens to a sense of his responsibility—but it is only upon Dos Passos' recognizance, not the reader's. We cannot believe that he would make this discovery, or that he would take decisive action. In part, this failure of credibility may be due to Dos Passos' exterior treatment. His brassy naturalism is embarrassed when required to exhibit moral crises and spiritual metamorphosis. Nothing so awkward as the use of the idea man's younger brother's letter— written from Spain in the course of the Civil War—as *deus ex machina* had appeared in Dos Passos' fiction. To communicate his new perception of individual responsibility and a morality that transcends the automatism of *U. S. A.*, Dos Passos would have to forsake his glossy reporting; he would have had to be convinced that he had really come around to a new way of judging men, to a sincere conviction that his old attitudes were false. The new do not sit comfortably in his lexicon, we are bound to feel. If, like Hemingway, he has come full circle from his early denials, to a complete acceptance, it has not yet been proven in his work. We still get the sense that he does not like the world, that his real judgment of it is negative, and that to approve and affirm is beyond his felt power—whatever may be the extent of his intellectual acceptance.

ERSKINE CALDWELL AND VARDIS FISHER
The Nearly-Animal Kingdom

EMERGING as a salient figure with extraordinary rapidity in the early '30's, Erskine Caldwell no doubt owed his popularity partly to fortuitous circumstances. Here was a writer concerned with the problems that engrossed all minds in those days of economic depression, and able to deal with such problems artistically; that is, in terms of human reactions. He could not only treat social issues artistically but extract what there could be of humor from them, a prodigious feat, it had seemed, since most of the fiction then current was solemn or hortatory or militant; a belly laugh was a prized rarity. He loomed on the scene quickly, portentously, and in the five years, 1931 through 1935, published seven books that established his reputation.

The son of a Presbyterian minister, Caldwell might have legitimately inherited his social conscience. Apparently nothing more strongly appealed to his imagination than the plight of the Southern sharecropper. Living among and observing these people, while the ferment of the time probably worked upon his mind, he was luckily so much of an artist that his portrayals did not suffer from untimely zeal but were tempered by a keen eye for the comic. His exigent pictures of human degradation were relieved, for artistic purpose and for the more ready assimilation by his comic sense. These creatures, a reader felt, were too pitiful to be merely pitied; one could not endure the pain of their situation unless one could laugh. For this reason Caldwell was not altogether *persona grata* with the militant literary leftists of the decade, who thought him sometimes lacking in serious-ness. Actually he was, with Dos Passos, the spearhead of "proletarian realism" in the early half of that decade of literary leftism, and was one of the most serious novelists in the era.

Besides his sudden emergence and universally acknowledged mastery, Caldwell was distinguished by his productiveness. Seemingly out of nowhere, with scarcely any observable apprenticeship, here was a major American writer pouring out in book after book a skillful, original kind of art and interpreting a phase of life in the United States that only Faulkner had previously investigated. If some readers saw a resemblance between the macabre humor in *As I Lay Dying* and that of some stories in *We Are the Living* (1933), it was only incidental, and the purport of the stories was positive, a call to an aroused social awareness, in a way and toward an end that no Faulkner story ever had been. There was no trace of the luxuriant prose, only the faint overtones of what was grotesquely comic in isolated gleams of the older writer's work. The Caldwell style was clean, terse, though often colloquial. It had the rhythms and repetitions of humble Southern speech, and it was the product of either a fortunate natural virtuosity or a cunning craftsmanship. The abrupt flowering as well as the fecundity of this new talent seemed to indicate that it was *au naturel*.

In the opening year of the depression decade two unpromising novels had inauspiciously appeared, *The Bastard* and *Poor Fool* (1930), and they have been allowed to go out of print. They show few of the Caldwellian characteristics, although their preoccupation is with degenerates and criminals. They have none of the essential naiveté, pureness of heart, and social consciousness of his other work, but seem rather forthright shockers of the subliterary school. The advance displayed in the first collection of stories, *American Earth*, which was published the next year, is almost as remarkable as that shown by *Tobacco Road* (1932) in the year following. In other words, only two years had elapsed between the publication of a juvenile work and the novel that is still Caldwell's masterpiece. We do not know when *The Bastard* or *Poor Fool* were written, but it is safe to assume that they were published very soon after composition.

The significance of this rapid increase in grasp and stature would be negligible but for the fact that we are still waiting, nearly fifteen years later, for a further advance, and there is little prospect of its coming. Caldwell, as novelist, has probably done his best work, unless he takes a quite new and different approach to his materials and experience (and *Georgia Boy* gave us some hope for this). As an artist in the short story, he has demonstrated that he is among our most accomplished. He is certainly among the major realists from Howells' time to the present, a most distinguished worker in the short story, but even here of late he has not kept pace with his achievements of the '30's. His energies during the war years tended to disperse themselves in journalism of various sorts and in editorial duties such as those connected with the American Folkways series.

In the short story Caldwell's famous "humor" seldom comes across. He has, in fact, nearly always used the short story as the vehicle for his most serious judgments of social inequities; and while the novels also levy a harsh verdict, they pronounce it through a waggish grotesquerie. The brevity of the form probably precludes an effective use of his kind of humor, which depends on droll repetitions, unexpected behavior and a picturesque idiom. On the other hand, the form is well adapted to his special use of incisive, shocking revelation, growing usually out of a set of conventional preconditions but developing in a way that is unexpected, most often brutal, or at best somehow harrowingly inhuman. He has used the short story with tremendous effect, but also he has written a good deal of very poor stuff. The four volumes of stories (later gathered into a mammoth compendium with the inspired title *Jackpot*) are very uneven. Reading through them, one does now and then hit the jackpot; and when that happens, the long stretches of lemons are quickly forgotten. From the earliest collection, *American Earth* (1931) to the latest, *Southways* (1938), the overall quality varies hardly at all, and if there is evident little growth there is also no decline. Two or three of the stories are undoubtedly the most powerful examples of the literature of social protest written in America. Without showing the technical virtuosity of Faulkner or the gemlike perfection of Hemingway, they exhibit a consummate, evidently natural, skill. And although written out of anger and compassion, they are most remarkable for a cool objectivity, which of course intensifies their final effectiveness.

The style in which Caldwell couches his stories and novels is certainly a contributing factor to their air of deft, childlike knowingness. It is, in a masterly way, as naive as the people it treats; and sometimes the narrative sections are as colloquial and simple-minded as the dialogue. The sentences are short, the words the very least complex, and there is always a rhythm of repetition in which phrases and whole sentences are repeated almost verbatim. It is all on a level with the subject matter, and excellently calculated to achieve its purposes, to sway the reader and lull his mind into the rhythms of the characters' thinking. Very little finally stands between the reader and Caldwell's meanings; it all seems to "come through" in a really extraordinary degree.

The irony which is the basis of Caldwell's humor[1] is absolutely never explicit; it is nearly always present, but brought actively to bear through the selection of event and the imagined responses of the characters. Never is the language ironical. In this matter Caldwell is clearly the master of all our humorous realists.[2]

A curious and yet typical example of this inherent irony and perfectly innocent handling of it is in the opening paragraphs of the story, "A Day's Wooing." "When Tuffy Webb woke up that morning, the first thing he saw was his new straw hat hanging on the back of the cane-bottomed chair beside the bed. The red, orange and blue silk band around the hat looked as bright in the sunshine as the decorations in the store windows in town on circus day. He reached out and felt the rough crown and brim, running his fingers over the stiff brown straw. He would never have to step aside for anybody, in a hat like that. That was all he needed, to get the world by the tail. 'Maybe that won't knock a few eyes out!' Tuffy said, throwing off the covers and leaping to the floor. 'They'll all be cross-eyed from looking at it.' "[3] Tuffy's main purpose in buying the hat was to capture the admiration and love of Nancy when he went to call on her. His call, though, only gained him the derision of Nancy's family, and he could not work up courage even to speak to her. Tuffy Webb is the personification of naiveté; and "A Day's Wooing" is one of the tenderest funny stories Caldwell has written.

On the whole, the humorous stories have a negligible importance, nor are they as numerous as the serious studies. When Caldwell is "serious" his concern is always with the plight of the poor whites and Negroes. Some of his finest stories spring from almost identical issues and seem to have been written as calls to social action. The seriousness of his theme does not mean, how-

---

[1] See note on page 280, Fisher's definition.

[2] Compare Vardis Fisher's attempt at a similar objective in *April;* here, while the irony is present in the action and character, it is *also* represented directly in actual phrasing and auctorial judgment; and thus, as humor, is comparatively ineffective.

[3] From "A Day's Wooing" in *Kneel to the Rising Sun* by Erskine Caldwell. © 1940 by Duell, Sloan & Pearce.

ever, that the tone is also serious; in most cases the situations are approached humorously; but the upshot of the action is always deadly in earnest. The excellent story, "Candy-Man Beechum", perfectly illustrates this typical Caldwell feat.

It is a pleasure to see Caldwell writing at the top of his form, as Candy-Man goes stepping across the Georgia gullies, high, wide and handsome. " 'Make way for these flapping feet, boy, because I'm going for to see my gal. She's standing on the tips of her toes waiting for me now.' The rabbits lit out for the hollow logs where those stomping big feet couldn't touch them." This big black boy, ready for a night with his yellow gal, in a few deft words is presented to us with all his good nature, explosive vitality and rhythm. He asks only to be on the move to where his gal is. When Little Bo hollers out to him not to tread on white folks' toes, Candy-Man says, " 'Me and white-folks don't mix, just as long as they leave me be. I skin their mules for them, and I snake their cypress logs, but when the day is done, I'm long gone where the white-folks ain't are.' " And he's as good as his word. He cuts across the country, as the "owls in the trees began to take on life. Those whooing birds were glad to see the setting sun." All he wants is to be let alone. "The big road was too crooked and curvy for Candy-Man. He struck out across the fields, headed like a plumb-line for a dishful of frying cat-fish. The lights of the town came up to meet him in the face like a swarm of lightning-bugs. Eight miles to town, and two more to go, and he'd be rapping on that yellow gal's door."

But this headlong, happy itinerary is abruptly halted, as Candy-Man reaches the fish-house door. The night policeman of the town senses the power and rhythm of the big black boy and says, " 'I reckon I'd better lock you up. It'll save a lot of trouble. I'm getting tired of chasing fighting niggers all over town.' " Candy-Man demurs. " 'I never hurt a body in all my life, white-boss. You sure has got me wrong. I'm just passing through for to see my gal.' " Such back talk is too much for the policeman, who forthwith fires at him. From the ground Candy-Man says, " 'White-boss, I sure am sorry you had to go and shoot me down. I never bothered white-folks, and they sure oughtn't bother me. But there ain't much use in living if that's the way it's going to be. I reckon I'll just have to blow out the light and fade away. Just reach me a blanket so I can cover my skin and bones.' "[4]

This perfect little story exhibits Caldwell at his best; he has given us a strong social argument, a fine character study, and a telling moral situation, in a story that embodies all the classical unities. Its merry rhythm collides sharply with its message. It is a memorable vignette and one of Caldwell's minor masterpieces.

His finest story to date, however, is a more ambitious undertaking, and one which has little of the humor and pace of "Candy-Man Beechum." It is a study of the cowardice growing out of hunger, of betrayal, and again, of social injustice. "Kneel to the Rising Sun" is one of the most powerful stories-with-a-message written by an American realist, and represents Caldwell's art in the short story at its zenith. As a study of racial conflict it is superb, holding up for our edification a balance of values in which the Negro comes off by far the best. It makes its points by the most vigorous and cold-blooded use of shock; it is purposely brutal and obscene on its surface, because its intention is so ethical. For a realist, there was no other way to write a story that would be sufficiently moving and horrible to induce conviction and impel action.

Lonnie Newsome, the sharecropper with a face sharp enough to split the boards for his own coffin, stands so in fear of his employer Arch Gunnard that he is afraid to ask for rations when his family is starving. But Clem, the Negro sharecropper, is not. Clem established his moral superiority by virtue of his courage; Lonnie, in the opening paragraphs, is demonstrated to have absolutely no bravery, as he makes no protest when Arch wantonly cuts off his dog's tail. Hunger and insecurity have robbed Lonnie of his manhood; he submits to Arch's cruelty almost as a matter of course.

When Lonnie's Pa, deaf and decrepit, wanders out into the night and can't be found, it is to Clem the Negro that Lonnie turns and from whom he gets assistance. The seven-hundred-

---

[4] From "Candy-Man Beechum" in *Kneel to the Rising Sun* by Erskine Caldwell. © 1940 by Duell, Sloan & Pearce.

pound hogs that Arch is fattening squeal and grunt all night long; and here we get the first intimation of what has happened to Pa. Unbelievable and shocking as such things may be, Caldwell lets us know he is not above having hogs devour a human being, if only to arouse us, to set the adrenalin loose in our bloodstream, so that his disposition of the problem will convince us. Clem is not afraid to accuse Arch of having in effect killed the old man by starving him into night-wandering; " 'You know good and well why he got eaten up by the fattening hogs,' Clem said, standing his ground. 'He was so hungry he had to get up out of bed in the middle of the night and come up here in the dark trying to find something to eat.' " And that of course is all Arch needs to hear. " 'Nigger, your time has come!' "[5] And though Clem darts off in the darkness, and Arch runs to the house for his gun, it is certain that Clem has overstepped the bounds and will pay with his life. He appeals uselessly to Lonnie for protection. Lonnie aids Arch and the neighbors in their hunt for the Negro who was his best friend, and only after Clem has been killed does he seem dimly to realize his guilt. We are not allowed, either, to forget the hogs. When Lonnie returns home his wife asks him to go up to the big house and get a little piece of streak-of-lean.

"He grabbed his wife about the shoulders.

" 'Meat?' he yelled, shaking her roughly.

" 'Yes,' she said, pulling away from him in surprise. 'Couldn't you go ask Arch Gunnard for a little bit of streak-of-lean?'

"Lonnie slumped down again on the steps, his hands falling between his outspread legs and his chin falling on his chest.

" 'No,' he said almost inaudibly. 'No, I aint hungry.' "[5]

This story depends upon three factors for its importance: first, the overall theme of racial inequality in the South; second, the degradation and degeneration of character attendant upon chronic hunger; and third, the purely physical violence and shock. All three are treated with almost complete effectiveness. On the realistic level the story is a total success; it does every-

---

[5] From "Kneel to the Rising Sun" in *Kneel to the Rising Sun* by Erskine Caldwell. © 1940 by Duell, Sloan & Pearce.

thing it sets out to do. There is no more to it than appears on the surface; it is a piece of documentary fiction, and a very good piece. It would have shocked Howells, no doubt, but it is the sort of realism he fostered.

The splendid promise Caldwell held out to us as novelist when *Tobacco Road* appeared has remained largely unfulfilled. Although he has published eight novels, only one of them seems to have such stature as to remain discernible for any length of time, and that of course is the earliest of his mature works, *Tobacco Road*. Two or three other Caldwell novels were sensations of their seasons, especially *God's Little Acre* (1934) and *Journeyman* (1935), but they were remarkable principally for their unashamed exploitation of erotic detail. Both contained essentially good workmanship, and both delved into the Georgia cracker milieu which Caldwell knows so well; but one sensed an incongruous sensationalism in passages dealing with fornication, and the novels seemed immature and boyish compared with their predecessor, *Tobacco Road*. Moreover, while *Journeyman* had a unity in its continuous sequence of sex activity, *God's Little Acre* seemed to fall apart by reason of its bifurcated theme. Ty Ty Walden's gold-fever and the antics of his sons and daughters are legitimately in the foreground; but Will Thompson's erotomania and his interest in the strike at the mill are diverse; and when the Ty Ty theme and the strike theme are mixed, the resulting amalgam cannot fuse. If Ty Ty had been shown as the exploited victim of capitalism, *God's Little Acre* would have cohered as *Tobacco Road* did; or if Will Thompson had been the focal center of the novel, Ty Ty's family relegated to a place in some subplot, the novel could have hung together.

Trouble in July (1940) and *All Night Long* (1942) are the weakest of all the novels, with the possible exception of the two early novels. The first of them tells a conventional story of a Negro lynched for a rape he did not commit. The second is a strange and stiff portrayal of Russian guerillas beating the Nazis back and is really less a novel than a fictionized companion volume to the "war correspondence" of *All-Out on the Road to Smolensk* and *Moscow Under Fire*. Of late years most of Caldwell's energies seem to have gone into his social-documentary studies and the travel books made jointly with the photographer, Margaret Bourke-White. There is, however, a gleam in the darkness that seems recently to envelop his creative genius. *Georgia Boy* (1943), while unimportant in itself, seemed to forecast a new orientation toward his experience and provided another point of departure for his art—the art which found its highest expression in *Tobacco Road.*

That novel is not to be confused with the play devised from it by another hand. That irresponsible farce in which almost any exaggeration was permitted if it would bring a laugh had little resemblance to the book in which the comic sense, though it reigns, does so only by sufferance. Thoughtful readers could laugh, but the echo was sober. With a group of characters differentiated from animals only in that they have speech, this novel succeeds in fascinating us and in bringing us to a more stringent awareness of the plight of impoverished families in the deep South than any sociological treatise could do. Lov Bensey is the first of these creatures we meet, as he comes upon the scene carrying a croker sack full of turnips. He stops before his father-in-law's house, being careful to sit down far enough away so that none of the Lester family can rush him and steal the turnips. He has a complaint to air to Jeeter, to Jeeter's wife Ada, and to the three other members of Jeeter's household: Ellie May, the hare-lipped daughter; Dude, the moronic adolescent son; and the old grandmother shriveled from hunger, whose habit it is to gather sticks and build a fire in the stove three times a day on the chance there will be something to cook. Lov's complaint has reference to Pearl, Jeeter's twelve-year-old daughter, Lov's wedded wife. " 'She aint never slept in the bed,' " Lov says. " 'It's that durn pallet on the floor that she sleeps on every night. Reckon you could make her stop doing that, Jeeter?' "[6] Jeeter is properly concerned at such behavior and promises to speak with Pearl if Lov will only let him have a few turnips to eat. But Lov sees no fairness in such a bargain. Meanwhile Ellie May begins to slide across the sandy yard toward him on her bare bottom, and before long Lov is more interested in her than in watching his sack of turnips. While they are "hugging and rubbing of the other" the Lesters all gang up on Lov, and Jeeter runs off with the turnips. Though he gains possession of the sack through the concerted efforts of the family, he does not divide with them. He eats his fill.

This is the opening action, and the rest of the novel is different not in kind but detail. Jeeter Lester himself, ignorant and outrageous, is yet a "good" man, as indeed are all the characters; we can hardly judge them by any human standards. Jeeter emerges as an individual largely because of his love for the land. At one time his forebears owned all the land thereabouts, but as they continued to plant tobacco until the soil would no longer produce, then switched to cotton and continued the depletion of the soil, they gave up parts of their holdings to satisfy taxes; and at last, in Jeeter's time, the land has passed entirely to other hands, while he remains as a sharecropper. Things have now reached a pass where he can no longer raise anything on the land, and he has exhausted his credit with the banks and stores in Marion. He and his family are slowly starving to death. They could go to the mills in Augusta and work, but Jeeter refuses to do that. He is a man of the soil; his love for the soil is the one abiding human attribute of the man.

It is unusual to find anything human about any of these people. Sister Bessie, who has set herself up as a woman preacher but who has mostly been a hussy, drops in on the Lesters and remains to marry Dude. She wins him by promising an automobile, which she buys with the insurance money left by her former husband. She spends the eight hundred dollars without regard for other contingencies, without once thinking that such a sum could ameliorate their lot, and without even inquiring about the value of the automobile she purchased, or knowing that one needed to protect oneself against sharp bargainers. Dude spends his time driving the car about and blowing the horn. At one point Bessie, Dude and Jeeter take a load of scrub oak down to Augusta, and they stay overnight in a cheap hotel. The hotel man interrupts Sister Bessie's sleep every hour all night long, taking her from one room to another, in which there is always a man sleeping. Recalling the pleasures of that night was a favorite pastime with her. " 'I want to go back some time and spend another night at that hotel,' Bessie said, giggling. 'I had the best time last night. It made me feel good, staying there. They sure know how to treat women real nice.' " [6]

We laugh at this behavior because it is so ludicrous; our sense of fitness and our expectations of human reaction are so thoroughly outraged and thwarted. These people act as we imagine apes might. They are on all-fours with the benighted Stone Age men of Vardis Fisher's *The Golden Rooms*, and more than one scene is suggestive of precivilized life. When Bessie and Dude bring their automobile home for the first time, the family greets them as Harg and his women might have done. "Ellie May and Ada stood at a safe distance so Dude would not run them away with a stick. The old grandmother had gone behind a chinaberry tree again, awed by the sight." [6]

Jeeter's sole desire in life, apart from eating, is to borrow enough money to buy some seed cotton and guano and to plant a crop. That he does nothing whatever to realize this dream does not invalidate his feeling about it. And as Dude and Bessie leave home, followed at last by Ellie May (the old grandmother had previously been run over and killed in the yard), Jeeter and Ada approach their own doom. It comes not in the shape of starvation, which probably otherwise lay ahead for them, but in the shape of an external calamity. At night a broom-sedge fire sweeps across the fields, and their house is burned before they can awaken. " 'Jeeter is better off now than he was,' " is the comment of a neighbor. " 'He was near about starved to death half the time and he couldn't raise no crops.' " Sister Bessie suggests that Jeeter would have been better off if he had gone to work in Augusta. But Lov disagrees: " 'I reckon Jeeter done right. . . . He was a man who liked to grow things in the ground. The mills aint no place for a human who's got that in his bones. The mills is sort of like automobiles—they're all right to fool around in and have a good time in, but they don't offer no love like the ground does. The ground sort of looks out after the people who keeps their feet on it. When people stand on planks in buildings all the time, and walk around on hard streets, the ground sort of loses interest in the human.' "[6]

It has been said that not only has Caldwell illegitimately exploited a social group, but that he deliberately exaggerated the degeneracy of the people. Yet unimpeachable sources have long since endorsed his reporting; the publications of research groups have underlined his findings and even exceeded them in tragic implication. The exploitation charge is certainly unjust, for after all, while we may laugh, we are left with a more lasting sympathy and a larger understanding as well as a desire to alter the conditions that brought about such degeneracy.

Undoubtedly the ferment of social protest in the '30's had something to do with Caldwell's success; he was at his best in the short story and novel when handling the "underprivileged." During the years since it became less necessary and altogether less fashionable to be concerned with social issues, Caldwell's grasp seems to have slackened. He has turned increasingly to straight reporting in travel books and "social studies." The novel, *Georgia Boy*, which in reality is a loosely connected series of sketches about the same characters, is not satisfactory but it may indicate a path for further advance. Superficially, it seems to be merely a group of anecdotes in which exaggeration is the medium through which humor is produced (in one chapter the characters are confronted with the problem of getting some goats off the roof of their house); but more importantly, it is a story of a Southern family very far removed in social strata from the Lesters and the Waldens. The Stroups are lower middle class, and Ma Stroup takes in washing, but they hire Negroes, and they live in town, and Pa is once even appointed dog-catcher. The humor is mellower in this book; we are no longer shocked by the degeneracy of the people; the comic effect does not depend on outrageous and subhuman contradictions. We laugh, but not at the odd reactions of the Stroups, only at the strange situations into which they very humanly get themselves. This is a total about-face for Caldwell, and it seems to suggest a new

[6] From *Tobacco Road* by Erskine Caldwell. © 1932 by Duell, Sloan & Pearce.

orientation toward his art. In addition, there has entered a tone of indulgent, almost affectionate regard for the characters, as if they might be out of the author's own past, as if he had begun to use autobiographical material for nearly the first time. If that is the case, he has only begun to work the mine that Wolfe exploited for an entire career; it could supply a second career for Caldwell. *Tragic Ground* (1944) and *A House in the Uplands* (1946) find Caldwell continuing to explore his subject matter, but the results are still tentative. He has not risen again to the level of *Tobacco Road.*

At first glance there would seem to be many correspondences between the work of Caldwell and Vardis Fisher. Both deal with bucolic subjects, both approach their material realistically, both depend heavily on colloquialisms in dialogue and narrative style, both have a "message," both are concerned with aspects of modern life that are brutal and raw, both are vigorously and uncompromisingly outspoken and, finally, both render a report on life that is, to say the least, unencouraging. But the divergences are equally marked. Caldwell maintains a rigidly objective attitude toward his characters and keeps himself out of his fictions. Fisher, as the creator, is always in attendance upon his portrayals; one feels his presence even though there are no overt auctorial asides. Caldwell is the mouthpiece for a philosophy of social amelioration, and leans toward the political Left; Fisher has a system of corrective psychology with which to save the human race, and is a conservative in politics. Caldwell's debt to predecessors outside the realistic stream seems greatest to Faulkner; Fisher's perhaps to Wolfe. Of the two men, one feels that Fisher is the more versatile and is still growing, while Caldwell has been the finer artist.

In the whole range of contemporary fiction there is not another career that parallels Vardis Fisher's. After publishing nearly twenty novels, he is still the least read of the major American literary artists. After winning one of the country's fattest novel prizes, which assured him at least one appearance at the top of best-seller lists, he went on to write books that had meager sales.

His name is seldom seen in popular critical surveys, though he has been hailed time and again as a great novelist. He has his zealous partisans and his equally outspoken enemies. But the reviewers and critics, by and large, have been content to dismiss him with faint praise.

There are various reasons for all this. Like Faulkner, Fisher has shunned the *soirées* and refused to help grease the machinery of publicity and "connections" that manufactures book sales. His flat refusal to compromise any of his convictions, and his intransigent stand regarding the treatment of sex in his novels, have probably cost him some favor with publishers. But we can have nothing but admiration for a writer whose serious regard for his work counsels him to spurn glittering Hollywood offers and to hold tenaciously to a high purpose through years of toil and begrudging public attention and relatively small emolument.

Fisher has been difficult to catalogue; his novels have fitted into no neat category; just as one believed he had emerged as a novelist of the recent frontier *(Toilers of the Hills)*, he became a Wolfean autobiographer (the Tetralogy); or he had just fixed himself as a psychoanalytical writer *(Forgive Us Our Virtues)* when he exfoliated as an historical novelist *(Children of God)*. No writer can be so Protean and still be first-rate, might be the dictum of Fisher's exasperated critics. And then, there is an extremism in Fisher's work which tends to alienate the average susceptibility. Like Wolfe, he has until recently seemed to make a fetish of force and power, and hence to exaggerate and distort. With him, a point had not been made until it had been doubly made. Wolfe's gigantism and Fisher's extremism sprang from the same power-fetish, but while in Wolfe one glimpsed an occasional sunny vista and an intermittent balance, in Fisher there is never a moment of equanimity; the conflicts and tortures of his protagonists are exhausting, as they are unresolved. The resulting overbalanced picture and the "life's not like that" effect it has upon the average reader is another reason for Fisher's lack of popular acceptance.

Caldwell, on the other hand, dealing with characters as near the animal level as any of Fisher's, and choosing them with as little regard for their representative norm as Americans, has always had a large audience. His people, starved and dull as they are, lewd and lusty as goats (whose sexual affairs are reported so exhaustively) appeal to us as being somehow human. We can laugh comfortably at them, since they are far enough removed from the conception we have of ourselves as civilized beings. We can feel sorry for them and even become militantly aroused by the injustice they suffer. But in Fisher's case we have none of this sense of removal; he insists that we identify ourselves with his people. His characters' ignoble patterns of thought and pretenses of superiority are presented as the norm for humanity. Our self-love is affronted, and we read insults into these books. That is exactly the trouble: we feel that this is precisely how Fisher wants us to react. It is as if he has a perverse wish to outrage us, as if in his desire to publish discoveries of our common frailty he stands in the position of prosecutor and accuses us of crimes.

For it is evident that Fisher's novels have sometimes cloaked a resurgent tractarian, and that the message has often gotten in the way of the story. The argument underlying several of his novels is that modern man can find salvation only when he knows himself and is willing to act on that knowledge. When we admit that we have animal impulses, and are not ashamed to act according to them, we will have gone a long way toward self-knowledge.[7] When we realize that we live largely by false moral standards and act out a lifelong drama of deceit and subterfuge by evading our ego-drives, we shall be in a position to develop our true humanity. The coexistent urges toward self-love and selflessness must find a happy balance before we can be delivered. "We are betrayed by what is false within," is the theme of the Tetralogy and of other novels; it even appears to be the central idea toward which the "ascent of man" series is shaping.

---

[7] This is the burden of Ty Ty Walden's philosophy too. "There was a mean trick played on us somewhere," he says. "God put us in the bodies of animals and tried to make us act like people. That was the beginning of trouble. If He had made us like we are, and not called us people, the last one of us would know how to live."—From *God's Little Acre.* by Erskine Caldwell. © 1933 by Duell, Sloan & Pearce.

To illustrate this argument seems to have been the principal intention of such novels as *No Villain Need Be* and *Forgive Us Our Virtues*. Even *April*, delightful as in many respects it is, is patently a satire and parable. And this is undoubtedly another reason why Fisher is not as widely read as some of his contemporaries.

Regardless of these handicaps, and they are serious ones, Fisher's position as novelist is certainly equal to that of Caldwell. For what he may lack in finesse and in artistic craftsmanship he easily makes up in scope and depth. As Caldwell is the spokesman for the Negro and the sharecropper of Georgia (less in his novels than in his documentary and travel books), so Fisher is the delineator of the Idaho farmer. Caldwell's few writings with a New England background and his one lamentable excursion into a portrayal of Russian life do not compare in any way with the extended scope of Fisher. Besides writing of the Idaho mountain man and his hard-bitten ways of life, Fisher made the American western hegira his province in one of the great historical novels of our day. Unlike others of our modern primitives, he has not hesitated to write "intellectual novels"; and finally he has embarked on the most dangerous of all novelistic seas, that of recreating Mankind—a task that has been tried before with dire results. Thus his scope is indubitable; whether he has "found himself" in any field is a question that concerns only his detractors. He has done distinguished work in all of these fields; and to the present time, he has made his greatest contributions in the realistic tradition in *Children of God* and *In Tragic Life*.

His two earliest novels, by themselves, would have been enough to make the reputation of an average novelist, who would have gone on repeating the formula until, by dint of sheer repetition, he had made his weight felt. *Toilers of the Hills* (1928) and *Dark Bridwell* (1931) are poignant, deeply beautiful novels of the Idaho soil in which Fisher paid tribute to the people and the acres of his youth. They are probably the most objective of his novels (before *Children of God*), and they have a freshness and a nascent power that is lacking in the later books. Opal and Dock

Hunter, the indomitable couple who cleared sagebrush and planted wheat on an Idaho homestead fifty years ago, are fine, original people. Charley Bridwell, whose dark destiny it was to play the role of a Lear when he was so obviously meant for a life of lazy philosophizing—his story is alternately tender and brutal. These novels are all story-telling; the preacher in Fisher never shows his zealot's face. Their characters are, like Caldwell's, childlike people in whom myth and lore are strong, since they live in a world tenanted by vast interrogations. Their knowledge is so limited and their animal power so great that, like Jeeter Lester and his family, they exist almost on a level of intuitive awareness. We pity them and are moved by the elemental sufferings they endure, but we do not closely identify ourselves with them and their misfortunes. There is seldom anything humorous about them; Charley Bridwell finds it comical to teach his three-year-old son Hamlin to chew tobacco and swear. ". . . he would stand up and curse with such deadly earnestness that his father would nearly fall off his rock with laughter. 'The God-damn trees!' Ham would shout, in his small enraged voice. 'Who put them there, I'd like to know! Christ and Jesus on them, the sons-of-bitches!' "[7] Jeeter's profanity ultimately becomes funny, but not so Ham's. That Fisher can write comedy is admitted; the second novel of the Tetralogy, *Passions Spin the Plot*, rises to heights of high comedy. Fisher believes that irony is the only source of humor[8] and it is true that "Forenoon" McClintock's escapades, Vridar Hunter's first experiences with drunkenness, are hilariously funny; but in a different sense from that in which Jeeter Lester's actions are funny. There is something wry in the response Vridar's pecadilloes wring from us, because we have a recognition of ourselves in him; we laugh at Jeeter largely because he is, to our sense, grotesque; we do not delight in his misery so much as find joy in his unusual reactions to environment. There is too much that is relevantly personal in Vridar's and "Fore-

---

[7] From *Dark Bridwell* by Vardis Fisher. © 1931 by The Caxton Printers, Ltd.
[8] "All genuine humor is ironic. It is not possible to conceive of any other kind."—From *The Neurotic Nightingale* by Vardis Fisher. © 1936 by The Casanova Press.

noon's" reactions. On the whole, there is not much humor in Fisher; his work is for the most part deadly earnest, extraordinarily "serious," and informed with an almost Calvinistic fervor to be truthful according to its own lights.

Only the short novel *April* (1937) besides *Passions Spin the Plot* has this lighter touch, the humor of irony, and it differs widely in tone and spirit from the Caldwellian comedy. In poking fun at the homely heroine, April, which was June Weeg's pet name for that lovely woman she knew her unseen inner self to be, Fisher far too much intellectualizes and explicates the situation, and what was evidently planned as comedy (and sometimes written in a style ponderously "comic")[9] turns finally to a dubious pathos. The novel remains an indeterminate entity, but it provides an interesting contrast to staple American humorous fiction as represented in Caldwell. June is not really funny; she is an interesting case of megalomania; perhaps with some justice a similar view could be taken of the mountebanks in *God's Little Acre* who are not really funny but are absorbing cases of erotomania.

Though it is probable that Fisher regards himself as a comic writer in the Meredithian sense, it is more likely that he will be remembered as an Ecclesiastes of modern life. He will be remembered also as a chronicler of the Mormon story, and perhaps as a fictioneering champion of philosophic naturalism. It is in these three aspects that one may most profitably consider his work through the most successful novels in each kind: *In Tragic Life* for the first; *Children of God* for the second; and the early panels of his anthropological series for the third. They are the summits of his achievement. The lesser novels have interest, and some of them easily exceed in value books far better known. In a sense,

---

9 June had a thigh "as large as the waist of many girls; . . . . she measured her hips and then upon the earth she drew the circumference and stood within. 'As big as a washtub or a sofa or a well. Just the size of a barrel,' she said. Her calf and her neck, they were the same size: two feet anybody might say and she would not say no, three feet or six feet, or half a mile. The distance around her was just about equal to that of the equator; and how could a man be expected to love that?"—From *April* by Vardis Fisher. © 1937 by The Caxton Printers, Ltd.

it may be unfortunate that *In Tragic Life* was the first section of the Tetralogy which included *Passions Spin the Plot, We Are Betrayed*, and *No Villain Need Be*, since it so clearly overshadowed them. They were anticlimactic, but any of them, by itself, was a respectable performance. Furthermore, the series did not add up to the excellence of its parts. In this respect the Vridar Hunter Tetralogy does not compare with *Studs Lonigan*, though the two epics are in other ways comparable. Among the historical novels, *Children of God* is easily superior to *City of Illusion* and *The Mothers. April* and *Forgive Us Our Virtues* were two excursions into abnormal psychology, and succeeded least as fiction. Finally we arrive at *Darkness and the Deep, The Golden Rooms*, and *Intimations of Eve*, where again one can only feel that Fisher is blazing a perilous trail but that he may with luck arrive at a safe destination.

Among autobiographical studies of adolescence in fictional form, *In Tragic Life* stands in a small and elect company. *Look Homeward, Angel, Young Lonigan*, the early volumes of *Jean Christophe*—it is only with works like these that it can be compared. This searing evocation of childhood is charged with a passion for truth, for the anatomical exposure of every hidden event in Vridar Hunter's formative years, told as if for cathartic value, as if to exorcise. This accounts for the Dreiserian doggedness in tracking down realistic detail and for the enormous and single-minded concentration on the harsh aspects of life as they impinge on the consciousness of a hypersensitive youth. Vridar's early years were filled with loneliness and terror. "He gathered from them a morbid fear of blood and death; he never looked back upon them without pain. He learned to hate, with intensity that shook him, all the brutal and ruthless forces of life. . . . When looking back, across a great surface of time, he felt most deeply the agony and fright. . . . It was the seared and blinded hours that rose out of darkness and lived again." Given this attitude, the recounting of childhood's experiences was bound to be a horrific tale, but it was equally certain to be an honest one, for Vridar not only hated brutality but despised all falsity and sham and regarded even the ordinary small pretenses, like the myth of Santa

Claus, as betrayals. His reactions to these betrayals are always extraordinarily violent; he retches, weeps, turns into the dark, or seeks escape in the hills. Upon the occasion when he learned the facts of birth, he "rose, feeling violently sick, and went into the bedroom. He lay on the bed and retched; and when his mother heard him and came, he turned from her and strove to hide his face." These remarkably strong reactions are those of an almost insanely sensitive individual; and the rendering of that individual's experience is done in like terms. Less highly organized beings, the rest of us may tend to feel that all these reactions are overwrought, that no childhood could be so harrowing, no environment so inimical as that of the black canyon of the Snake River in which Vridar grew up.

Joe and Prudence Hunter, his parents, were stern, puritanical Mormons, and they knew nothing of child psychology. Their lack of understanding helped warp and distort Vridar's view of life; every natural discovery and inclination of his youth and young manhood was blighted by parental indifference or proscription; his native environs and the playmates of his childhood were primitive or savage; life became a nightmare to be endured. The burgeoning of sexual instinct and interests in the boy, more powerful than in most, received preternatural repressions. When Vridar persuaded his little sister to expose herself before him, and his mother discovered what he had done, she spoke quietly first, then flogged him with a chokeberry limb, and "it wrought upon his soul a violent distortion; it laid a lonely estrangement between mother and son. Because from every burning stroke, he took into his heart, not a clear sense of error, but a ghastly dread of the beautiful, the sweet, and the unexplained. Nothing was right, nothing was godly, except pain and solitude and hard ways. That was the meaning, that was the lesson, of the chokeberry limb. The soft, the alluring, and all the tenderness of rapture: these were of the devil, these were to be cast out. There was sin in the world, there was guilt, and it was decoyed in everything of loveliness and light; and virtue, upon which God alone smiled, was to be found in the stern and the austere."

There were few interludes in which life took on any brighter raiment. On the whole "when he looked back . . . his adolescence seemed to have been a dreary autumn, with little in it of light and hope. It was a gray time, a time of despair." He believed that all the world was bad, but curiously, that "nearly all the people in the world were honest, wise, and brave." Only he was vile. Yet at times even he felt stirrings of greatness, and from determining to be a prophet, he resolved to be a great poet or a teacher. His brother, Mertyl, a couple of years younger, reacted more equably to this harsh life; and we are never in any doubt as to the really exceptional quality of Vridar or of his exceptional response to life. The boy is by no means average; he is a genius. It is only when we understand this fundamental circumstance that we can account for the agony and terror with which Vridar's story is filled. It is Vridar's agony we are meant to feel; life is "tragic" for him; it is much less so for everyone else in his world.

And yet the picture we get of the two little boys, lost like waifs in this cruel outpost of the Idaho hills, is a moving one; we cannot help suffering with them, and we feel pity and tenderness as they creep through this amazingly brutal scene, each with such infinite potential capacity for absorbing love and beauty and a little understanding, yet condemned to wander, strangers and afraid, beneath the dark sky of a benighted childhood.

In its technical aspects *In Tragic Life* shows flaws, but the novel triumphs over them by the sheer power and intensity of its manner. Fisher is constantly holding up bait before our eyes: he prefixes each scene with a signal. "The first crucial period of Vridar's life fell between the April and the October of his ninth year. Twice, during this while, his spirit was desolated by his father's wrath. ¿ . . Joe's first rage fell in the month of June. It came about this way."[10] These stage settings and incantations are superfluous when they do not actually detract from the effectiveness of the drama. In scene after scene Vridar is shown as reacting with almost identical outward effect, as mentioned above. These repetitions are annoying; but they cannot materially harm the novel. It sweeps through and beyond such flaws in the mighty tide of its vigor, thoroughness and passionate honesty.

Certain scenes are unsurpassed for raw outspoken power, as

that of the disemboweled horse, or of Vridar in the flume, or of the innumerable bloody fights. The Fisher style, tending to nervous effects and a Wolfean rhetoric, is fully adequate, although there is often a feeling of language being pushed to its extremes. And there are passages of remarkable beauty, as when Vridar responds to the burgeoning year. "He walked in fancy, and beauty clothed him. Beauty gave him golden trousers of sunlight, hats of cloudscarf, and shoes of odorous soil. In a later time he traveled far on land and sea; he awaited spring in many places; but he never saw it shower such wealth, such mammoth armfuls of loveliness, as it bestowed with blind extravagance upon this sunken bottomland, this well of winter that was his home. Summer he had learned to fear because of its murmuring flies, the passionless aloofness of its zenith, the quiet fixed insanity of its heat; autumn because of its carpets of desolate frost, the naked bones of its trees, and its loneliness; winter because of its white deserts and screaming winds. But spring was all tenderness and faith. Its great pulse gushed and ran and out of everything came beauty. The sky was a blue allegory, each tree was a green parable; the sun was a warm legend out of Palestine. He loved it. He trusted it. April and violet and bluebird: it was a time to smell and breathe and feel. Ah, Spring! Spring!"[10]

Stylistically, *Children of God* (1939) is in all respects on a par with the Tetralogy, but it is worlds removed in tone, spirit and method. The often tortured and neurotic self-obsession of the Vridar Hunter books led some to believe that Fisher was a novelist with but one story to tell. *Children of God* prodigally proved them wrong. It is wholly objective in its dramatization of the Mormon movement, a saga that encompasses scores of characters, literally hundreds of fantastic events, and nearly a century of time. It adheres faithfully to the historic facts; one of Fisher's boasts is that in his historical fiction he has never imagined a basic fact or event; and still *Children of God* is selective and, in its mass, a balanced artistic whole. Its three sections center attention first upon Joseph Smith, founder of the religion, then upon Brigham Young, its consolidator, and lastly upon a group of fictional

---

[10] From *In Tragic Life* by Vardis Fisher. © 1932 by The Caxton Printers, Ltd.

third generation Mormons who are symptomatic of the spiritual deliquium and ultimate disintegration of the church. If the first two sections seem more vivid and better realized than the concluding one, it is upon history and not the novelist's handiwork that the blame must be laid. No historical novelist ever built more closely upon the records; it may be a limiting factor in Fisher's case that his conception of such fiction excludes the license Tolstoy allowed himself in *War and Peace* and fixed his boundaries so straitly in the tradition of *Henry Esmond*. However that may be, *Children of God* is all drama and has the pace and color of its epoch, a straightforward chronology, and it eschews auctorial asides. Its Esmond is Brigham Young, who breathes with sturdy life in an interpretation that is more satisfactory than any biographer's; its Beatrix is Amelia, the only one of more than twenty wives who fathomed the heart of that desert statesman. Numerous others are limned with nearly equal insight.

Caldwell's use of colloquialisms is one of his more distinguishing practices; Fisher, too, has a remarkably accurate ear for speech, and he has reproduced the racy Rocky Mountain dialect in all of his books. *Children of God* is especially rich in it, though one sometimes wonders if all of the "westernisms" were current during Joseph Smith's time. Mormon lore, because of its Western pioneer associations, is replete with wonderfully expressive epithets and figures of speech; Fisher dug into a mine of them in his researches for this novel. "Mouth-almighty," "hog-intogs," "pack up your daisy kickers," "send you to hell across lots," "devil-dodgers," and scores more, besides the insane rhetoric of a Parley Pratt or a Sidney Rigdon, strengthen the picturesque realism of a historical novel planted firmly in a great tradition.

For the present, at least, Fisher has given up historical fiction, as it is usually defined; but he has launched upon an undertaking of literally unlimited scope: a novelized reconstruction of man's growth from the prehuman stage to his present degree of civilization. *Darkness and the Deep* (1943), the first volume, established the cosmic beginnings, described our universe according to Jeans and Whitehead, and traced the slow ascent of life from protoplasm to the first prehistoric man who learned to use a club. *The Golden Rooms* (1944) and *Intimations of Eve* (1946) continued the evolutionary epic. At the outset having the aspect of a *tour de force*, the series as it progresses promises to shape toward a greater achievement, but it is still too early to prophesy. One feels that, so far, an incredible amount of ingenuity and steady artifice were required to make the subhuman figures and their poor, beastlike reactions to environment sufficiently dramatic to hold attention. With material such as this, a novelist, whose business is to portray human beings in conflict, with their retinue of ideas and customs and morals, is very nearly hamstrung. Yet *The Golden Rooms* manages the feat of dramatizing the discoveries and awakenings of these insapient beings in a striking degree. We see Harg, the Stone Age man, surrounded by his females and children, learning almost by chance, yet with some vestige of intelligent direction, to make a fire with sticks. We follow him as he discovers that with fire he can hold off the terrors of night and the cold. We enter with him into the "golden rooms" of firelight in those long prehistoric nights when the world was young and infinitely terrible for ignorant, animallike men. We see him strut and become a tyrant through his superior claims as a fire-maker. It cannot be said that we identify ourselves with him, but we cannot help feeling sympathy and some vicarious terror as this ancient life impinges on the imagination.

We have had similar experiments in fiction before, from Jack London's lamentable *Before Adam* to Johannes V. Jensen's trilogy, *The Long Journey*. I doubt if any novelist, working in the realistic tradition, and positing a naturalistic view of the universe, will ever have done as thorough a job as Fisher's when his series is completed. The project promises to be a multiple-volumned series; it may telescope eons and it may lavish details in the life of a single figure, Christ, let us say. This is historical fiction on a vaulting scale, and that is the measure of Vardis Fisher's ambition. It is a talisman of his scope and resources; and it is doubtful if any other naturalist, literary or philosophical, among his contemporaries, will hew more closely to the naturalistic line, and work with more patience and fortitude. The series, at this late date in his development, shows a continuing improvement in technique. In the marshaling of narrative, in sheer story-telling, *The Golden Rooms* is superior even to *Children of God;* and in style it is more direct, simple and effective than any writing he has so far done. From these facts one might easily see an augury of greater work to come. If, as can hardly be doubted, it is the duty and the glory of the novelist to illumine life's meanings by dealing with our common humanity, then Fisher must soon turn his attention not to man the puppet of history, but to man the social being who suffers and rhapsodizes in his full stature upon the summit of all his inheritance. That he is equipped to do this, *In Tragic Life* showed. The answer to whether he will do it again, and with universal meaning, waits upon the completion of his experiment-in-progress.

JAMES T. FARRELL

And the Poverty of Spirit

THE YOUNGEST writer in the gallery of American realists, and the most productive of them all, James T. Farrell has established himself in the vanguard of present-day naturalism. Born in 1904, Farrell became at thirty the acknowledged peer among our so-called "hard-boiled" novelists, for he had by then completed the *Studs Lonigan* trilogy and proved himself capable of sustained flight in a realm of high literary worth. Here was a young writer with the utmost seriousness of purpose, determined to make a veracious comment on life as he had seen it, and, most remarkable of all, able to write with absolute convincingness about something other than himself. In other words, here was a novelist who did not offer his autobiography as fiction. This alone was evidence that Farrell had a staying power transcending that of his only other rival of a like age, Thomas Wolfe. In complete contrast to Wolfe, he held an ideal of the strictest possible objectivity, and his commentary on the world pictured in his work

invariably emerged from the artistic presentation of its dramatized action. Like Dos Passos, he has been concerned with social
issues and placed reliance upon some form of collectivism for
the improvement of man's lot on earth. In his novels, however,
he has been careful never to propagandize, and is content to allow his pictures of spiritual and material degradation to speak
for themselves.

Of all the contemporary novelists, Farrell is probably the most
knowing as regards his own artistic intentions. Like Zola, whom
he admires and has often quoted, he has drawn up his own plan
of action. He has written a good deal of criticism and in it repeatedly formulated his literary philosophy, evincing that he
understands what he is about. He is the most "serious" novelist
of them all, and shows a doggedness, a determination to write in
his own way in spite of every criticism and exhortation, to map
his own campaign and stick to it, come hell and high water. Like
Frank Norris, he believes in the novelist's responsibility to offer
a serious criticism of life, to educate and enlighten by means of a
truthful representation of human experience. He believes that a
novelist's work, if properly done, creates [1]"the consciousness of
an epoch, and is thus one of the instruments that work toward
the molding and remolding of the human consciousness."

As early as 1929 Farrell had in mind the entire structure of his
Studs Lonigan trilogy. He had written a story entitled "Studs"
which described a wake attended by a group of the dead young
man's friends, their desultory and banal conversation, puerile observations on death, irrelevant comments on the deceased. The
story pictured the spiritual poverty of young poolroom sharks in
a Chicago Fifty-Eighth Street neighborhood. In this microcosm
was latent the whole saga of Studs, later to be written in a thousand pages of the most frank and detailed naturalistic writing
our literature has ever seen. The story of this boy became, in
Farrell's mind, a social manifestation. It was to be written entirely within the framework of a mental cast that should reflect

---

[1] From *A Note on Literary Criticism* by James T. Farrell. © 1936 by Vanguard Press.

Studs' own feelings and pattern of thinking. Farrell was trying to "recreate a sense of what life meant to Studs Lonigan,"[2] and above all not to formulate conclusions from his story. The story should stand by itself, and the alert reader would be able to compare his own life-attitude with that of Studs. Thus would emerge a truly objective picture of a social and moral milieu that would shape the reader's consciousness by helping him pass value judgments on this world of the Chicago lower middle class—this limited, purblind, and in the end horrifying pattern of American city life.

The dominant impression made by *Studs Lonigan* is of the waste and tragedy caused by spiritual poverty. These Chicago youths are, to begin with, normal healthy boys, and they have access to all the avenues of useful living, for they are by no means products of the slums. But they do not take advantage of their opportunities; they are spiritually unequipped to do so. Instead, they have held up to them, by the older members of their own gangs, moral codes that exclude any really rewarding or lasting values. To speak of "love" in any but the physical sense is beneath their contempt. They are pariahs if they take books seriously. Only prowess with their fists, and drink and sexual promiscuity are looked upon with approbation. To be important and worthwhile citizens of this jungle one must be tough, hardboiled, contemptuous of established morality. These youths are, of course, constantly at odds with their elders, who hold no such beliefs. But the elders do not know how to persuade their children against immorality. These oldsters are Irish immigrants who have worked and sacrificed to gain some measure of material competency and ease; they are often bigoted Catholics and they cannot understand their adolescent sons and daughters. They inveigh against their moral looseness but are as blind as any in trying to find an adequate motivation for improvement. The home is no longer an important fact in educating the young; instead, the streets and the poolroom become the institutions of

---

[2] From "How 'Studs Lonigan' Was Written," in *The League of Frightened Philistines* by James T. Farrell. © 1945 by Vanguard Press.

educative importance. Left to themselves, these youngsters turn to liquor and sex, and with all taboos relaxed, waste their potential humanity. Like Studs, many of them whose ambition it was to become "strong and tough and the real stuff" ended by dying of the results of youthful excesses, or sank into a humdrum middle age of physical corpulence and spiritual vacuity.

The poignancy of this tragedy lies in the fact that these boys do have, at the outset, potentialities for development into human beings of stature and worth. They even feel intimations of some future state of grace, and are not without sensitivity, gratitude, honesty, and a sort of idealism. Studs frequently as a boy has these moments of wonder, when he believes that some day good, true and beautiful things will happen to him, that he is marked for a special destiny, and that happiness lies ahead. But as he grows older he knows these moments less often, and of course at last realizes that he will never know anything better than what life up until then has vouchsafed him; that in fact all the good things, such as they were, are already in the past. It is this leading motif which Farrell has pointed up in his selection of John Dewey's observation as a motto for the work: "The poignancy of situations which evoke reflection lies in the fact that we do not know the meaning of the tendencies that are pressing for action."

It would be a great mistake to imagine that Farrell is exclusively, or even chiefly, a naturalist of the Zola order. If he had been, he would have maintained that Studs' tragedy was the result wholly of an adverse environment. And yet, there were others living in the same neighborhood who did escape its stultifying effects. And why? Farrell gives us the clue when he says, "*Studs Lonigan* was conceived as the story of an American destiny in our time. It deals with the making and education of an ordinary American boy. My attitude toward it and toward my character here is essentially a simple one. 'There but for the grace of God go I.' . . . 'There but for the grace of God go'—many others."[3] So it is some intangible difference that causes some to go the way of Studs, and others to go the way of Farrell himself.

---

[3] *Ibid.*

The Fifty-Eighth Street gang of which Farrell was very nearly a member did not turn him into a wastrel. Instead, it taught him the dangers of its code. But again, why? Farrell's only answer is on the level of pure idealism: because it was willed otherwise. I suppose Farrell's explanation would be that there was some quirk of circumstance, chance, or hereditary grace which led some to more worthy goals. At any rate, it was for a reason that cannot be scientifically ascertained.

In 1932 the first volume of the trilogy was published: *Young Lonigan: a Boyhood in Chicago Streets.* We meet Studs as a boy of fourteen, and at the end of the novel he has not quite turned sixteen. Between those two milestones he has the usual experiences of adolescence, including his first real attraction to a girl, Lucy Scanlan, his long thoughts of life and death, and, more unusually for his age, liquor and the sex act. It is a long, circumstantial record, reporting conversations with painstaking accuracy (and Farrell has an almost phonographic ear for speech), cataloguing at length the minor affairs that concern young boys everywhere. The episode in which Studs and Lucy go for a walk, climb a tree, and think tenderly of each other, is a landmark in his fiction for sensitivity and the evocation of youthful love. But Studs cannot hold to this dream of love, for the code of his tough companions excludes it. He must learn the supposed delights of sexual intercourse with a "bad" girl, and then boast of his prowess to impress the gang. The values he is taught to cherish are nearly all antisocial. To "be somebody" in his world he must fight, swagger, shoot pool, and disclaim any interest in intellectual affairs. He wants to be a man among men; the only way to be the "real stuff" is to meet the gang's concept of what maturity means: to be able to drink bootleg whiskey, and to fornicate. All the softness in his nature must be rigidly suppressed; whenever he has feelings of tenderness or impulses to poetry or dutiful emotions toward his family or the Church, these must be evicted and replaced by a hard cynicism. Otherwise his meaning would be lost; he would be branded a sissy or a weakling.

And yet in the opening volume, we constantly are made to feel that here is a good boy, a youth worth saving, and we observe him becoming more deeply entrenched in youthful cynicism with a sense of horror and fear. Where will it all end? The ominous note of Death is sounded now and again. In the second volume, *The Young Manhood of Studs Lonigan* (1934) one of Studs' best friends, Paulie Haggerty, dies—and at his funeral Studs is terrified by the prospect of his own end. He constantly resolves to do better, to forsake his sinful ways—for in moments he does recognize sin, the hell of the Church, where "all the heads of the damned kept bobbing up, bobbing up. And everybody there was damned for eternity, damned to moan and burn, with only their heads now and then bobbing up out of the flames." But needless to say his resolutions are shortlived, for to hold to them he would have to sacrifice all standing in his world.

More and more the future looms without fulfillment of the rosy promises of his boyhood. Studs goes to work for his father as a painting contractor, and he notices that he is not as fast or as strong as he once was. "He hated to think of going on, painting walls day after day after day, risking lead-poisoning too, until he got old and a big belly like his old man, and then to go around bossing other guys who painted walls day after day after day. Goddam it, yes, there was something more to life. There had to be." But all he can find is drunken parties and "batting the breeze" with his cronies. He does not even fall in love, for the episode with Lucy has faded away, and she had disdained the tough that he had become. In *Judgment Day* (1935) Studs, fifteen years older than when we first met him, is definitely on the down grade. He is almost prepossessed with thoughts of his own death, and he remembers others of his gang who have died. He notices that his heart is acting up, that his wind is going, that he is getting stout around the middle. He becomes preoccupied about his health. And at other times he still cherishes the illusion that life has welcome surprises in store, that one day he will be a more important man, for instance, than Red Kelly, who has gone in for ward politics. Nostalgically he remembers Lucy, magic name, and he can never find again the poetry of that afternoon with her. "And still he would always love Lucy, who had sat with him in a tree in Washington Park, kissing him, shy, swinging her legs, talking about little things that meant more than the mere meaning of the words, swinging her legs with her blue-wash-bloomers showing a little, a girl at the stage when she is starting to get breasts and a figure, and she is gay and laughs, and has imps in her eyes, swinging her legs, singing, *In the Blue Ridge Mountains of Virginia.*"[4]

Studs' last days are spent in the midst of the depression, and he is of course one of the "lumpen-proletariat," completely un-class-conscious, opinionated, fascist-minded, a perfect product of the jingo press. He is nevertheless caught in the economic collapse, is out of work, and meets his death as the result of exposure while seeking a job. Studs Lonigan goes to his death, a shattered middle-aged man, the pathetic product of a time and place in American life which is authentically drawn in one of the monuments of naturalistic fiction.

What seems perhaps to have been a work antedating the first of the Lonigan books is *Gas-House McGinty,* published in 1933. This novel, one of the least important of Farrell's books, stems largely from Joyce in that it employs a long dream sequence, an amalgam of thoughts and reported conversations, and is not reportorial in its methods. It is disconnected and impressionistic, and has all the aspect of an immature effort. But it does provide a ground of comparison with the solid achievement of the Danny O'Neill tetralogy which in part uses the same material. Gas-House McGinty is boss of an express company's call office where Jim O'Neill, father of Danny, also works. So we have the background in which Jim and later Danny appear. But the slapdash of the early book scarcely brings out the importance of industrial conditions as they affect the worker; it does not begin to give the full and real sense of the influence of employment upon thinking and action that we get from the same material treated in the manner of *Father and Son.*

The Danny O'Neill tetralogy includes *A World I Never Made* (1936), *No Star is Lost* (1939), *Father and Son* (1940), and *My Days of Anger* (1943). A more ambitious undertaking

---

[4] From *Judgment Day* by James T. Farrell. © 1935 by Vanguard Press.

even than *Studs Lonigan*, this long series has for its central character a boy glimpsed occasionally in the earlier work, but a child of far different potentialities from Studs. Danny, too, is the product of lower middle-class Irish in Chicago, but he has a fey quality, a seriousness of mind, a receptivity to ideas lacking in most of his companions. Younger than Studs, he starts by looking up to the hard-boiled youth, and desiring to emulate him. But either because he is physically frailer, or has to wear glasses, or finds books interesting, he does not follow in Studs' footsteps. He graduates from high school and even attends college. He dabbles in some of the dissipations of the Fifty-Eighth Street gang, but they do not particularly reward him, and furthermore he has never been admitted wholeheartedly into the gang, so their standards of value are not so precious to him. Danny suffers far more than Studs from a sense of the inferiority, the spiritual emptiness, of his family life. Danny is sensitive and, as he grows older, becomes more so rather than less. The standards of his middle-class home weigh heavily on him; he must make a clean break with all that is atrophying in his home environment before he can begin to live a larger and freer life. It takes him long to do this, but eventually he succeeds.

The real interest, however, and the prime focus of the tetralogy, is not Danny but his family. Family life, both on the really proletarian level of his father and mother, and on the petty bourgeois level of his Grandmother O'Flaherty, with whom he goes to live when very young because his parents cannot afford to keep him—this life is the primary subject of the series. The O'Flahertys, Uncle Al, Aunt Margaret and Grandma, are exceptional people in their energy, their individuality, and their desire to rise above the lowly status of plain working people. Jim O'Neill and his wife Lizz are on the lowest rung of the economic ladder; Lizz is a slattern and she has too many children; Jim is forced to work day in and day out all of his life, and scarcely makes enough for their subsistence. Young Danny and his small sister Margaret live alternately in these two households until Grandmother O'Flaherty takes them in permanently. It is the picture of group living in these homes that gives the tetralogy its strength, provides it with pathos, such drama as there is, and its overall significance.

It is not an engaging picture, and while Danny emerges at the end free of the superstitions, the curses, the pettiness and bickerings, his soul is no doubt permanently scarred. But the great thing is, he does escape, through enlightment achieved in school and through the arts.

With less social significance than *Studs*, and probably less force because of that, the Danny O'Neill series succeeds magnificently in one office of the novel; namely, character creation. Uncle Al O'Flaherty, Aunt Margaret, Jim O'Neill, Grandmother—these are memorable portraits. Who can forget Al's cheerfulness, his humble and real desire to help Danny escape the poverty of his home, his Babbitt-like precepts which are nevertheless worthy attributes at his level? Aunt Margaret's own story is a moving one: infatuation with a man who betrays her, and subsequent decline through drink and self-pity to a tragic end. The father-and-son relationship between Danny and Jim is a finely wrought saga of human intercourse, a beautiful story, deeply probing in its truth and eternally sad, as must always be the story of disparity between the aspirations of the older and the younger generation.

What one regrets in this tetralogy is the overlavish documentation, the repetition of incident, the piling up of detail, which though present were less noticeable in the trilogy, because, first, the story took less time to tell, and second, the chief character was usually the focus of interest. A lack of selectivity is probably the worst fault of Farrell's fiction; but that seems to be one of the attendant factors in naturalistic writing. Undoubtedly the impressiveness of the work depends to a great degree upon its massing of detail. As in the case of Dreiser and Dos Passos, it is next to impossible for Farrell to get his effects in a short space of time. He must heap up scenes and incidents until the total weight of his material finally makes itself felt. For this reason he has written few if any short stories of value, though he has published a great many. His collections include *Calico Shoes, Guillotine Party, Can All This Grandeur Perish?, To Whom It May Con-*

cern, $1000 a Week and *Tommy Gallagher's Crusade,* but almost all are mere transcripts of events, seldom with sufficient subtlety or point to be memorable.

It is far otherwise when he essays full-length fiction, and to date, exclusive of the immature *Gas-House McGinty,* he has written two excellent novels unrelated to the personae of the two long series. These are *Ellen Rogers* (1941) and *Bernard Clare* (1946); the latter, however, may be the beginning of another series.

Ellen Rogers, as a fictional creation, is not unworthy to set beside Carrie Meeber; unlike Carrie, however, she has a capacity for love that exceeds her perception of self-interest. Ellen, a product of the same sort of environment out of which Studs Lonigan came, is essentially an amoral youngster; but she is as greatly wronged as Roberta Alden. Like Roberta, her end comes tragically. Ed Lanson, whom she loves, has something in common with Clyde Griffiths; they are both men of no principle, the products of an age in which social taboos no longer have sufficient authority to prevent them from committing the crime of murder.

Ellen Rogers' tragedy comes as the result of her love for a man incapable of anything but self-love. To be sure, Ellen is no saint. At nineteen she had had affairs, and they bored her. She knew she possessed beauty and appeal, was altogether too conscious of it, and to assuage her boredom enmeshed young men in the toils of passion. But, lacking principle herself, she met Ed Lanson, a man of even less moral responsibility. His charm, his superficial acquaintance with the great poets and philosophers, his flowery language, made him irresistible.

In fact, Ed's trouble was that no woman could resist him. He had glanced through Nietzsche and imbibed at that fount of amorality; he identified himself with the Superman ideal. His acts were, he told himself, beyond good and evil. Besides, whenever a problem became too abstruse he turned his attention to easier subjects, in his case, women. And thus it happened that Ellen found herself in the very position in which she had often placed her victims. She overlooked, for a long time, Ed's impecuniosity, faithlessness and dishonesty, but finally she had to admit that he didn't love her. Still she would not give him up and used every conceivable device to hold him. When she failed, she walked into the cold waters of Lake Michigan. And Ed dismissed the episode of Ellen as lightly as he had dismissed those before her; as the train which carried him away rushed by the shores of the lake where she had drowned herself, he was already preparing a new conquest.

In this novel, as cannot be said even for *Studs Lonigan,* Farrell's choice of incident is unerringly apposite. The story moves forward with brief, telling episodes, each of photographic clarity and truthfulness. His dialogue, as always, is superb. Farrell never once interposes comment. Ellen and Ed and the many secondary characters are shown from without, yet their inmost being is illuminated. The exterior treatment of Farrell's characters, unlike that of the people of Dos Passos' *Number One,* successfully portrays their interior life, perhaps because these people are intrinsically shallow. At any rate, here is a case in which slow-footed naturalism engages to deliver the whole of the story, and succeeds.

It is evident that Farrell's work contains an enormous amount of moral judging. Or rather, we are made to judge; for Farrell never points to crises or explains them. And if the novels through *Ellen Rogers* had not convinced them, *Bernard Clare* should once and for all have silenced those who complained that Farrell writes merely photographically. For this story, he went back to his early memories as an aspiring writer, alone and friendless in New York. The time of action is the summer and fall of 1927, when Bernard Clare, a young man of twenty-one, had come from Chicago to find freedom and to write the great American novel. His attempts to write in the quiet of the New York Public Library were foiled by his wandering interest in girls and his thoughts of sex. Too, he had to earn his living, and he took odd jobs, as counterman in a cigar store, later as classified ad salesman for a telephone directory. In these jobs he was quite successful, but he was always contemptuous of such success, as it represented in his mind the cheap commercialism of American culture. But as a writer he seemed to get nowhere.

In the course of his search for a girl, he accidentally met a married woman, Eva Stone, with whom he slept on the afternoon of their first meeting. He eventually became involved with her in a way that threatened to destroy the freedom he was jealously guarding. He had often declared that if he was ever to write, he must dedicate his life to his art. Eva, more sensibly than he, actually believed this, and declared they must give each other up. Bernard was unwilling to make this sacrifice, and finally was caught *flagrante delicto* by Eva's husband. Whereupon a moral choice was forced, and Eva made it. She elected to stay with her complaisant husband; while Bernard descended into a state of despair, alleviated only by drunkenness.

Now, such a story, baldly outlined, seems trite enough. But Farrell has handled it freshly. There are few stereotypes of action or phrase, no romantic agonizing, no rhetoric. It is all immediate, lifelike, matter-of-fact. It is even Dreiserian. Not only in this novel but throughout all his work, Farrell's tenderness, compassion, pity for the purblind creatures whose little lives are wasted on treadmills, whose aspirations are small but doomed never to materialize, and his robust anger at the harm done by false social concepts, are reminiscent of Dreiser. But also Farrell has what Dreiser did not have, a thorough-going knowledge of what he is about as a craftsman. *Bernard Clare* shows that Farrell's progress continues, that he is becoming more selective, and that story involvement, almost in the sense of plot, is not altogether beyond him. *Ellen Rogers* and *Bernard Clare* are "plotted" more than any of his novels, and are therefore the most easily read of them all.

The style of James T. Farrell has often been characterized as wanting in grace and incisiveness; it has been compared to Norris' and Dreiser's as sprawling and a-tonic, a prose that jangles upon the ears. Yet it is not out of harmony with its subject matter. A nice, orderly instrument might very well lose for us the impact of Farrell's material. And it is apparent, in *Bernard Clare*, that he is sharpening his style to his peculiar uses as an ever better medium for conveying his story. To be convinced that he can write superlatively well, one need only consider such a passage as is contained in Bernard's diary: "Memory, the bones of our past, tells us that one day we shall all be bones and decay. And nothing will remain of us, not one thought, not one word, not one recollection. Time, memory, everything in this world is a prophecy of the ending, and our own ending is the prophecy of the ending of all. All, all leads to the triumph of universal ice. Even the atoms will die. Between the fires of the beginning and the frozen dead atoms of the end, I loved you, Eva. But each ending, each parting, each time we clung and our hearts fell in beating unison, and we limply and warmly lay together, this led to and prophesied the end of our love, and the end of our love promised the end of our lives, and the end of our lives foretold the end of the world."[5]

With Hemingway and Steinbeck, Farrell is one of our few major novelists still likely to produce important fiction; in fact, Farrell perhaps has the best chance of all, for he is not only the youngest but seems to have treasured up the greatest store of material in a memory that is little short of prodigious. There is little doubt but that he will continue to work in the naturalistic vein; but he may very well go on to even more significant treatment of the lower middle-class lives he knows so well, to illumine our understanding of them with a more disciplined art. Meanwhile he has taken his place in the vanguard of American novelists, and emphatically vindicated the naturalism upon which he has insisted.

A FORECAST

ON THE BASIS of what American writers of fiction have done in the past one hundred and fifty years, by the several dominant types of fiction they have produced, is it possible to draw any conclusions from which to predict future trends? Of one thing we may be sure: for a long time to come there will be novelists and short-story writers to turn out their special idealizations of real experience against the demands of the "average reader." We will have "historical novels" from time to time which rise above

---

[5] From *Bernard Clare* by James T. Farrell. © 1946 by Vanguard Press.

the ruck of such fiction, but which will not be entitled to a place beside the novels of Cooper. We will have sentimental stories praising various aspects of our conventional life, acceptable to wide portions of the reading public; but they will not be literature. Of romanticizing there will be no end; but the line of inheritance drawn from Cooper seems artistically almost to have ended with him.

Those present-day writers who stem from the Irving tradition are fairly numerous, and they continue to produce fiction of a considerable stature. It is not too fanciful to see in the stories of Katherine Anne Porter some of the shadowy substance and the love of allegory introduced by Hawthorne; or to find that Henry James has wielded his influence upon such sensitive, highly involute and distinguished work as *Noon Wine* and the stories in *Pale Horse, Pale Rider*. Miss Porter, from whom critics have been expecting greater things, seems still on the threshold of real achievement, and the short forms in which she has worked have not given room for the full display of her talent. Eudora Welty, a younger writer whose work has many similar characteristics, may yet outdistance Miss Porter in the revelations of a temperament that provides an unusual refraction of her peculiar Southern world.

These, however, are but two harbingers, and the lesser writers who have preempted the mantle of the Temperamentists hardly constitute a sufficiently numerous school upon which to place any reliance for the future. There have been writers, like Glenway Wescott and Kay Boyle, who indicated in some of their works a derivation from this line, but many of them have failed to fulfill their early promise. Whether the vein has run out is impossible to say; at any rate it does not seem to be the main source of current fictional creation. In recent years the renewed vogue of James (largely, one imagines, a critical enthusiasm) may bring an increased activity upon the part of young writers, and in some of our academic magazines short stories in the Jamesian style are almost the only kind printed.

Since writers are creatures of their times, regardless of the type of imagination they possess, it is always instructive to regard the milieu in which they write. The character of American life in the coming decades will determine, to a great extent, the kind of fiction we will have. We know that during the first World War many of our novelists engaged in writing novels to exemplify the values of patriotism, while others turned to fantasy, and still others became silent. During periods of great spiritual stress it is not unusual for writers to reflect the tensions. Frequently they lose their bearings, just as other people do. Such gifted writers as Edith Wharton and Dorothy Canfield can, in time of war, produce novels glorifying destruction. The air is electric with false shibboleths; a mind-cast is prevalent that distorts our view of reality. And when war is ended, the illusions of a frenetic time seem to have been the results of betrayal. Then we have fiction which condemns the attitudes previously extolled and reflects hostility to all idealism—a hostility that is almost as disproportioned as the former zeal. Few indeed are the writers who can take the long view.

During the second World War, of course, there was on the whole a more temperate enthusiasm for bloodshed. Our writers did not expect Utopia to emerge from the last battle. Even so, there were many who, during the interim between wars, had renounced all idealism, and had been, like Dos Passos and Hemingway, the evangels of disillusion; yet upon the incidence of the second war, they had almost unanimously recanted their former attitudes and began praising the virtues of a society and a culture they had formerly anathematized. Dos Passos, Hemingway, Van Wyck Brooks, Sinclair Lewis, MacLeish—the list is very long. In fact, a whole generation of writers either ascended a bandwagon upon which to wave a flag, or found refuge in some cloister (as, in T. S. Eliot's case, the Church of England), or turned to neo-humanism, to the Catholic Church, or descended into silence. Younger writers of World War II often wrote fantasies, or imitated Franz Kafka and established a cult of violent symbolism in which to express their parables of modern life's paradoxes.

But, regarded in its widest perspective, American fiction produced between wars, as well as during the conflict, was broadly in the Howells tradition. The writers of the interim period who gave promise of forging distinctive utterance often seemed to have lost their way or could not make the final expression. Casualties were many, and those who had expected good things from such realists as Albert Halper, Robert Cantwell and their brothers-at-arms in the proletarian camp were disappointed. Others, like William Saroyan and Jesse Stuart, went on essentially repeating what they had said earlier. Saroyan, one of the most gifted writers of his generation, made his greatest contribution in the drama. Such plays as "The Time of Your Life" and "My Heart's in the Highlands" blew fresh currents into our theatre; his short fiction likewise created a new style in the American story form; but his novels have not been so successful. Walter Van Tilburg Clark, Robert Penn Warren and Wallace Stegner continue to work in the realistic vein, but none of them has so far shown evidence of first-rate ability. We are probably still too close to the last war to have been given its Hemingways and Dos Passoses, but such novels as those by John Hersey, Harry Brown and Frederick Wakeman show that its fictional treatment may well be based in realism.

Novelists of the future will no doubt avail themselves of the many resources introduced to their craft by the shapers. A combination of the old techniques may produce new ones. The novelists will probably attempt to reflect their times, and they will try to show how human beings have thought and acted in their own milieu. It seems most likely that, to do this, they will draw upon the life they have known. As Howells long ago said, the faithful portrayal of life in fiction lifts us to an interest in the meaning of things. To cast new light upon existence and help us, as human beings, to get around life's obstacles, is the real duty and the crowning achievement of the novelist. The writers whose perception of reality is equal to these ends will produce the great fiction of the future.

INDEX

INDEX

I 3